MAKING HEALTHY SAUSAGES

Stanley Marianski, Adam Marianski

Bookmagic, LLC.
Seminole, Florida

Making Healthy Sausages
Stanley Marianski, Adam Marianski

ISBN: 978-0-9836973-0-5
Library of Congress Control Number: 2011913523

Bookmagic, LLC.
http://www.bookmagic.com

Printed in the United States of America.

Contents

Introduction

There has never been a greater consumer awareness about the food we eat. In December 2010 CNN news reported that in 2020 about 50% of the American population will suffer from some form of diabetes. High blood pressure and cholesterol levels are increasing and obesity is a huge concern. Until one reaches the age of 50, these problems generally lay hidden, with the exception of being overweight, but for many of us there comes a moment when our body starts to react in a threatening way. The only way to compensate this imbalance and remain healthy is to pay attention to the foods we eat.

Sausages have always been one of our favorite foods, but they are not the healthiest product. They contain a significant amount of fat and salt, the latter often added not for flavor, but for preservation purposes. Some sausage types are better suited for making low salt or low fat sausages, others contain more salt for safety reasons and should not be interfered with. The book reinvents traditional sausage making and introduces a completely new way of thinking. The sausage is not spiced hamburger meat anymore, but rather a "package" which contains meat plus other ingredients. All those ingredients acting together create a nutritional and healthy product.

It is only recently that we have seen an incredible progress in the technology of making reduced fat products. The trend started with low fat milk, then yogurts, sour cream, cheeses, dressings, soups, snacks and then reduced fat hot dogs. Making those products required a knowledge of new ingredients which were invented only in the last 30 years. For example, first starter cultures for making fermented sausages were discovered about 70 years ago, but only in the last 5 years have become commonly available. The path is always the same: a new product is discovered, then it is used by the commercial industry, and finally it becomes available for the general public.

Most reduced fat products require the addition of hydrocolloids which in most cases are naturally derived products, for example carrageenan gum or konjac flour. Those additives are applied in miniature doses yet are able to greatly change the characteristics of the product.

Until recently only professionally trained food technologists or chemists were applying those ingredients to food products. Then professional cooks discovered that those new additives offered many benefits and the products became accepted in the restaurant industry. Finally, the ever growing online industry started to sell those items to the general public. Those products come with instructions on how to use them and this is how new technology becomes available to all of us in time. Highly technical and expensive textbooks are replaced with easier to understand guides and finally a hobbyist can make new products at home.

The purpose of the book is to educate the reader how to use those new additives that the food industry has embraced for so long. How to apply less salt and fat and produce a sausage that will be flavorsome, healthy and safe to eat. After reading this book he should be able to create his own recipes or modify any existing recipe to make a healthier sausage without compromising the flavor. There are thousands of recipes on the Internet and many sausage making sites. Anybody can copy down a recipe and make a sausage, but that does not make him any wiser. And how do we distinguish a good recipe from a mediocre one? The collection of 80 recipes provides a valuable reference on the structure of reduced fat products. Each recipe contains less than 200 calories per 100 g serving.

The book teaches the basics of sausage making and includes all advice and tips that will make a reader a proficient and smart sausage maker. He will be able to control the amount of calories the sausage contains and decide what ingredients will go inside. After studying the book he will be the modern sausage maker.

Stanley Marianski

Chapter 1

Principles of Meat Science

Meat is composed of:
- water - 75%
- protein - 20%
- fat (varies greatly) - 3%
- sugar (glycogen, glucose) - 1%
- vitamins and minerals - 1%

Different animals or even meat cuts from the same animal exhibit *different proportions of the above components.* The animal's physical activity and type of diet influence those components and the color of the meat as well. Meat contains about 75% of water but fat contains only 10-15%. This implies that a fatty meat will lose moisture faster as it has less moisture to begin with, a fact which is important when making air dried or slow fermented products. As the animal matures, it usually increases in fatness, which causes a proportional loss of water.

pH of the meat

When an animal is alive the pH (acidity) value of its meat is around 7.0 (neutral point). After the slaughter and bleeding the oxygen supply is interrupted and enzymes start converting glycogen (meat sugar) into lactic acid. This lowers the pH (increases acidity) of the meat and the process is known as glycolysis. Understanding pH of meat is quite important as it allows us to classify meats by the pH and to predict how much water a particular type can hold. We are all familiar with the acidic taste of lemon juice and vinegar. Gentle foods such as milk will be found on the opposite end of the scale. How fast and low pH drops depends on the conditions that the animal was submitted to during transport and before slaughter. The factors that affect meat pH are genetics, pre-slaughter stress and post-slaughter handling.

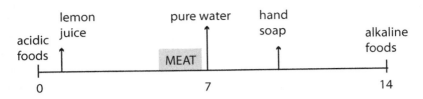

Fig. 1.2 General pH scale.

Water holding capacity is related to the pH of the meat. As the pH decreases so does the water holding capacity of the meat. At the isoelectric point (pH around 5.3), meat has the minimum strength to hold water and drying is fastest. This relationship is of great advantage when choosing meats for making dry products whose technology depends on water removal. On the other hand when making a boiled ham, we want it to be juicy and meat with a higher pH will be chosen. The meat with a higher pH binds water very well and inhibits drying. This can affect the safety of a drying product as more moisture creates better conditions for the growth of bacteria.

Extra amounts of water are pumped into hams or added to emulsified sausages during the chopping process. To increase meat's water holding capacity, phosphates are added. Phosphates are *alkaline* with pH 7.3 - 9.8 and will increase pH of the meat. This will allow meat to hold a larger amount of water.

Meat	pH	Description
Live animal	7.2	
Normal	5.8 (24 hours after slaughter)	typical red color, good water binding
PSE (Pale, Soft, Exudative)	5.5 (60 minutes after slaughter)	pale color, very soft, poor water binding
DFD (Dark, Firm, Dry)	6.2 (24 hours after slaughter)	dark red color, very good water binding

Proteins. Proteins are very important molecules to all forms of life. They are one of four of life's basic building blocks; the other three are carbohydrates (sugars), lipids (fats), and nucleic acids (DNA and RNA). Proteins make up about 15% of your body weight, and serve all kinds of functions. They are large molecules made up of hundreds of atoms of carbon, hydrogen, oxygen, and nitrogen. A scientist can separate those proteins from one another. Then he can break them down into smaller parts and finally arrive into what is defined as amino acids. By studying those amino acids and the rules that govern their behavior we learn about proteins. There are many proteins and they don't look alike or taste alike. Meat proteins coagulate when heated to 135-155° F (58-131° C). They can be divided into:

- Sarcoplasmic (plasma) - water soluble.
- Myofibrillar (contractile) - or salt soluble.
- Stromal (connective) - relatively insoluble.

Sarcoplasmic proteins are commonly extracted with curing solutions and help emulsify fat, the factor which is crucial when making emulsified sausages. They are already soluble in the muscle cells, hence called water soluble proteins. The fluid (meat juice) that drips from thawed meat contains these proteins. They also help convert glycogen (meat sugar) into lactic acid which contributes to stronger fermentation when making fermented products. *Myoglobin*, which gives meat its color belongs to this group.

Myofibrillar proteins are responsible for the contraction ability of living muscle. *They are soluble in high salt solutions* which allows them to retain water and encapsulate fats, thus preventing separation during cooking. The most important proteins in this group are *myosin* and *actin*; they contribute to the water holding and emulsifying capacity of meat with **myosin** being the most important. By needle pumping meat with a curing solution (salt, water, nitrite, phosphates, erythorbate) and applying mechanical action (cutting, tumbling) we can extract these proteins. The resulting solution is the "exudate" which acts as a glue and holds individual meat particles together, the important property when making formed hams. This extraction becomes much stronger when meat is cut in a bowl cutter in the presence of salt, phosphate and water. As a result an emulsified meat paste is obtained which may be added into the sausage mass or be frozen for later use. The leanest and the most expensive meats generally contain the highest level of these proteins.

Connective tissue proteins function as a supporting structure for the body of an animal. They transmit the movement generated by contraction of the myofibrillar proteins to the skeleton of the body. The most important proteins in this group are *collagen* and *elastin*.

Exudate - *the glue that holds sausages or reformed meats together.* Exudate is the solution of meat proteins with salt. Protein extraction during mincing/cutting or by mechanical action of massaging and tumbling is the main factor that determines the binding strength of the sausage emulsions or restructured meats. *On heating, exudate becomes a solid gel* helping to bind meat parts together. Extracted proteins form more cohesive bonds between the protein matrix and the meat surface. Many sausage recipes include the following sentence: mix all ground meat with spices until the mixture becomes sticky (gluey). After a few minutes of mixing and kneading by hand, the loosely held meat mass starts to stick together and becomes one solid mass. This is due to the binding properties of exudate. Meat proteins were extracted during cutting and combined with salt to form exudate. As mentioned earlier, the leaner the meats used, the more exudate is extracted. This is a logical statement as exudate is a solution of meat proteins with salt and less noble cuts such as connective tissue and fats contain less protein. *Exudate forms on surfaces which are cut.* If the connective tissue on the meat surface is intact, the surface should be cut or scored to facilitate exudate extraction and subsequent binding. One of the purposes of massaging and tumbling is to solubilize and extract *myofibrillar* proteins to produce exudate on the surface of the meat.

Sources of Meat

The main sources of manufacturing meats are:

- Cattle - beef, veal
- Pig
- Sheep
- Poultry - chicken, turkey, goose and duck.

In many areas goat and horse are consumed too. In addition, hunting enthusiasts bring meats such as deer, wild boar, bear, small game and wild birds to the dinner table. To a large extent the quality of meat relates to the type of feed the animal consumes. Cattle eat grass, hay and grains and their digestive system breaks down those feeds into amino acids and proteins that create a characteristic texture and flavor. Such foods do not contain much fat and consequently beef fat is concentrated in muscles.

Pigs, in contrast, eat a variety of foods and their diet contains more fat. They eat a lot of corn which produces a softer meat. English producers feed their hogs with barley instead as this produces harder bacon which is preferred by the local consumer. In the Eastern part of the USA, hogs were often fed peanuts which resulted in a soft meat and fat that will melt at lower than usual temperatures. Famous Spanish Serrano dry hams are made from hogs that graze freely in oak forests and consume a lot of oak corns. This diet imparts a characteristic texture and flavor to the meat. Polish Kabanosy were originally made from fat pigs that were fed mainly potatoes. The type of animal diet is very instrumental in producing meat that displays an original flavor and character. Pigs of today are fed commercially prepared foods enriched with antibiotics. They spend their entire life in movement restricted pens that affect the texture of the meat. To satisfy the low fat expectations of a consumer, the fat content of pork meat is much lower than before. The animals are much smaller today compared to the giants that freely walked only 100 years ago.

Meat Cuts

Short of being a farmer, a person living in a large city has little choice but to purchase meats in a local supermarket. Individuals who keep on winning whole hog barbecue contests purchase their pigs from selected farmers. From a manufacturing point of view available meat cuts can be divided into two groups:

- Noble cuts.
- Less noble cuts.

Noble cuts are those cuts which are highly regarded by chefs as:

- They consist almost entirely of desirable lean meat.
- Are easy to prepare as they contain small amounts of bone.
- Contain outside fat which is easy to remove.
- Include little connective tissue.
- Are simple to cook.

They are highly regarded by a consumer as:

- They can be cooked using simple methods.
- Are tender when cooked.
- Taste good.

Noble cuts come from the parts of the animal that exercise less frequently such as beef round, rump, sirloin, loin or pork ham, loin and belly. Less noble cuts exhibit opposite characteristics and come from the parts of the animal that exercise frequently such as the neck, chuck, shoulder, shin or pork shoulder, picnic and hocks. Such cuts contain many bones, smaller muscles and more connective tissue. As there is a finite number of noble parts the animal carries, the less noble and smaller parts are used for making sausages. This includes cuts and trimmings removed from the more noble cuts and parts such as liver, kidney, heart, tongue, jowls and skin. The only instance when noble meat cuts will be used for making sausages is the shortage of less noble cuts or a recipe such as ham sausage that calls specifically for lean ham.

There is a unique meat classification system in the USA:

1. Acceptable grade - the only fresh pork sold in supermarkets.

2. Utility grade - used in processed products and not available in supermarkets for purchase.

Pork meat is divided into five prime areas:

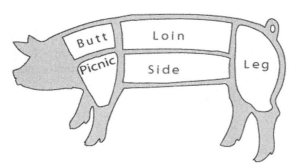

1. Shoulder butt
(Boston butt).
2. Shoulder picnic.
3. Loin.
4. Ham.
5. Side (bacon,
spare ribs).

Photo 1.1 Pork prime cuts.

Those main cuts are further broken down to additional parts. They all have unique names and numbers and are listed in trade catalogs. These five primary cuts come from the meat that a home sausage maker will be able to purchase in a supermarket. There are many meat products and known sausages that require meats from other parts of the hog's body than those five primary cuts mentioned above. To make liver sausages you need liver, fat, meat from heads, brains, kidneys, hearts, back fat, lungs, tripes, etc. To make head cheese you need head meat, shank (hocks) and skins. These parts are rich in collagen and will form a gelatin which will hold the meat ingredients together. Blood is of course needed for blood sausages. Meat processors dealing with slaughter houses have access to those meats and they use them to manufacture different sausages. A person living on a farm will be able to obtain a hog without much difficulty, a person living in a large city is facing some obstacles but can make substitutions.

The factors that are of special interest to us when processing meats are:

- **Moisture.** Meat contains about 75% water but more water can be added during the manufacturing process. This water should be retained by the meat which is especially important for commercial producers as it amounts to higher yields and profits.
- **Fat.** Fat contains about 10-15% water. Proper fat selection is important when making fermented sausages.
- **Connective tissue.** Selective meat rich in connective tissue is important when making head cheeses.
- **Cohesion.** Allows binding meat pieces together, for example when making hams.

Moisture. The ability of meat to absorb and hold water is an important factor when making meat products, especially when producing formed hams or emulsified sausages such as frankfurters or bologna. The leaner the meat, the stronger binding capacity it possesses. The finer comminution of the particles, the higher degree of protein extraction and the stronger water-binding capacity of the meat. Meat coming from different animals exhibits different water binding properties. For example, beef binds water much better than pork.

1. Adding water. When a piece of meat is cooked it will lose some of the water, fat and juices. Adding water to meat helps offset some of this loss. Meat will lose some of this water anyhow, but because it contained more water when the cooking started, the cooked product will lose less of its original weight as some of the added water would be retained.

2. Adding water and salt. Adding salt into meat extracts meat proteins which form a solution with salt and water inside. This solution acts like glue holding individual pieces of meat and water together. This further improves the meat's water binding properties and results in a smaller cooking loss.

3. Adding water, salt and phosphates. When phosphates are used alone they are less effective, but when applied with salt they force meat to bind water in a formidable way. They accelerate the salt effects allowing the same results to occur sooner.

In other words the combined action of salt and phosphates is greater than the combined efforts of salt and phosphates if used individually. Around 0.3% phosphate is a typical dose. The maximum allowed is 0.5% but note that they are quite bitter and adding more than 0.3% may affect the product's flavor. Phosphates commonly used in making meat products are: pyrophosphates and tripolyphosphates. An important function of phosphates is their ability to accelerate the extractability of meat proteins. This leads to a uniform, interwoven matrix which entraps water and fat during comminution and holds it together during heat treatment. To increase and accelerate the distribution of a salt and phosphates solution within meat a physical action is employed. This is accomplished by massaging or tumbling machines designed for this purpose.

Fat influences flavor, juiciness and texture of the product. It also impacts shelf life and profits. Melting of fat begins at 35-40° C (95-104° F) depending on the type of fat. The type of food a particular animal eats will influence the texture and the melting point of its fat. The molten fat is able to escape from the damaged fat cells. Once the temperature falls into the range 40-80° C (104-176° F), the fat cells start to break down rapidly. For those reasons fatty products such as sausages should not be smoked or cooked at high temperatures for longer periods of time as the fats will melt affecting the texture of the sausage.

Melting and solidifying temperature of some fats		
Meat	Melting	Solidifying
Pork	82 - 104° F (28 - 40° C)	71 - 90° F (22-32° C)
Beef	104 - 122° F (40 - 50° C)	86 - 100° F (30 - 38° C)
Lamb	110 - 130° F (44 - 55° C)	93 - 113° F (34 - 45° C)
Chicken	~75° F (24° C)	< 50° F (10° C)

An interesting relationship exists between the texture of the fat and its distance from the center of the animal. The internal body fats are hardest, for example kidney fat. By the same token, *the outer layer of back fat is softer than the inside layer*, a fact that should be noted when choosing the hardest fat for making salami.

The color of fat depends on the type of animal and to a smaller degree its age and diet. For example, in colder climates in the summer when animals graze on grass, the fat is more yellow than when the animals are fed a prepared diet in the winter.

Generally the color of fat among animals follows these guidelines:
- Goat - white.
- Pig - white.
- Cattle - light yellow.
- Sheep - white to creamy.
- Horse - yellow.
- Buffalo - yellow.

Pork fat is the best for making sausages as it is white and tastes the best. It exhibits different degrees of hardness depending on which part it comes from. Back fat, jowl fat or butt fat (surface area) have a very hard texture and higher melting point. They are the best choices to use where we expect to see individual specks of fat in a finished product such as dry salami. Soft fat such as bacon fat is fine for making fermented spreadable sausages such as mettwurst or teewurst. *For most sausages any fat pork trimmings are fine* providing they were partially frozen when submitted to the grinding process. This prevents fat smearing when the temperature increases due to the mechanical action of knives and rotating worm on fat particles.

Beef fat has a higher melting temperature than pork but is yellowish in color which affects the appearance of the product where discrete particles of fat should be visible.

Connective Tissue

The connective tissue consists mainly from fibres of collagen and to a smaller extent from fibres of elastin. *Collagen* is much more prevalent and is found in bone, ligaments, skin, tendon, jowls and other connective tissues. It accounts for about 20% of the total protein. It is a framework that holds the individual muscles fibres and the bundles of muscles together. This function requires connective tissue to be tough and strong. *Collagen* is characterized by inter and intramolecular cross-links, whose number increases with the animal's age. *Collagen* water holding power is weaker than that of protein solution extracted from lean meat, and some of the water is returned during heating. *Collagen* is a tough tissue but becomes a tender meat when cooked for a few hours on low heat. *Collagen* is insoluble in water, but upon heating, *collagen* turns into gelatin, which forms a gel upon cooling. On heating to 148° F (65° C) *collagen* fibers start to shrink and if the heat continues, they form a gelatin. Fat that comes from part of the animal not supported by skeleton framework, such as the belly must have some connective tissue in order to support the weight above. It can be generalized that the softer the fat, the more *connective* tissue present. In air dried products such as country ham or prosciutto, collagen becomes tender in time due to natural reactions taking place inside the meat. *Elastin* is found in ligaments of the vertebrae and in the walls of large arteries. It has a yellow color and is of minor importance for making sausages.

Meat Binding

Understanding cohesion forces which are responsible for binding meats is important when making formed meats that consist of smaller meat cuts. Those pieces whether stuffed in a large casing or placed in a form, must bind together otherwise the slice of the finished product will not hold together and little holes will be visible inside. The best example is formed boiled ham which is made of smaller cuts. Such cuts must be carefully selected not only by the size and fat content, but by the meat color as well. And they must bind together so that the fully cooked product will look as if made from one solid chunk of meat. *The binding is improved if pressure is applied to meat pieces.* The binding will also be stronger if *exudate* has formed on the meat surface and the meats are heated to 149° F (65° C) or higher. A classical example is formed boiled ham where meat cuts are enclosed in a form and pressure is applied. Then the form is immersed in hot water and the ham is cooked. After cooling the form is opened, the meat is removed and what was a combination of individual meat cuts before has become a one solid block of ham. An egg white is often used as a binding aid to bind different ingredients together, for example in Bockwurst sausage. Gelatin powder will help to bind larger meat cuts. The strongest binding agent is relatively new product called transglutaminase, commonly called the "meat glue."

Water Holding Capacity

Different meats exhibit different capacity for binding water. Understanding this concept is important for making sausages where we can decide which meats will be used to produce a sausage.

Water binding quality of different meats	
Excellent	**Beef**: Hot bull meat, chilled bull meat, beef shank meat, beef chucks, boneless cow meat
Good	**Beef:** head meat, cheeks **Veal**: boneless veal, calf head meat **Pork**: trimmings-extra lean, trimmings-lean, head meat, cheeks (jowls)
Poor	**Beef**: hearts, weasand meat, giblets, tongue trimmings **Pork**: regular trimmings, hearts, jowls, ham fat **Sheep**: cheeks, hearts
Very poor	Ox lips, beef tripe, pork tripe, hearts, pork snouts, pork lips. These cuts although nutritious, exhibit little water binding properties and are mainly used as filler meat. Pork tripe, snouts and lips should be limited to 25% of the meat total
Hot bull meat: meat from a freshly slaughtered animal. The above data adapted from: *Sausage and Ready to Eat Meats, Institute of Meat packing, The University of Chicago.*	

The best quality emulsified sausages always incorporate beef as it easily binds water that has formed from the ice that is added during the cutting process. There are other factors that influence the water holding capacity of meat but they are difficult to control. These factors are:

- The age - the older the animal, or the longer it has been stored, the poorer its binding qualities.
- Acidity of meat (pH).
- Freezing meat - frozen meat is not as good as fresh meat, since the muscle fibres are broken by ice crystals.

Meat Color

The color of *fresh meat* is determined largely by the amount of *myoglobin* a particular animal carries. The more *myoglobin* the darker the meat, it is that simple. Going from top to bottom, meats that contain more *myoglobin* are: horse, beef, lamb, veal, pork, dark poultry and light poultry. The amount of *myoglobin* present in meat increases with the age of the animal. Different parts of the same animal, take the turkey for example, will have a different color as well. Muscles that are exercised frequently such as legs need more oxygen. *As a result they develop a darker color* unlike the breast which is white due to little exercise. This color is pretty much fixed and there is not much we can do about it unless we mix different meats together.

Meat Color	Dark red	Red	Light red	Pink	Light pink	Pale pink
Bull	x					
Cow			x			
Young cow				x		
Veal					x	
Old Sheep	x					
Adult sheep			x			
Young sheep				x		
Old goat	x					
Adult goat		x				
Young goat			x			
Pig				x		
Young pig						x
Buffalo						
Rabbit	x					x
Horse	x					

The color of *cooked* (uncured) meat varies from greyish brown for beef and grey-white for pork and is due to denaturation (cooking) of *myoglobin*. The red color usually disappears in poultry at 152° F (67° C), in pork at 158° F (70° C) and in beef at 167° F (75° C). The color of *cured* meat is pink and is due to the reaction between nitrite and *myoglobin*. The color can vary from light pink to light red and depends on the amount of *myoglobin* a particular meat cut contains and the amount of nitrite added to the cure. Curing and nitrates are covered in details in the chapter on curing.

Meat Tenderness and Flavor

Tenderness of meat depends on the age of the animal, methods of chilling and meat acidity. The way the meat is cooked is another important factor that must be considered and here the cook decides the tenderness of the final product. Meat flavor increases with the age of the animal. The characteristic flavors of a particular animal are concentrated more in the fat than in the lean of the meat. Low fat meats exhibit weaker flavors. Freezing and thawing has little effect on meat flavor, however, prolonged frozen storage can effect meat's flavor due to rancidity of fat. Rancidity is created by meat's reaction with oxygen which is accelerated by exposure of meat to light.

Chapter 2

Food Safety and Meat Microbiology

Meat of a healthy animal is clean and contains very few bacteria. Any invading bacteria will be destroyed by the animal's immune system. Once the animal is slaughtered these defense mechanisms are destroyed and the meat tissue is subjected to rapid decay. Although unaware of the process, early sausage makers knew that once the animal was killed, it was a race between external preservation techniques and the decomposition of the raw meats to decide the ultimate fate of the issue.

Most bacteria are present on the skin and in the intestines. In a stressed animal bacteria are able to travel from the animal's gut right through the casing into the meat. The slaughtering process starts introducing bacteria into the exposed surfaces. Given time they will find their way inside anyhow, but the real trouble starts when *we* create a new surface cut with a knife. This creates an opening for bacteria to enter the meat from the outside and start spoiling it. We must realize that they don't appear in some magical way inside of the meat, they always start from *the outside and they work their way in.*

Meat Surface Area and Volume Relationship

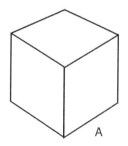 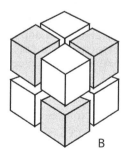

Fig. 8.1 Relationship of surface area and volume.

A. Cube A is 1 inch on each side and has a volume of 1 cubic inch and a surface area of 6 square inches. **B.** Three complete cuts (two vertical and one horizontal) produce eight small cubes with a volume of 0.125 cubic inch. Total *volume remains the same* - 1 cubic inch, but total *surface area has doubled* and is 12 square inches.

This is what happens when the meat is cut, the surface area increases. Now imagine what happens when the grinder cuts meat through a 1/8" (3 mm) plate, it creates an infinite number of small particles. The more cuts, the more spoils of meat, the more air and free water available to bacteria. This is the reason why *ground meat has the shortest shelf life*. In a large piece of meat the outside surface serves as a natural barrier preventing access to bacteria. *They have a long distance to travel to reach the center of the meat.* Meat muscles are surrounded with a connective tissue which also *acts as a protective sheath and so does the outside skin.* Duties like cutting meat, grinding, mixing or stuffing all increase meat temperature and should be performed in the kitchen at the lowest possible temperatures as fast as possible. Otherwise we create conditions for the growth of bacteria and that will decrease the shelf life of the product.

All About Bacteria

Food safety is nothing else but the control of bacteria and to do it effectively first we have to learn how bacteria behave. Once one knows what bacteria like or dislike, it will be very simple to produce safe products with a long shelf life. Let's make something clear: it is impossible to eliminate bacteria altogether, life on the planet will come to a halt. They are everywhere: on the floor, on walls, in the air, on our hands and all they need to grow is moisture, nutrients and warm temperature.

All microorganisms can be divided into the following classes:

- Bacteria
- Yeasts
- Molds

They all share one thing in common: they want to live and given the proper conditions they will start multiplying. They don't grow bigger, they just divide and divide and divide until there is nothing for them to eat, or until conditions become so unfavorable that they stop multiplying and die.

Meat contains about 75% of water and this moisture is the main reason that it spoils. Bacteria love temperatures that revolve around the temperature of our body (36.6° C, 98.6° F). Holding products at higher temperatures (greater than 130° F, 54° C) restricts the growth of bacteria. Increasing temperatures over 60° C (140° F) will start killing them. Most bacteria need oxygen (aerobic), others thrive without it (anaerobic). All of them hate cold and around 32° F (0° C) they become lethargic, and when the temperature drops lower they become dormant. *Keeping them at low temperatures does not kill them, but only stops them from multiplying.* Once when the conditions are favorable again, they will wake up and start growing again. Some bacteria tolerate the presence of salt better than others and we take advantage of this when curing meats. Other bacteria (e.g. *Clostridium botulinum*) are able to survive high temperatures because they form spores. Spores are special cells that envelop themselves in a protective shell and become resistant to harsh environmental conditions. Once conditions become favorable, the cells return to their actively growing state.

Given favorable conditions bacteria can double up in numbers every 20 minutes. In a refrigerator their number will also grow, albeit at a reduced pace, but they can double up in 12 hours. Short of deep freezing, it is impossible to stop bacteria from contaminating meat, but we can create conditions that will slow down their growing rate. At room temperatures bacteria will grow anywhere they have access to nutrients and water. Microorganisms which are of special interest when processing meats:

- Food spoilage bacteria.
- Dangerous (pathogenic) bacteria.
- Beneficial bacteria.
- Yeasts and molds.

Food Spoilage Bacteria

Spoilage bacteria break down meat proteins and fats causing food to deteriorate and develop unpleasant odors, tastes, and textures. Fruits and vegetables get mushy or slimy and meat develops a bad odor. Most people will not eat spoiled food. However, if they did, they probably would not get seriously sick. Bacteria such as *Pseudomonas spp.* or *Brochotrix thermosphacta* cause slime, discoloration and odors, but don't produce toxins. There are different spoilage bacteria and each reproduces at specific temperatures. Some can grow at low temperatures in the refrigerator or freezer.

Pathogenic Bacteria

It is commonly believed that the presence of bacteria creates an immense danger, but this belief is far from the truth. The fact is that a very small percentage of bacteria can place us in any danger, and most of us with a healthy immune system are able to fight them off. *Pathogenic bacteria cause illness.* They grow rapidly in the "Danger Zone" - the temperatures between 40 and 140° F - and *do not generally affect the taste, smell, or appearance of food.* Food that is left too long at warm temperatures could be dangerous to eat, but smell and look just fine. *Clostridium botulinum, Bacillus cereus* or *Staphylococcus aureus* infect food with toxin which will bring harm to us in just a few hours. Still others, like *Salmonella* or *Escherichia coli* will find their way with infected meat into our intestines, and *if present in sufficient numbers*, will pose a serious danger. Pathogenic bacteria hate cold conditions and lie dormant at low temperatures waiting for an opportunity to jump into action when the conditions get warmer again. They all die when submitted to the cooking temperature of 160° F (72° C), but some sausages are never cooked and different strategies must be implemented to keep them at bay. Fighting bacteria is a never ending battle, but at least we can do our best to turn the odds in our favor.

Beneficial Bacteria

Without beneficial bacteria it will not be possible to make fermented sausages. They naturally occur in meat but in most cases they are added into the meat in the form of starter cultures. There are two classes of beneficial (friendly) bacteria:

- Lactic acid producing bacteria - *Lactobacillus, Pediococcus.*
- Color and flavor forming bacteria - *Staphylococcus, Kocuria* (previously known as *Micrococcus*).

Although lactic acid producing bacteria are used mainly to produce fermented products, color and flavor forming bacteria are needed to brake Nitrate into nitrite and are often added to develop a stronger red color of meats.

Yeasts and Molds

Yeast and molds grow much slower than bacteria and they develop later in the drying process. This means they are normally part of the traditionally made sausage process. Yeasts need little oxygen to survive, and live near the surface inside of the sausage. Molds are aerobic (need oxygen) and will grow on the surface of the sausage only. On fermented European sausages, the development of mold is often seen as a desired feature as it contributes to the flavor of the sausage. Smoking sausages during or after fermentation, will prevent the growth of mold. If mold develops and is not desired, it can be easily wiped off with a cloth saturated in vinegar. Because molds can grow only on the outside of the sausage, there is nothing wrong with the meat itself.

Effects of Time and Temperature on Bacteria Growth

Under the correct conditions, spoilage bacteria reproduce rapidly and the populations can grow very large. Temperature and time are the factors that affect bacterial growth the most. Below 45° F bacteria grow slowly and at temperatures above 140° F they start to die. In the so called "danger zone" between 40-140° F (4-60° C) many bacteria grow very well. Most bacteria will grow exponentially at temperatures between 70° F and 120° F. When bacteria grow, they increase in numbers, not in size. Let's see how fast bacteria grow at ideal temperature:

Number of bacteria	Elapsed time
10	0
20	20 minutes
40	40 minutes
80	1 hour
160	1 hour 20 min
320	1 hour 40 min
640	2 hours
1280	2 hours 20 min
2560	2 hours 40 min
5120	3 hours
10,240	3 hours 20 min
20,480	3 hours 40 min
40,960	4 hours
81,920	4 hours 20 min
163.840	4 hours 40 min
327,680	5 hours
655,360	5 hours 20 min
1,310,720	5 hours 40 min
2,621,440	6 hours

Now it becomes evident what happens to a piece of meat left out on the kitchen table for many hours on a beautiful and hot summer day. The thermometer drawing that follows below has been compiled from the data we found at the College of Agriculture, Auburn University, Alabama. It shows the time that is required for one bacteria cell to become two at different storage temperatures. Looking at the drawing we can see that once the temperature rises above 50° F (10° C), bacteria will double up every time we raise the temperature by about 5° F. From the above examples we can draw a logical conclusion that if we want to process meats we should perform these tasks at temperatures not higher than 50° F (10° C). And those are the temperatures present in meat processing plants. You might say that lowering the temperature of the room will be better still. Of course it will be better, but people working in such conditions for 8 hours a day will find it very uncomfortable.

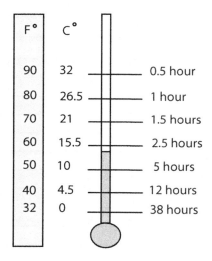

It can be seen that at 32° F (0° C) bacteria needs as much as 38 hours to divide in two. That also means that if our piece of meat had a certain amount of bacteria on its surface, after 38 hours of lying in a refrigerator the amount of bacteria in the same piece of meat will double. If we move this meat from the refrigerator to a room having a temperature of 80° F (26.5° C) the bacteria will double up every hour (12 times faster). At 90° F (32° C) they will be dividing every 30 minutes.

Fig. 8.2 Bacteria growth with temperature.

After cooking, meats are free of bacteria, but leaving them warm for an extended time *will invite new bacteria* to settle in and start growing. For this reason smoked and subsequently cooked meats are submitted to cold showers to pass through the "danger zone" as fast as possible.

Destruction of Bacteria

Most pathogenic bacteria, including *Salmonella, Escherichia coli 0157:H7, Listeria monocytogenes,* and *Campylobacter,* can be fairly easily destroyed using a mild cooking process. Maintaining a minimum temperature within the range of 130-165° F (54 -74° C) for a specific amount of time will kill them. However, cooking at low temperatures will not destroy these toxins once they have formed in food. Spoilage bacteria (*Pseudomonas* spp.) need oxygen to survive and applying a vacuum (removing air) during mixing and stuffing is an effective way to inhibit their growth. At home, a precaution must be made so that the sausage mix is stuffed firmly and any air pockets which are visible in a stuffed casing are pricked with a needle. Oxygen also affects the development of proper curing color and promotes rancidity in fats.

Toxins

Toxins of most concern are produced by *Clostridium botulinum, Clostridium perfringens, Bacillus cereus*, and *Staphylococcus aureus*. All are the result of the growth of bacteria in foods that have been mishandled. These bacteria are common in the environment and are often found on carcasses. Proper cooking, fermentation, cooling, and storage of food can prevent the growth of these bacteria and more importantly, the production of their toxins. Thermal processing (canning) at temperatures of greater than 240° F (115° C) for a specific amount of time is necessary to destroy most spores and toxins.

What is Botulism?

Botulism, once known as a sausage disease, is a rare but serious food borne disease that can be fatal. The symptoms of botulism include difficulty swallowing, talking, breathing, and double vision. Without medical care, respiratory failure and death are likely. Botulism symptoms typically appear within 18 to 36 hours of eating the contaminated food, although it can be as soon as four hours and last up to eight days. Food borne botulism can be especially dangerous because many people can be poisoned at once. Sausages are the second biggest source of food contamination and food poisoning, second only to home-canned food products. The optimal temperature range for the growth of botulinum bacteria is 78-95° F (26-35° C) and it significantly slows down at 118° F (48° C). When these bacteria feel threatened, they envelop themselves in protective shells called "spores" which can only be killed by boiling at 212° F (100° C) for at least 10 minutes. At 140° F (60° C), botulinum spores do not develop into toxins, although they are heat resistant.

Where Does Botulism Come From?

C. botulinum is found in soil and aquatic sediments all over the world. Like plant seeds, they can lie dormant for years. They are not threatening until they encounter an adequate environment for growth. The spores that germinate produce the deadly botulinum toxin. To grow, these bacteria require a slightly acidic, oxygen free environment that is warm and moist. That is exactly what happens when smoking meats:

1. First of all, meats contain a lot of moisture. Water is then also added to sausages to facilitate stuffing. Hams and other meats are pumped up with water.

2. Lack of oxygen – when smoking we intentionally decrease the amount of available air. This allows our sawdust or wood chips to generate lots of smoke.

3. Temperatures between 40° and 140° F - most smoking is done at this temperature range. The most dangerous range is from 78-95° F (26-35° C), and that fits into the "warm smoking" method. Bacteria thrive at this temperature range. It looks like we have created ideal conditions for botulin toxin. Clearly, we have to come up with a solution.

How to Prevent Botulism

The answer lies in the use of *Nitrates/nitrites*. When present, they prevent the transformation of *C. botulinum* spores into toxins. It is almost like applying a vaccine to eliminate a disease. By curing meats with nitrites, we protect ourselves from possibly contracting a deadly disease. Nitrites are cheap, commonly available, and completely safe in amounts recommended by the Food and Drug Administration. So why not use them? All commercial plants do. Nitrites are needed only when smoking meats or making fermented sausages. You don't need nitrites when barbecuing or grilling, as the temperatures are high enough to inhibit the development of botulinum spores into toxins.

Trichinae

There are some cold smoked pork sausages and loins that will not be submitted to the cooking process and raw pork or wild game meat can be at risk of being infected with trichinae. Trichinae is an illness caused by the consumption of raw or under cooked meat infected with *"trichinella spiralis"*. It is a round worm that can migrate from the digestive tract and settle in the form of cysts in various muscles of the body. The disease is almost non-existent in American pigs due to their strictly controlled feed, but it can still be found in meats of free roaming animals. The illness is not contagious, but the first symptoms appear within 1-2 days of eating contaminated meat. They include nausea, diarrhea, vomiting, abdominal pain, itchy skin, and may be mistaken for the flu. Trichinae in pork is killed by raising its internal temperature to 137° F (58° C). The U.S. Code of Federal Regulations requires pork to be cooked for 1 minute at 140° F (60° C). Traditionally made fermented sausages also called dry or slow-fermented sausages, are normally never cooked and the heat treatment does not apply here. They are cured with a higher percentage of salt which kills *trichinae* too. Fortunately, *storing pork at low temperatures also kills trichinae.* The U.S. Department of Agriculture's Code of Federal Regulations, Title 9, Volume 2, Cite: 9 CFR318.10 requires that pork intended for use in processed products be frozen at:

Group 1 - comprises product in separate pieces not exceeding 6" (15 cm) in thickness, or arranged on separate racks with layers not exceeding 6" (15 cm) in depth, or stored in crates or boxes not exceeding 6" (15 cm) in depth, or stored as solidly frozen blocks not exceeding 6" (15 cm) in thickness.

Group 2 - comprises product in pieces, layers, or within containers, the thickness of which exceeds 6" (15 cm) but not 27" (68 cm) and product in containers including tierces, barrels, kegs, and cartons having a thickness not exceeding 27" (68 cm).

Table 1. Required Period of Freezing Indicated			
Temperature		Days	
° F	° C	Group 1	Group 2
5	-15	20	30
- 10	-23.3	10	20
- 20	-28.9	6	12

Microwaving, curing, drying or smoking is not effective in preventing Trichinae. It should be noted that *freezing may not kill larval cysts in bears and other wild game that live in Northwestern U.S. and Alaska.* That meat has to be cooked to 160° F (72° C) internal temperature. Pork products which are not cooked such as slow fermented and dried sausages are at risk of being infected with *trichinae*. Those products are cured with salt and the USDA lists detailed procedures.

Good Manufacturing Practices that Can be Applied in the Everyday Kitchen

Home made sausages are subject to the ambient temperature of the kitchen and a dose of common sense is of invaluable help:

- Take only what you need from the cooler.
- When meat has been processed, put it back into the cooler.
- Keep your equipment clean and cold.
- Work as fast as possible.
- Try to always keep meat refrigerated.
- If your premises are not temperature controlled, limit your production to late evening or early morning hours.
- Wash your hands often.

Storing Meat

All uncooked meats or sausages should be treated as fresh meat. We can keep on hand an amount that will be consumed within a few days and the rest should be frozen. A ready to eat product should not be stored for more than 7 days if held at 41° F, or 4 days at 45° F. This practice will help control the growth of *Listeria monocytogenes*, a harmful bacteria. Meats should be stored at 32-40° F (0-4° C). We should bear in mind that there are differences between home and commercial refrigerators and freezers:

Home refrigerator	Butcher's cooler
36° - 40 F° (2° - 4° C)	32 F ° (0° C)
Home freezer	Butcher's freezer
0° F (-18° C)	-25° F (- 32° C)

Meat products stored for a long time in a freezer will start developing an inferior taste due to the oxidation of fat. Those chemical changes known as "rancidity" occur spontaneously and are triggered by light or oxygen. Meats stored in a freezer will turn rancid more slowly than meats stored in a refrigerator. Rancid meat is noticeable more with frozen meat than chilled meat because bacteria can spoil meat in a refrigerator well before rancidity begins. To prevent fat oxidation and to prolong the shelf-life of the product, antioxidants such as BHA, BHT, TBHQ and rosemary extracts are commonly used.

Chapter 3

USDA Dietary Guidelines

In 1980, the U.S. Department of Agriculture (USDA) and the U.S. Department of Health and Human Services (HHS) released the first edition of *Nutrition and Your Health: Dietary Guidelines for Americans*. By law (Public Law 101-445, Title III, U.S.C. 5301 et seq.), the *Dietary Guidelines for Americans* is reviewed, updated if necessary, and published every 5 years. Because of their focus on health promotion and disease risk reduction, the *Dietary Guidelines* form the basis for nutrition policy in Federal food, education, and information programs.

Its recommendations accommodate the reality that a large percentage of Americans are overweight or obese and/or at risk of various chronic diseases. The most recent data indicate that 72 percent of men and 64 percent of women are overweight or obese, with about one-third of adults being obese. Approximately 32 percent of children and adolescents ages 2 to 19 are overweight or obese, with 17 percent of children being obese.

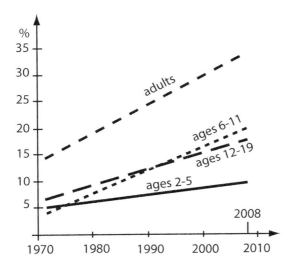

Fig. 3.1 Obesity in America... then and now.

Poor diet and physical inactivity are the most important factors con-
tributing to an epidemic of overweight and obesity affecting men,
women, and children in all segments of our society. Americans currently consume too much sodium and too many calories from solid
fats, added sugars, and refined grains (grains and grain products miss-
ing *the bran, germ, and/or endosperm*; any grain product that is not a
whole grain).

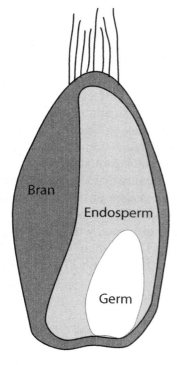

Bran is an outside beneficial fiber. It
accounts for about 14.5% of the kernel
weight.

Endosperm is a source of white flour.
It accounts for about 83% of the kernel
weight.

Germ is the embryo of the seed and
accounts for 2.5% of the kernel weight.

Whole grains foods are made with
flour that contains all three parts of the
grain.

White flour is made from endosperm
only. To compensate for the nutrients
that were in bran and in germ, but were
milled out, new nutrients are mixed
with white flour and the product becomes **enriched white flour.**

USDA guidelines recommend that
at least half of our daily grains come
from whole grains.

Fig. 3.2 A kernel of wheat.

2011 USDA Food Recommendations

- Balancing Calories to Reduce Weight.
- Prevent and/or reduce overweight and obesity through
improved eating and physical activity behaviors.
- Control total calorie intake to manage body weight. For people
who are overweight or obese, this will mean consuming fewer
calories from foods and beverages.
- Increase physical activity and reduce time spent in sedentary
behaviors.

- Maintain appropriate calorie balance during each stage of life - childhood, adolescence, adulthood, pregnancy and breast-feeding, and older age.

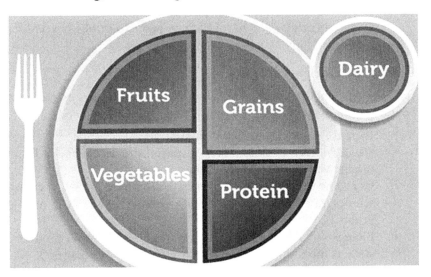

Photo 3.1 ChooseMyPlate.gov

Foods and Food Components to Reduce

- Reduce daily sodium intake to less than 2,300 milligrams (mg) and further reduce intake to 1,500 mg among persons who are 51 and older and those of any age who are African American or have hypertension, diabetes, or chronic kidney disease. The 1,500 mg recommendation applies to about half of the U.S. population, including children, and the majority of adults.
- Consume less than 10 percent of calories from saturated fatty acids by replacing them with monounsaturated and polyun-saturated fatty acids.
- Consume less than 300 mg per day of dietary cholesterol.
- Keep *trans* fatty acid consumption as low as possible by limit-ing foods that contain synthetic sources of *trans* fats, such as partially hydrogenated oils, and by limiting other solid fats.
- Reduce the intake of calories from solid fats and added sugars.

- Limit the consumption of foods that contain refined grains, especially refined grain foods that contain solid fats, added sugars, and sodium.
- If alcohol is consumed, it should be consumed in moderation - up to one drink per day for women and two drinks per day for men - and only by adults of legal drinking age.

Foods And Nutrients to Increase

Individuals should meet the following recommendations as part of a healthy eating pattern while staying within their calorie needs.

- Increase vegetable and fruit intake.
- Eat a variety of vegetables, especially dark-green, red and orange vegetables and beans and peas.
- Consume at least half of all grains as whole grains. Increase whole-grain intake by replacing refined grains with whole grains.
- Increase intake of fat-free or low-fat milk and milk products, such as milk, yogurt, cheese, or fortified soy beverages.
- Choose a variety of protein foods, which include seafood, lean meat and poultry, eggs, beans and peas, soy products, and unsalted nuts and seeds.
- Increase the amount and variety of seafood consumed by choosing seafood in place of some meat and poultry.
- Replace protein foods that are higher in solid fats with choices that are lower in solid fats and calories and/or are sources of oils.
- Use oils to replace solid fats where possible.
- Choose foods that provide more potassium, dietary fiber, calcium, and vitamin D, which are nutrients of concern in American diets. These foods include vegetables, fruits, whole grains, milk and milk products.

Recommendations For Specific Population Groups

Women capable of becoming pregnant

- Choose foods that supply heme iron, which is more readily absorbed by the body, additional iron sources, and enhancers of iron absorption such as vitamin C rich foods.

- Consume 400 micrograms (mcg) per day of synthetic folic acid (from fortified foods and/or supplements) in addition to food forms of folate from a varied diet.

Women who are pregnant or breastfeeding

- Consume 8 to 12 ounces of seafood per week from a variety of seafood types.
- Due to their high methyl mercury content, limit white (albacore) tuna to 6 ounces per week and do not eat the following four types of fish: tilefish, shark, swordfish, and king mackerel.
- If pregnant, take an iron supplement, as recommended by an obstetrician or other health care provider.

Individuals ages 50 years and older

- Consume foods fortified with vitamin B12, such as fortified cereals, or dietary supplements.

Building Healthy Eating Patterns

- Select an eating pattern that meets nutrient needs over time at an appropriate calorie level.
- Account for all foods and beverages consumed and assess how they fit within a total healthy eating pattern.
- Follow food safety recommendations when preparing and eating foods to reduce the risk of foodborne illnesses.

Cook and eat at home more often, preferably as a family

When preparing meals, include vegetables, fruits, whole grains, fat-free or low-fat dairy products, and protein foods that provide fewer calories and more nutrients. Experiment with healthy recipes and ingredient substitution.

The Heavy Toll Of Diet-Related Chronic Diseases

Cardiovascular Disease

- 81.1 million Americans - **37** percent of the population - have cardiovascular disease. Major risk factors include high levels of blood cholesterol and other lipids, type 2 diabetes, hypertension (high blood pressure), metabolic syndrome, overweight and obesity, physical inactivity, and tobacco use.
- 16 percent of the U.S. adult population has high total blood cholesterol.

Hypertension

- 74.5 million Americans - 34 percent of U.S. adults - have hypertension.
- Hypertension is a major risk factor for heart disease, stroke, congestive heart failure, and kidney disease.
- Dietary factors that increase blood pressure include excessive sodium and insufficient potassium intake, overweight and obesity, and excess alcohol consumption.
- 36 percent of American adults have pre-hypertension - blood pressure numbers that are higher than normal, but not yet in the hypertension range.

Diabetes

- Nearly 24 million people - almost 11 percent of the population - ages 20 years and older have diabetes. The vast majority of cases are type 2 diabetes, which is heavily influenced by diet and physical activity.
- About 78 million Americans - 35 percent of the U.S. adult population ages 20 years or older - have pre-diabetes. Pre-diabetes (also called impaired glucose tolerance or impaired fasting glucose) means that blood glucose levels are higher than normal, but not high enough to be called diabetes.

Cancer

- Almost one in two men and women - approximately 41 percent of the population - will be diagnosed with cancer during their lifetime.
- Dietary factors are associated with risk of some types of cancer, including breast (postmenopausal), endometrial, colon, kidney, mouth, pharynx, larynx, and esophagus.

Osteoporosis

- One out of every two women and one in four men ages 50 years and older will have an osteoporosis - related fracture in their lifetime.
- About 85 to 90 percent of adult bone mass is acquired by the age of 18 in girls and the age of 20 in boys. Adequate nutrition and regular participation in physical activity are important factors in achieving and maintaining optimal bone mass.

Balancing Calories

- Enjoy your food, but eat less.
- Avoid oversized portions.

Foods to Increase

- Make half your plate fruits and vegetables.
- Make at least half your grains whole grains.
- Switch to fat-free or low-fat (1%) milk.

Foods to Reduce

- Compare sodium in foods like soup, bread, and frozen meals - and choose the foods with lower numbers.
- Drink water instead of sugary drinks.

Understanding calories

The main sources of calories are:

- Carbohydrates - provide 4 calories per gram and are the primary source of calories for most Americans. Carbohydrates are classified as simple, including sugars, or complex, including starches and fibers.
- Proteins - provide 4 calories per gram. Protein is found in animal-based foods such as seafood, meat, poultry, eggs, milk and milk products. Plant sources of protein include beans and peas, nuts, seeds, and soy products.
- Fats - provide 9 calories per gram, which is more calories per gram than any other food product. Some fat is found naturally in foods, and fat is often added to foods during preparation.

Alcohol - provides 7 calories per gram and is a top calorie contributor in the diets of many American adults, but provides few nutrients. On average one drink provides as many calories as a slice of pizza. If you drink just one beer (250 ml) a day (150 calories), you will gain 150 x 7 = 1050 calories in a week. In 23 days you may gain one pound of fat, which will grow to 15 pounds in a year. This will surely happen if you cannot burn those beer calories as they will push your daily calories over your daily limit. Unfortunately, this is a common case and in a few years you will carry an unsightly belly.

The total number of calories a person needs each day varies depending on a number of factors, including the persons's age, gender, height, weight, and level of physical activity. If you consume more calories than you burn, you are gaining weight. If you lose more calories than you consume, through dieting, physical exercise or both, you are losing weight.

Estimated Calorie Needs per Day by Age, Gender, and Physical Activity Level				
Gender	Age (years)	Physical Activity Level		
		Sedentary	Moderately Active	Active
Child (female and male)	2-3	1,000-1,200	1,000-1,400	1,000-1,400
Female	4-8	1,200-1,400	1,400-1,600	1,400-1,800
	9-13	1,400-1,600	1,600-2,000	1,800-2,200
	14-18	1,800	2,000	2,400
	19-30	1,800-2,000	2,000-2,200	2,400
	31-50	1,800	2,000	2,200
	51+	1,600	1,800	2,000-2,200
Male	4-8	1,200-1,400	1,400-1,600	1,600-2,000
	9-13	1,600-2,000	1,800-2,200	2,000-2,600
	14-18	2,000-2,400	2,400-2,800	2,800-3,200
	19-30	2,400-2,600	2,600-2,800	3,000
	31-50	2,200-2,400	2,400-2,600	2,800-3,000
	51+	2,000-2,200	2,200-2,400	2,400-2,800

One pound of fat is equal to about 3500 calories. One calorie is the amount of energy that is required to raise the temperature of 1 liter (1 kg) of water by 1 degree Celsius.

Burning Calories Through Exercise

Eating one value meal (double burger, large fries and soda) in a fast food restaurant will pump over 1000 calories into your body. To lose one U.S. pound (.454 kg), you must burn 3,500 more calories than you take in as food.

It takes a lot of sweat to burn it all up:

Exercise	Duration	Energy spent
Bicycling, leisure	60 min	324 cal
Bicycling, 12-14 mph	60 min	713 cal
Swimming, moderate	60 min	497 cal
Weight lifting, regular pace, with breaks	60 min	250 cal
Weight lifting, fast pace	60 min	450 cal
Walking, 3 mph	60 min	356 cal
Running, 5.2 mph	60 min	734 cal
Running, 8 mph	60 min	1,102 cal
		Above figures based on 180 lb weight.

Salt and Hypertension

Sodium is an essential nutrient but is needed by the body in relatively small quantities. The higher an individual's sodium intake, the higher the individual's blood pressure. Salt added at the table and in cooking provides only a small proportion of the total sodium we consume. Most sodium comes from salt added during food processing. Virtually all Americans consume more sodium than they need. The estimated average intake of sodium for all Americans ages 2 and older is approximately 3,400 mg per day.

As sodium is found in almost all foods, the calorie intake is associated with sodium intake, i.e., the more food one eats, the more sodium one consumes. By the same token, eating less food lowers calorie intake and the amount of sodium we consume. Because a Recommended Dietary Allowance for sodium could not be determined, the Institute of Medicine (IOM) set Adequate Intake (AI) levels for this nutrient. The sodium Adequate Intake is based on the amount that is needed to meet the sodium needs of *healthy and moderately active individuals*. It covers sweat losses in unacclimatized individuals who are exposed to high temperatures or who become physically active, and ensures that recommended intake levels for other nutrients can be met.

For adolescents and adults of all ages (14 years and older), the Institute of Medicine set the **Tolerable Upper Intake Level (UL)** at **2,300 mg** per day. *The UL is the highest daily nutrient intake level that is likely to pose no risk of adverse health effects (e.g., for sodium, increased blood pressure) to almost all individuals in the general population.*

Adequate Intake Sodium Level	
Age (in years)	**Sodium (in mg per day)**
1-3	1,000
4-8	1,200
9-50	1,500
51-70	1,300
71+	1,200

The UL was based on several trials, including data from the Dietary Approaches to Stop Hypertension (DASH)-Sodium trial.

The IOM noted that in the DASH-Sodium trial, *blood pressure was lowered when target sodium intake was reduced to 2,300 mg per day, and lowered even further when sodium was targeted to the level of 1,200 mg per day.*

Americans should reduce their sodium intake to less than 2,300 mg or 1,500 mg per day depending on age and other individual characteristics. *African Americans, individuals with hypertension, diabetes, or chronic kidney disease and individuals ages 51 and older, tend to be even more responsive to the blood pressure-raising effects of sodium than others*; therefore, *they should reduce their intake to* **1,500 mg** per day.

Fats

Dietary fats are found in both plant and animal foods. Fats supply calories and essential fatty acids, and help in the absorption of the fat-soluble vitamins A, D, E, and K. Fats contain a mixture of saturated, monounsaturated, or polyunsaturated fatty acids. *Trans* fatty acids are unsaturated fatty acids. However, they are structurally different from the predominant unsaturated fatty acids that occur naturally in plant foods and have dissimilar health effects. The types of fatty acids consumed are more important in influencing the risk of cardiovascular disease than is the total amount of fat in the diet. Animal fats tend to have a higher proportion of saturated fatty acids (seafood being the major exception), and plant foods tend to have a higher proportion of monounsaturated and/or polyunsaturated fatty acids (coconut oil, palm kernel oil, and palm oil being the exceptions). Most fats with a high percentage of saturated or *trans* fatty acids are solid at room temperature and are referred to as "solid fats," while those with more unsaturated fatty acids are usually liquid at room temperature and are referred to as "oils." The body uses some saturated fatty acids for physiological and structural functions, but it makes more than enough to meet those needs. People therefore have no dietary requirement for saturated fatty acids. Higher intake of most dietary saturated fatty acids is associated with higher levels of blood total cholesterol and low-density lipoprotein (LDL) cholesterol. Higher total and LDL cholesterol levels are risk factors for cardiovascular disease. Consuming less than 10 percent of calories from saturated fatty acids and *replacing them with monounsaturated and/or polyunsaturated fatty acids* is associated with low blood cholesterol levels, and therefore a lower risk of cardiovascular disease.

To reduce the intake of saturated fatty acids, many Americans should limit their consumption of the major sources that are high in saturated fatty acids and replace them with foods that are rich in monounsaturated and polyunsaturated fatty acids. For example, when preparing foods at home, solid fats (e.g., butter and lard) can be replaced with vegetable oils that are rich in monounsaturated and polyunsaturated fatty acids. In addition, many of the major food sources of saturated fatty acids can be purchased or prepared in ways that help reduce the consumption of saturated fatty acids (e.g., purchasing fat-free or low-fat milk, trimming fat from meat). Oils that are rich in monounsaturated fatty acids include canola, olive and safflower oils. Oils that are good sources of polyunsaturated fatty acids include soybean, corn, and cottonseed oils.

A number of studies have observed an association between increased *trans* fatty acid intake and increased risk of cardiovascular disease. This increased risk is due, in part, to its LDL cholesterol-raising effect. Therefore, Americans should keep their intake of *trans* fatty acids as low as possible. To reduce the intake of solid fats, most Americans should limit their intake of sources that are high in solid fats and/or replace them with alternatives that are low in solid fats (e.g., fat-free milk). Reducing these sources of excess solid fats in a diet will result in reduced intake of saturated fatty acids, *trans* fatty acids, and calories. Common solid fats include butter, beef fat (tallow), chicken fat, pork fat (lard), stick margarine, and shortening. In addition to being a major contributor of solid fats, moderate evidence suggests an association between the increased intake of processed meats (e.g., franks, sausage, and bacon) and increased risk of colon cancer and cardiovascular disease.

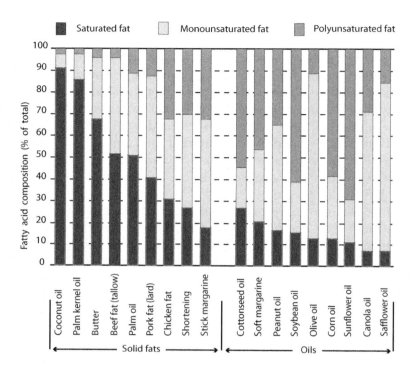

Fig. 3.3 Fatty Acid Profiles of Common Fats and Oils.

Cholesterol

The body uses cholesterol for physiological and structural functions, but it makes more than enough for these purposes. Therefore, people do not need to eat sources of dietary cholesterol. Cholesterol is found only in animal foods. Dietary cholesterol has been shown to raise blood LDL cholesterol levels in some individuals. However, the effect is reduced when saturated fatty acid intake is low, and the potential negative effects of dietary cholesterol are relatively small compared to those of saturated and *trans* fatty acids. Consuming less than 300 mg per day of cholesterol can help maintain normal blood cholesterol levels. Consuming less than 200 mg per day can further help individuals at high risk of cardiovascular disease. Cholesterol intake by men averages about 350 mg per day. Average cholesterol intake by women is 240 mg per day.

Nutrient Rich Foods

Milk and Milk Products

Milk and milk products contribute many nutrients, such as calcium, vitamin D (for products fortified with vitamin D), and potassium to the diet. Choosing fat-free or low-fat milk and milk products provides the same nutrients with less solid fat and thus fewer calories.

Protein Foods

Protein foods include seafood, meat, poultry, eggs, beans and peas, soy products, nuts and seeds. In addition to protein, these foods contribute B vitamins (e.g., niacin, thiamin, riboflavin, and B_6), vitamin E, iron, zinc, and magnesium to the diet. Plant sources of protein don't rank as high in protein as animal or seafood sources.

Some protein rich foods:

Protein rich foods, 100 g serving			
Name	Protein (g)	Fat (g)	Energy (cal)
Egg	12.56	9.51	143
Cheese, muenster	23.41	30.04	368
Chicken breast tenders,	14.73	15.75	263
Beef, ground (85% lean)	18.59	15.00	215
Tuna, yellowfin, raw	24.40	0.49	109
Peanut butter	25.09	50.39	588
Beans, kidney, red	22.53	1.06	337
One medium egg weighs about 50 g.			

Seafood

Seafood contributes a range of nutrients, notably the omega-3 fatty acids, eicosapentaenoic acid (EPA) and docosahexaenoic acid (DHA). Moderate evidence shows that consumption of about 8 ounces per week of a variety of seafood, which provide an average consumption of 250 mg per day of EPA and DHA, is associated with reduced cardiac deaths among individuals with and without pre-existing cardiovascular disease.

Oils

Fats with a high percentage of monounsaturated and polyunsaturated fatty acids are usually liquid at room temperature and are referred to as oils. Oils contribute essential fatty acids and vitamin E to the diet. Replacing some saturated fatty acids with unsaturated fatty acids lowers blood cholesterol levels. Oils are naturally present in foods such as olives, nuts, avocados, and seafood. Many common oils are extracted from plants, such as canola, corn, olive, peanut, safflower, soybean, and sunflower oils. Coconut oil, palm kernel oil, and palm oil are high in saturated acids and partially hydrogenated oils contain *trans* fatty acids. For nutritional purposes, they should be considered solid fats.

Dietary Fiber

Dietary fiber is the non-digestible form of carbohydrates. Dietary fiber naturally occurs in plants, helps provide a feeling of fullness, and is important in promoting healthy laxation. Some of the best sources of dietary fiber are beans and peas. Additional sources of dietary fiber include other vegetables, fruits, whole grains, and nuts. Dietary fiber that occurs naturally in foods may help reduce the risk of cardiovascular disease, obesity, and type 2 diabetes. The Adequate Intake (AI) for fiber is 14 g per 1,000 calories or 25 g per day for women and 38 g per day for men.

Sugars

The major sources of added sugars in the diet are soda, energy drinks, and sports drinks, grain-based desserts, sugar-sweetened fruit drinks, dairy-based desserts and candy. Most of those products supply calories, but few or no essential nutrients and no dietary fiber. Reducing the consumption of these sources of added sugars will lower the calorie content of the diet, without compromising its nutritional adequacy.

Beans and Peas are Unique Foods

Beans and peas are the mature forms of legumes. They include kidney beans, pinto beans, black beans, garbanzo beans (chickpeas), lima beans, black-eyed peas, split peas, and lentils. Beans and peas are excellent sources of protein. They are excellent sources of dietary fiber and nutrients such as potassium and folate, which also are found in other vegetables. Because of their high nutrient content, beans and peas may be considered both as a vegetable and as a protein food. Green peas and green (string) beans are not considered to be "Beans and Peas." Green beans are grouped with other vegetables such as onions, lettuce, celery, and cabbage because their nutrient content is similar to those foods.

Chapter 4

Fats-Oils-Fat Replacers-Additives

Fats

Currently, Americans derive about 36% of calories from fat which is more than the 30% maximum recommended by a number of health organizations. The easiest method to decrease the percentage of intake calories is to substitute low-fat foods for high-fat foods. However, it is easier said than done, because high fat foods taste so good. One of the characteristics of fat is that it acts as a flavor intensifier and with reduced fat, the flavor suffers. Fat provides a pleasant mouthfeel which is hard to replace with fat substitutes. People find a low-fat diet bland and have difficulty to maintain it over a period of time.

Fat is not the enemy, calories are.

To function properly, our body needs fat. It maintains cell membranes, absorbs vitamins, carries food flavors and provides energy. It is difficult to realize the huge amount of fat that we consume, as we don't consume it in pure form, instead, we consume fat in meat, cheese, milk, pizza, fries, snacks etc. Vegetables, fruits, diet soda, skim milk and low fat dairy products are low in fat but rank at the bottom of the preferred list of foods most people like to consume. A fat rich snack is great food for a hiker embarking on 6 months long Appalachian trail hike from Georgia to Maine, but for most people cutting down on fat results in weight loss and improvement of health.

Calorie Equivalent of High Energy Products	
Carbohydrates	4 cal/g
Protein	4 cal/g
Alcohol	7 cal/g
Fat	9 cal/g

Fats can be classified as;

- Saturated - found mainly in animals (meat and poultry, butter, cheese and milk products). The exceptions are cocoa butter, coconut oil and palm oil. Saturated fats are solid at room temperature: lard, butter, suet. Saturated fats are "bad fats."
- Monounsaturated fat - found in plants, but also in animals. Olive, canola and peanut oil. These are "good fats."
- Polyunsaturated fat - plants. Corn, olive, canola, peanut, sunflower, soybean, safflower, cotton seed. Also present in fish. These are "good fats."

Most fats contain a proportion of each of the three basic types of fat, but are named according to the dominating type. There is also *trans* fat (made from partially hydrogenated vegetable oils-stick margarine, shortening). Trans fats may significantly increase the risk of coronary heart disease and are considered "bad fats."

Increasing the proportion of *polyunsaturated and monounsaturated* fats *(good fats)* plays a protective role against chronic heart disease (CHD). *Saturated fats (bad fats)* tend to increase levels of LDL (low-density-lipoproteins) cholesterol which is associated with promoting cardiovascular disease. The strongest evidence about the benefits of polyunsaturated fat comes from the fact that Eskimos are on a high fat fish diet, yet are less prone to heart disease than other ethnic groups that consume regular foods. Depending on their structure and composition fats can be classified as:

- Solid fats - these fats are solid at room temperature and high in saturated fatty acids. The fats in meat, poultry, and eggs are considered solid fats. Any significant consumption of those fats should be avoided as they increase cholesterol levels and may lead to cardiovascular diseases. For those reasons meat and poultry should be consumed in lean forms to decrease the intake of solid fats.

- Oils - fats which are liquid at room temperature and low in saturated fatty acids. *Oils are generally much healthier* and contain less saturated acids. The fats in seafood, nuts, and seeds are considered oils. The exceptions are coconut oil and palm oils which are highly saturated. Natural oils: soybean, canola, olive, peanut, cottonseed, sunflower, corn, palm (50% saturated), coconut (92% saturated).

Lard

Lard has always been an important cooking and baking staple in cultures where pork is an important dietary item, the fat of pigs often being as valuable a product as their meat. During the 19th century, lard was used in a similar fashion as butter in North America and many European nations. Lard was also held at the same level of popularity as butter in the early 20th century and was widely used as a substitute for butter during World War II. Toward the late 20th century, lard began to be regarded as less healthy than vegetable oils (such as olive and sunflower oil) because of its high saturated fatty acid and cholesterol content.

However, despite its reputation, *lard has less saturated fat, more unsaturated fat, and less cholesterol than an equal amount of butter by weight.* Unlike many margarines and vegetable shortenings, unhydrogenated lard contains no trans fat (the consumption of trans fats increases the risk of coronary heart disease). It has also been regarded as a "poverty food". Many restaurants in the western nations have eliminated the use of lard in their kitchens *because of the religious and health-related dietary restrictions of many of their customers.* Many industrial bakers substitute beef tallow for lard in order to compensate for the lack of mouthfeel in many baked goods and to free their food products from pork-based dietary restrictions.

However, in the 1990's and early 2000's, the unique culinary properties of lard became widely recognized by chefs and bakers, leading to a partial rehabilitation of this fat among professionals. This trend has been partially driven by negative publicity about the trans fat content of the partially hydrogenated vegetable oils in vegetable shortening.

Lard is one of the few edible oils with a relatively high smoke point, attributable to its high saturated fatty acids content. Pure lard is especially useful for cooking since *it produces little smoke when heated* and has a distinct taste when combined with other foods. Many chefs and bakers deem lard a superior cooking fat over shortening because of lard's range of applications and taste. Because of the relatively large fat crystals found in lard, it is extremely effective as a shortening in baking. Pie crusts made with lard tend to be more flaky than those made with butter. Many cooks employ both types of fat in their pastries to combine the shortening properties of lard with the flavor of butter.

Butter consists mostly of *saturated fat* and is a significant source of dietary cholesterol. For these reasons, butter has been generally considered to be a contributor to health problems, especially heart disease. For many years, vegetable margarine was recommended as a substitute, since it is an unsaturated fat and contains little or no cholesterol. Although in recent decades it has become accepted that the trans fats contained in partially hydrogenated oils used in typical margarines significantly raise undesirable LDL cholesterol levels as well.

A higher proportion of monounsaturated fats in the diet is linked with a reduction in the risk of coronary heart disease. This is significant because olive oil is considerably rich in monounsaturated fats, most notably oleic acid. *Lard contains more monounsaturated fats than butter or tallow.* Lard is one of the great products that is largely misunderstood today and has developed an undeserving reputation as an unhealthy product. To set the record straight we have listed some USDA data and statistics about lard and other animal fats. The conclusion is simple: *pork fat (lard) is much heathier than butter or tallow (beef or sheep fat).* Save on butter, eat more lard and you will live longer.

Comparative properties of common cooking fats per 100 g (3.5 oz)						
	Total Fat	Saturated Fat	Monoun-saturated Fat	Polyun-saturated Fat	Protein	Choles-terol
Vegetable shortening	71 g	23 g	8 g	37 g	0 g	0
Olive Oil	100 g	14 g	**73 g**	11 g	0 g	0
Butter	81 g	**51 g**	21 g	3 g	1 g	**215** mg
Tallow	100 g	50 g	42 g	4 g	0 g	109 mg
Lard	100 g	39 g	**45 g**	11 g	0 g	95 mg

Lard is rendered (heat melted) pork fat.
Tallow is a rendered suet.
Suet is a fresh beef or sheep fat.   *Source: USDA Nutrient database.*

Oils

The polyunsaturated fat (PUFA) and monounsaturated fat (MUFA) are known to lower the risk of heart disease. The Omega-6 (nuts, seeds, vegetable oils, sunflower, safflower, soybean oil) and Omega-3 (fatty fish, shell fish, flax seeds, walnuts, canola) oils are polyunsaturated fats and are essential for heart and brain function. All latest research demonstrates that *polyunsaturated fat* provides most benefits in decreasing the risk of coronary heart disease. Vegetable oil can be used to replace animal fat in processed meats.

Comparative properties of common cooking oils per 1 Tbsp (14g)				
	Total Fat	Saturated Fat	Monounsaturated Fat	Polyunsaturated Fat
Canola	14 g	1.0 g	8.0 g	4.0 g
Corn	14 g	2.0 g	4.0 g	8.0 g
Olive	14 g	2.0 g	10.0 g	1.5 g
Soy	14 g	2.2 g	3.20 g	8.0 g
Sunflower	14 g	1.5 g	3.0 g	9.0 g
Peanut	14 g	2.5 g	6.0 g	5.0 g
None of the oils contain trans fat, sodium, protein or cholesterol.				

The data in the above tables demonstrate that all vegetable oils are superior to animal fats. Although olive oil costs on average 3 times more than canola, both oils display similar characteristics. Besides being the richest source of energy, fats perform many important functions:

- Transport fat-soluble vitamins (A,D,E and K) and are a source of essential fatty acids.
- Provide a pleasant mouthfeel.
- Affect appearance, color and texture.
- Intensify flavor.

Dietary Recommendations

- Fats should not account for more than 30% of total calories.
- Saturated fats should make up less of 10% of calories.
- Monounsaturated fats should make up 10-20% of calories from fat.

As a food ingredient in meat products, fat plays an important role because it provides flavor, texture and a pleasant mouthfeel. Unfortunately it goes "rancid" (deterioration of flavor) in meat products that are frozen for extended periods of time. The removal of fat in food products results in products with inferior texture. The challenge is to produce sausages that will conform to customer expectations. Low fat sausages must feel like regular sausages so some clever substituting must be implemented. A sausage made from lean meat only will not have the right texture and mouthfeel so these characteristics must be addressed. A good example is hamburger that has been greatly over-cooked, its texture is gone and the mouthfeel is inferior, it is like eating a piece of bread crumbs. To make a sausage with little fat and to preserve its good mouthfeel we have to make it juicier and this is accomplished by increasing its water content. This extra water is mixed with ingredients that bind it, otherwise water will leak out and that will not look appetizing.

In 1994 in the USA, the Nutrition Labeling and Education Act was introduced which made it mandatory to list on product labels the amount of calories from fat in addition to the total amount of calories present.

Fat Labeling

Fat-free: less than 0.5 g fat/serving and /reference amount.
Low-fat: 3 g or less fat/serving size.
Reduced or less fat: 25% or less fat/serving than regular (full fat) product.
Percent fat-free: This defines how many calories come from fat, for example, 95% fat free means that only 5% of calories come from fat.

For meat, poultry, seafood and game meats:

Lean: less than 10 g fat, 4.5 g or less saturated fat and less than 95 mg cholesterol/serving and /100 g.
Extra Lean: less than 5 g fat, less than 2 g saturated fat and less than 95 mg cholesterol/serving and/100 g.

Calories

Calorie-free: less than 5 calories/serving and reference amount.
Low-calorie: 40 or less calories/reference serving size.
Reduced or fewer calories: 25% or less calories/serving than regular product.
Light: 1/3 fewer calories or 1/2 the fat of the reference food. If the food derives 50% or more of its calories from fat, the fat must be reduced by 50%.

Fat Replacers

Fat replacers, also called fat substitutes, fat mimetics, fat extenders, and fat analogues are ingredients that provide some or all of the functions of fat, *yet introduce fewer calories than fat.* The main bulk of fat replacers is not used by the meat industry, but by general foods, as fat replacers were originally designed for making low fat ice creams, yogurts, cheese cakes, cheeses, spreads, sauces, salad dressings, potato chips and other snacks. Such fat replacers had to exactly mimic characteristics and sensory qualities of the products that were very familiar to a customer. There is not one universal fat replacer that is ideal for all uses, furthermore, most replacers contain calories as well, although to a smaller degree than regular fat.

There are many commercially produced fat replacers in the USA and Europe, but they are available in large quantities to *large producers only.* Online distributors of sausage equipment and supplies keep on adding new products, for example The Sausage Maker Inc., is offering a fat replacer blend that consists of microcrystalline cellulose, Konjac gum and xantham gum. However, the largest selection of fat replacers is offered by online distributors of baking supplies as the majority of fat replacers are used in baking and general cooking. The Links of Interest section of the book provides some useful addresses. To cover the subject thoroughly we mention all types of fat replacers that are on the market, even those which are hard to obtain by a hobbyist. However, the recipes include only those fat replacers that are commonly obtainable. Fat replacers can be classified into three categories:

◊   *Carbohydrate-based*

◊   *Protein-based*

◊   *Fat-based*

Carbohydrate-Based Fat Replacers

Carbohydrate-based fat replacers are derived from starches, wood, plant roots, fruits and seaweeds. They are able to hold substantial amounts of water and by forming gels, mimic some of the sensory and textural characteristics of fat. Being carbohydrates, they can theoretically provide up to 4 cal/g, but, because they are usually mixed with water they provide only 1 to 2 cal/g. Cellulose, which mimics fat sensory qualities very well, provides 0 calories as its particles are too large to be absorbed and digested by our intestinal tract.

The most popular carbohydrate-based fat replacers are:

- Starch and starch derived products.
- Starch sugars - dextrins and maltodextrins.
- Gums.
- Pectin
- Cellulose.
- Fiber.

Starch and Starch Derived Products

Starch is the most common carbohydrate in the human diet and is contained in many staple foods, including meat products. Both cost and functionality are primary reasons for its popularity. The major sources of starch worldwide are corn, wheat, potato and tapioca. Ready to eat foods containing starch are bread, pancakes, cereals, noodles, pasta, porridge and tortilla. All starches are good thickeners and are used to thicken soups or gravies. The main advantage that cornstarch offers is that it has a neutral flavor. Another advantage is that unlike flour-thickened sauces it doesn't separate when frozen. Starch has the ability to swell and take on water. The swelling of the starch occurs during the heating stage. A combination of *starch and carrageenan* produces a synergistic effect. Most commercial fat replacers derived from starch carry label designations of either *modified starch, dextrin or maltodextrin.*

Modified starch

Properties of starch can be altered by physical, enzymatical or chemical processes to obtain a modified starch that will be more suitable for a particular application. Modified starches are used in practically all starch applications, such as in food products as a thickening agent, stabilizer or emulsifier; in pharmaceuticals as a disintegrant; or in paper as a binder. Modified starches remain stable at many temperatures, allowing foods to be frozen and then thawed without losing texture and taste. Because of that modified starches are used in frozen and instant foods. A suitably-modified starch is used as a fat substitute for low-fat versions of traditionally fatty foods, e.g., reduced-fat hard salami having about 1/3 the usual fat content.

When using corn starch, first mix it with cold water (or another liquid) until it forms a smooth paste, then add it to whatever is being thickened. Adding starch directly into the cooking food will form lumps that are then difficult to mash out. A good idea is to put starch and cold water into a jar with a screw on lid and vigorously shake the sealed jar until the solution is smooth. This method can be applied to a flour/water mixture. It allows greater control when slowly adding it to a soup, sauce, or gravy.

Potato starch is a very refined starch extracted from potatoes. The cells of the root tubers of the potato plant contain starch grains. To extract the starch, the potatoes are crushed; and the starch grains are released from the mashed potatoes. The starch is then washed out and dried to powder. Potato starch and its derivatives are used in noodles, potato chips, *sausages*, bakery cream and instant soups and sauces, in gluten-free recipes in kosher foods for Passover and in Asian cuisine. The superior water binding of potato starches improves moisture retention and increases yield while providing juiciness in processed meats.

Is Potato Starch the Same as Potato Flour?

Potato starch	Potato Flour
A very fine flour, neutral taste, made by removing potato skin, then made into a watery slurry, and dehydrated to form potato starch powder. It is not cooked and it *does not absorb much water, unless it is heated.* When heated with liquid, it will make an excellent sauce or gravy.	Potato flour is made from the potato, including the skin, and it is cooked. It has a slight potato flavor. Potato flour contains protein, the starch does not. It can absorb large amounts of liquid. Adding small amounts of potato flour (2%) to a sausage mix helps to increase the water holding capacity and hold the product together.

In food applications a starch is twice as effective as the flour it was made from.

100 g serving	Protein (g)	Fat (g)	Carbohy-drates (g)	Salt (mg)	Energy (cal)	Choles-terol (mg)
Potato flour	8.82	1.47	79.4	0	353	0
Potato starch	0	0	83.3	0	333	0
						Source: Bob's Red Mill Natural Foods

Flours

Adding 2-3% of potato flour to minced meat was widely practiced in the past and it offered many advantages. It made sausages cheaper

what was important after the II World War ended and it improved the
mouthfeel of low fat products.

Nutritional Values of Different Flours (100 g serving)						
Name	Protein (g)	Fat (g)	Carbo-hydrates (g)	Salt (mg)	Fiber (g)	Cal-ories (cal)
Soy, full-fat	34.54	20.65	35.19	13	9.6	436
Soy, low-fat	45.51	8.90	34.93	9	16.0	375
Soy, de-fatted	47.01	1.22	38.37	20	17.5	330
Wheat, whole grain	13.21	2.50	71.97	2	10.7	340
Wheat, white,	10.33	0.98	76.31	2	2.7	364
Potato	6.90	0.34	83.10	55	5.9	357
Rice, white	5.95	1.42	80.13	0	2.4	366
Corn, whole grain, white	6.93	3.86	76.85	5	7.3	361
Semolina	12.68	1.05	72.83	1	3.9	360
Chickpea (besan)	22.39	6.69	57.82	64	10.8	387
Source: USDA Nutrient database						

From the above data it is conclusive that de-fatted soy flour clearly is
the nutritional winner. It contains the most protein and dietary fiber,
and it is the lowest in calories. The reason that its use in meat products
is not widespread is that it has a little "beany" flavor. Its derivative
- Textured Vegetable Protein is used in processed meats as it has a
neutral flavor, particle size similar to minced meat and its texture and
bite resemble those of real meat.

Semolina is the coarsely ground endosperm of durum, a hard
spring wheat with a high-gluten content and golden color. It is hard,
granular and resembles sugar. Semolina is usually enriched and is used
to make couscous and pasta products such as spaghetti, vermicelli,
macaroni and lasagna noodles. Except for some specialty products,
breads are seldom made with semolina. Durum wheat is considered
the gold standard for pasta production; the wheat kernel's density and
high protein and gluten content result in firm pasta with a consistent
cooking quality and golden color. Semolina has been used as a filler in
many European sausages, for example Polish Semolina Liver Sausage.

Starch Sugars - Dextrins and Maltodextrins

Starch can be hydrolyzed into simpler carbohydrates known as *dextrins* by acids, various enzymes, or a combination of the two. The extent of conversion is typically quantified by dextrose equivalent (DE), which is roughly the fraction of the glycosidic bonds in starch that have been broken. These starch sugars include:

- *Dextrose* (DE 100), commercial glucose, prepared by the complete hydrolysis of starch. This is the simplest form of sugar and is the preferred sugar for making fermented sausages (salami) as bacteria can feed on them without a delay. Dextrins provide 4 cal/g of energy.
- Various glucose syrup / *corn syrups* (DE 30–70), viscous solutions used as sweeteners and thickeners in many kinds of processed foods.
- *Maltodextrin*, a lightly hydrolyzed (DE 10–20) starch product used as a bland-tasting filler and thickener.

Dextrose equivalent (DE) is the relative sweetness of sugars, *compared to dextrose*, both expressed as a percentage. Dextrose is about 70% as sweet as common sugar (sucrose). For example, a maltodextrin with a DE of 10 would be 10% as sweet as dextrose (DE = 100), while sucrose, with a DE of 120, would be 1.2 times as sweet as dextrose. For solutions made from starch, it is an estimate of the percentage reducing sugars present in the total starch product.

Dextrose Equivalent (DE) of Different Carbohydrates	
Starch	0
Dextrins	1 - 11
Maltodextrins	3 - 20
Dextrose (glucose)	100
Sucrose (sugar)	120

Maltodextrins

Maltodextrin is produced by *cooking the starch*, also known as hydrolysis of starch. During the cooking process, natural enzymes and acids break down the starch further. The result is easy to digest white powder that contains around four calories per gram and very small amounts of fat, protein, fiber and carbohydrates. In the USA, maltodextrin is generally made from corn, potato or rice, while in Europe, wheat is commonly used. It can be made from tapioca as well. Malto-dextrin has a dextrose equivalent (DE) of less than 20 and it exhibits an excellent ability to mimic the functional properties of fat and oil. For solutions made from starch, DE is an estimate of the percentage reducing sugars present in the total starch product. Low DE maltodex-trin add creaminess, and a fatty mouthfeel to processed meats. The higher the DE, the stickier the maltodextrin will be. As the DE increases, the viscosity decreases and the maltodextrins behave more like a corn syrup solid. Very high DE maltodextrin will become almost solid and will make the sausage too hard.

Maltodextrin has wide range of applications as a food additive. It is usually sweet or without any flavor. *Maltodextrin has the property of attracting water from the environment.* The characteristic of malto-dextrin varies to some extent depending on the source of starch, i.e., whether it is produced from rice, wheat, corn or potato. Maltodextrin can also be added to protein drinks to increase the amount of calo-ries. It is used in many energy drinks for being easily digestible. After heavy exercise or any other strenuous activity, if maltodextrin is taken along with other nutrients, it speeds up the transportation of nutrients to the muscle tissues and cells. Because of this, it is widely used by bodybuilders who take it along with whey protein. Maltodextrins are all natural food ingredients that have not been chemically modified.

The U.S. Food and Drug Administration classifies potato starch maltodextrin as a direct food ingredient. *There are no limits to the concentrations of maltodextrins allowed in foods.* As other carbohydrates they provide 4 cal/g. However, when used as fat replacements, they are mixed with a water to maltodextrin ratio of 3:1, which reduces the calories further to 1 cal/g.

1 Maltodextrin + 3 Water = 4 Fat

One part of a low DE (dextrose equivalent) maltodextrin and three parts of water can often replace four parts of fat or oil. This can reduce the calories originally provided by fat to as little as 11%. However, it must be noted that in very few cases can all of the fat or oil in a formu-lation be substituted by low DE maltodextrins without changing the texture and flavor characteristics of the food substantially.

Preparing maltodextrin

Maltodextrins are very easy to dissolve in cold water and are clear in solution. Making maltodextrin gel is quite easy: to make 20% maltodextrin gel, place 400 ml (400 g) of cold tap water in a blender and apply low speed. Slowly add 100 g of maltodextrin until a smooth, low viscosity solution is obtained. After cooling in a refrigerator, a white spreadable gel is obtained. Maltodextrin gels display fat-like characteristics, and are thermoreversible, which means that as temperature changes, they melt and solidify again without loss of quality. Low DE maltodextrins can be added directly as powders or be prepared as gels. It is easier to calculate the amount of powder and water when making gel as a separate processing step. Low DE maltodextrins provide some characteristics of fat and are well suited for making low fat sausages:

- Add viscosity. Viscosity describes a fluid's internal resistance to flow and may be thought of as a measure of fluid friction. Thus, water is "thin", having a lower viscosity, while honey is "thick", having a higher viscosity.
- Don't contribute sweetness.
- Retain moisture.
- Contribute to good texture.
- Reduce calories.

Maltodextrins can be used alone or in combination with other fat replacers such as starches and gums. This can often bring synergistic results (the combined action of all components is stronger than if the components were used alone). Maltrodextrin are often used as fat replacers in meat products such as hamburgers and frankfurters. Corn derived maltodextrins with DE from 4 to 8 are recommended for low fat mayonnaise, *sausages*, confectionery creams, and ice cream.
Note: keep in mind that many maltodextrins that are sold on the internet do not gel.

Gums

Gums, technically referred to as hydrocolloids, originate from different sources. They can immobilize water and contribute viscosity. Two gums that are pretty familiar are gelatin and corn starch. If you look at processed food, you see all sorts of other gums like carrageenan, xanthan gum, cellulose gum, locust bean gum, gum arabic, agar, and so on. The value of gums is not as a fat replacer but as a thickener which can combine with water and create gel. Gums fulfil several functions in food products:

1. They thicken things - ice cream, syrups.
2. They emulsify things - mixed liquids stay together without separating.

3. They change the texture - a gum will make something thicker.
4. They stabilize crystals - a gum might help prevent sugar or ice from crystallizing.
5. They help to reduce cooking loss which results in a higher yield and more succulent product.

The most popular carbohydrate-based fat replacers are:

- Agar
- Alginate
- Carrageenan
- Gum Arabic
- Guar Gum
- Locust Bean Gum
- Konjac Gum
- Xantham Gum

While at first glimpse, such exotic names may discourage consumers from ever considering such products, the truth is that they are natural products which we consume all the time. The are added to ice creams, puddings, sauces and processed foods that require a creamy texture. Without gums sugar crystals will separate from ice cream and many products would turn into a watery mess.

We take for granted that manufactured foods should always look good and taste well, but there is more to that than meets the eye. Food products are made in one location, then stored in a different one, and then transported many miles to a supermarket where they will sit on a shelf for some time. Gums hold those products together. The reason that we dedicate so much space to gums is that they become more popular every day. Originally, only food technologists understood the subject and they were the ones to add them into food products. Today gums are commonly available and used in general cooking. For example traditional jams were made by stirring the mixture of fruit and sugar for hours until it lost enough moisture to gel. Pectin shortens the process to minutes and the product looks better and has a better consistency.

Let's make something clear-an occasional cook or a sausage maker does not need to use things like carrageenan, Konjac flour or xanthan gum because the sausage needs a superior texture. Commercial producers need to use gums, as their products, for example thinly sliced and packaged ham, must hold its shape together for a long time. A hobbyist can also use less expensive things like gelatin, flour, eggs or protein concentrate, because the time between making the product and consumption is usually very short. Nevertheless, the information presented in this chapter, will enable the reader to have a better understanding of the subject and will make it easier to further expand his knowledge by reading more technical books.

Agar - is made from the same family of red seaweeds as carrageenan. Agar is a natural *vegetable gelatin counterpart*. White and semi-translucent, it is sold in packages as washed and dried strips or in powdered form. Agar is approximately 80% fiber and is a very popular product in Asia. It can be used as an addition or as a replacement to pectin in jams and marmalades, as a substitute to gelatin for its superior gelling properties, and as a strengthening ingredient in souffles and custards. Agar is rather expensive.

Alginate - alginic acid, also called algin or alginate, is an anionic polysaccharide distributed widely in the cell walls of brown algae, where it, through binding water, forms a viscous gum. In extracted form it absorbs water quickly; *it is capable of absorbing 200-300 times its own weight in water.* The chemical compound sodium alginate is the sodium salt of alginic acid. Sodium alginate is a flavorless gum, used to increase viscosity and to act as an emulsifier.

Carrageenan is a natural extract from red seaweeds used in processed foods for stabilization, thickening, and gelation. During the heating process carrageenan can absorb plenty of water and trap it inside. This results in a higher cooking yield and less purge during storage. About 0.01% (1 g per kg of meat) can increase the yield of the finished product up to 8%. Usually, up to 1.0% (10 g/kg) of carrageenan is added to processed meats. Carrageenan forms a solid gel during cooling and improves sliceability. Many vegetarians use carrageenan in place of products like gelatin, since it is 100% vegetarian.

There are three types of carrageenan employed in the food industry:
- Kappa - meat products, very strong gel. It is currently the most used type of carrageenan in low fat sausages.
- Iota - meat products, medium strong gel.
- Lambda - sauces and dressings. Does not gel.

Kappa carrageenan gels better in the presence of alkali agents such as potassium chloride (KCL). Enough potassium chloride is usually added to the carrageenan blend to create a strong gel. Potassium chloride is the same salt that is added to Morton's Low Salt, at 50% level, thus the salt itself promotes the development of strong gel. In addition milk protein is a strong promoter of carrageenan gels. Adding caseinate (milk protein) or non-fat dry milk will assist in the development of strong carrageenan gel. Kappa and Iota carrageenan are only partially cold water soluble and need to be heated for full activation. Lambda carrageenan is fully cold water soluble.

Gum Arabic

Gum arabic is the hardened sap of the Acacia senegal tree, which is found in the swath of arid lands extending from Senegal on the west coast of Africa all the way to Pakistan and India. It's a natural emulsifier, which means that it can keep together substances which normally would not mix well. Pharmaceutical companies use it to keep medicines from separating into their different ingredients, and a dab of gum arabic makes newspaper ink more cohesive and permanent. Coca-Cola uses gum arabic to keep the sugar from precipitating to the bottom of its sodas. Gum arabic is tasteless and edible. As a food additive, it has been extensively tested and is considered to be one of the safest additives for human consumption.

Gum arabic has many non-food uses as well. It is used in paints, inks, glues, printing, cosmetics, photography, incense cones, shoe polish, postage stamps, cigarette paper adhesive, and pyrotechnic operations. In beverages, gum arabic helps citrus and other oil-based flavors remain evenly suspended in water. Gum arabic can be completely dissolved in its own volume of water. In confectionery, glazes and artificial whipped creams, gum arabic keeps flavor oils and fats uniformly distributed, retards crystallization of sugar, thickens chewing gums and jellies, and gives soft candies a desirable mouth feel. In cough drops and lozenges, gum arabic soothes irritated mucous membranes. Many dry-packaged products, such as instant drinks, dessert mixes and soup bases, use it to enhance the shelf life of flavors. The gum is used in soft drink syrups, chocolate candies, gummy candies, and marshmallows. Like gelatin and carrageenan, gum arabic can be used to bind food substances as well as to smoothen textures, or to hold flavoring.

Guar gum - made from the seeds of a plant that grows in India and Pakistan. When placed in contact with water, guar gum will gel even at low concentrations (1% to 2%). Guar gum has been used for centuries as a thickening agent for foods and pharmaceuticals.

Locust bean gum - locust bean gum, also known as carob gum, carob bean gum, and carobin is a galactomannan vegetable gum extracted from the seeds of the Carob tree, mostly found in the Mediterranean. The taste of locust bean powder is similar to ground cocoa powder, but it contains less fat and calories than cocoa. It is dispersible in either hot or cold water. Locust bean gum is used in food products, cosmetics and other products.

Note: guar gum and *locust bean gum* belong to a group of gums that are known as *Galactomannans.*

Both gums are excellent thickeners and are added to low fat products to bind water. They are used in sausages to soften the texture and to facilitate stuffing. The clear advantage of both gums is that they can hold water at high temperatures, for example during the baking process, which results in a better product.

Xanthan Gum

Xanthan gum is produced by *fermentation* of glucose, sucrose (corn sugar), or lactose by bacteria. During fermentation, a strain of bacteria (*Xanthomonas campestris*) turns sugar into a colorless slime called xanthan gum. Xanthan gum is most often found in salad dressings and sauces. It helps to prevent oil separation by stabilizing the emulsion, although it is not an emulsifier. Xanthan gum also helps suspend solid particles, such as spices. Also used in frozen foods and beverages, xanthan gum helps create the pleasant texture in many ice creams, along with guar gum and locust bean gum Xanthan gum is soluble in cold water but in order to eliminate lumps, it should be well agitated.

Xanthan gum does not gelatinize when used alone, but it can form gel at any pH when used with konjac gum. At a ratio of 3 (xanthan) : 2 (konjac) the strongest gel is obtained. The gel is thermo-reversible: it is in solid state at temperatures below 40° C (104° F), but it will be in a semi-solid or liquid state at temperatures of 50° C (122° F) or above. When the temperature drops back to the ambient temperature <40° C (<122° F), it will resume the solid state.

Gellan Gum

Gellan gum is a high molecular weight polysaccharide (i.e., complex sugar) gum produced as a fermentation product by a pure culture of the microbe *Sphingomonas elodea*. Gellan gum is a food additive that acts as a thickening or gelling agent, and can produce gel textures in food products ranging from hard and brittle to fluid. Gellan is used in bakery fillings, confections, dairy products, dessert gels, frostings, glazes, jams and jellies, low-fat spreads, and other products.

Konjac Gum

Konjac flour also called konjac gum or konjac glucomannan is produced from the konjac plant root and can form meltable or heat stable gels. Konjac flour is rich in soluble fiber, but does not contain starch or sugar so it does not have calories. It is also gluten free. Its thickening power is 10 times greater than cornstarch. Konjac has the highest water holding capacity of any soluble fiber-up to 100 times its own water weight. One part of glucomannan can absorb 50 parts of liquid. About one teaspoon of konjac flour can gel about one cup of liquid, which may be water, meat stock or wine. Konjac powder can be used as a thickener for smooth gravies, sauces, glazes, soups, stews and casseroles. Konjac interacts synergistically with carrageenan, xanthan gum, locust bean gum. Konjac interacts with most starches increasing viscosity and allowing improvement of texture.

As a gelling agent, konjac exhibits *the unique ability to form thermo-reversible and thermo-irreversible gels under different conditions:*

- Reversible gum- konjac mixed with xanthan gum.
- Non-reversible gum-when heated at a pH of 9-10.

With addition of a mild alkali such as calcium hydroxide, Konjac will set to a strong, elastic and thermo-irreversible gel. This gel will remain stable even when heated to 100° C and above. Konjac will form a reversible gel when it is mixed with xanthan gum. Due to the thermo-irreversible property of the konjac gum, it has become popular to make a great variety of foods such as konjac cake, konjac noodles, and *foods for vegetarians.*

Preparing Konjac gel:

If konjac flour is added directly to food it may create lumps. Konjac powder thickens slowly when mixed with cold water, but quickly thickens when it's heated. Mix konjac flour with cold water or other liquid first, stirring often until fully dissolved. Then add konjac flour to a hot liquid or food that is cooking. It has no taste of its own so it inherits the flavor of the product. Konjac flour can be mixed with other gums or starches. If you have not used konjac powder as a thickening agent before, it is best to experiment with it by beginning with lesser amounts, and adding as necessary until the desired consistency is reached. The addition of 0.02-0.03% konjac to 1% xanthan gum will raise its viscosity by 2-3 times under heating. Konjac is usually added at 0.25-0.50%.

Gum Blends

It is often desirable to use a combination of gums to create a synergistic effect. Synergy means that a combined effect of two or more ingredients is greater than it would be expected from the additive combination of each ingredient. In this case the viscosity or gel strength will be greater if the following combinations are created:

- Xantham gum with guar gum.
- Xantham gum with bean gum.
- Konjac with carrageenan.
- Konjac with xanthan.

The above combinations may be used at a one-to-one ratio with each other. The synergistic effect is also present when a gum is combined with starch.

- Konjac with starch.
- Carrageenan with starch.

Adding modified starch and gum to food produces a similar effect. However, modified starch is less expensive than a gum. Adding starch to ground meat is a universally accepted method. On the other hand 1 part of gum will produce a similar effect as 10 parts of starch, so the result balances out. Using gum is more crucial in fine products like yoghurt or pie filling where the change in flavor and mouthfeel is easy to notice. Synergistic results of combining different gums are based on liquid gels. Those combinations may behave differently when added to ground meat. They will definitely bind water and create gels, but they may exhibit a weaker synergistic effect. The gums most often used in processed meats are: *carrageenan, xanthan and konjac.*

Pectin

Anybody who has recently made jams or jellies at home is familiar with pectin. Powdered or liquid pectin can be found in every supermarket. In the past jellied products were made by manually stirring fruit pulp until enough moisture was removed in order for the product to gel. Today pectin is added and the cooking process is cut down to a minute. The cooking loss is smaller and the product has more natural color. Pectin occurs in varying accounts in all plants and fruits. It is not found in animal tissues. The skins, cores, and peels are a particularly rich source of pectin. Pectin is one of the most versatile stabilizers available. Its gelling, thickening and stabilizing attributes makes it an essential additive not only in jams and jellies but in the production of many other food products, as well as in pharmaceutical and medical applications. The FDA recognizes pectin as GRAS (generally recognized as safe). It may be used in all non-standardized foods. Commercially prepared pectin is a natural and safe product. It is an extract from apples or citrus fruits and being tasteless it doesn't change the flavor of the food it is added to. Use of pectin offers many advantages:

- Drastically shortens cooking time. This results in more product as there is lesser amount of evaporated water. These two advantages greatly offset the initial cost of pectin.
- Allows for making jellied products from fruits that are pectin poor. Juice from such fruits will not produce jelly, unless a commercial pectin is added.
- The final product displays a much lighter color as due to a shorter cooking process, there is no time for sugar to caramelize.
- Some pectins allow for using a small amount to no sugar.

Although pectin can easily be made at home from apples or citrus fruit, it needs a significant amount of sugar to produce a gel. This restricts its use to making sweet fillings, jams, ice cream and other spreadable products, but not sausages, which in most cases do not contain sugar. The average store-bought pectin is a '*high-methoxyl*' product that requires at least a 55% sugar concentration to gel properly and obviously cannot be used in sausages.

Low methoxy amidated pectin is a modified pectin that requires only a calcium source to gel and is used for making sugar free jams and jellies. Low methoxy amidated pectin creates a thermoreversible gel. This type of pectin is calcium sensitive, it will gel without the use of sugar, although the addition of sugar will not affect the gelling process. It is activated by monocalcium, which is a rock mineral calcium source. There is calcium in the pectin mix. Monocalcium is also a yeast nutrient for baking, in baking powder as an acidulant (for adding the necessary acidic quality) and also a mineral supplement, which is perfectly safe for human consumption. Along with sugar, Splenda can also be used with this low-methoxyl pectin. Low-methoxyl pectin is commonly used in a large number of sugar-free products such as: aspic, jams, yogurts, jelled pies, jelled milk puddings and candies, and jello. It will also gel fresh, canned, or frozen fruits and juices. *Low-methoxyl pectin does not require sugar and can be used with meat products.* Pectin is available from online suppliers, in health food stores and in local supermarkets.

In emulsified meat products, such as sausages, pates and meat spreads, pectin enables fat reduction and by *adding carrageenan in edition to pectin* a superior texture may be obtained. Hydrating in water prior to mixing with the meat would be best - use 1 part pectin to 5 parts water. In jam making you would take the total weight of the batch and multiply it by 5% to get your pectin usage amount.

Cellulose - *Food That Isn't Food*

Cellulose is the most abundant organic compound on Earth. About 33% of all plant matter is cellulose (the cellulose content of cotton is 90% and that of wood is 40–50%). It is found in fruits, vegetables, leaves, trunks and barks of plants. The following are the main cellulose products that are used in food industry:

- Microcrystalline cellulose
- Methyl cellulose
- Carbomethyl cellulose
- Methyl ethyl cellulose

Microcrystalline cellulose (cellulose gel) can function as an anticaking agent, bulking agent, foaming agent, glazing agent, carrier, emulsifier, stabilizer, and fat replacer. The most common form is used in vitamin pills or tablets. Many commercial microcrystalline cellulose products, for example Avicel by FMC BioPolymer, have been specifically developed for low fat applications. Those fat replacers are used in salad dressings, bakery products, dairy products, ice creams, spreads, cheeses and *processed meats*. The average amount used varies from 0.4 to 3%. This free flowing powder becomes slippery when wet. Microcrystalline cellulose is one of the ingredients of the fat replacer blend, that has been recently introduced online for the home market by The Sausage Maker, Buffalo, NY.

Methyl cellulose functions as a bulking agent, emulsifier, glazing agent, stabilizer and thickener. It is a white powder derived from cellulose. It dissolves in cold (but not in hot) water, forming a clear viscous solution or gel. It is a vegetarian alternative to the use of gelatin. It is sold under a variety of trade names and is used as a thickener and emulsifier in various food and cosmetic products, and also as a treatment of constipation. Like cellulose, it is not digestible, not toxic, and not allergenic. Methyl cellulose is also an important emulsifier, preventing the separation of two mixed liquids. When eaten, methyl cellulose is not absorbed by the intestines but passes through the digestive tract undisturbed. It attracts large amounts of water into the colon, producing a softer and bulkier stool. It is used to treat constipation, diverticulosis, hemorrhoids and irritable bowel syndrome. It should be taken with sufficient amounts of fluid to prevent dehydration.

Methyl ethyl cellulose functions as an emulsifier, foaming agent, stabilizer, and thickener. Used in many products including pasteurized products, ice-creams, cheeses, dairy products, batters, baked emulsions and spreads, breakfast cereals, and bakery goods etc.

Carbomethyl cellulose functions as a stabilizer and thickener. It is known for its excellent water retaining capacity. It is used in food science as a viscosity modifier or thickener, and to stabilize emulsions in various products including ice cream. It is also a constituent of many non-food products, such as toothpaste, laxatives, diet pills, water based paints, detergents, textile sizing and various paper products. It is used primarily because it has high viscosity, is non-toxic, and is non-allergenic. In laundry detergents it is used as a soil suspension polymer designed to deposit onto cotton and other cellulosic fabrics creating a negatively charged barrier to soils in the wash solution. Carbomethyl cellulose is used as a lubricant in non-volatile eye drops (artificial tears).

Protein-Based Fat Replacers

Protein based food replacers are made from whey, soy, legumes, protein or milk and egg protein, and can provide 1 cal/g - 4 cal/g of energy. They are easy to use and what is important, they are easily available from distributors of sausage making supplies on the Internet. They hold water well, provide a good mouthfeel and help to stabilize emulsions.

Sodium caseinate, a milk protein, is an excellent emulsifier that was commonly used to stabilize fat and water emulsions. Caseinate allowed to emulsify different types of fats from different animals. However, the price of milk proteins was increasing and soy proteins took over the dominant spot. Caseinate is about 90% protein and is added at 1-2% per kg of meat. Milk protein will lighten up the sausage and will make it slightly softer. It is added to meat batter as dry powder or as prepared emulsion. The emulsion is usually set at milk protein/fatty trimmings/water in the ratio of 1:5:5.

Non-fat dry milk is produced by removing fat and water from milk. Lactose (milk sugar), milk proteins, and milk minerals are present in the same relative proportions as in fresh milk. Non-fat dry milk powder is an extender that binds water very well and is often used in making sausages. Dry milk powder contains 50% lactose (sugar) and is used in fermented sausages as a source of food for lactic acid producing bacteria.

Ingredient (100 g serving)	Protein (g)	Fat (g)	Carbo-hydrates (g)	Salt (mg)	Energy (cal)
Non-fat dry milk	36.16	0.77	51.98	535	362
					Source: USDA Nutrient database

Dry milk powder greatly *improves the taste of low fat sausages*. Non fat dry milk powder is a good natural product and it does not affect the flavor of the product. It is added at about 3% and effectively binds water and emulsifies fats. Its action is very similar to that of soy protein concentrate.

Whey protein is made by drying liquid whey, which is a byproduct obtained during cheese making. Similarly to soy products, whey protein comes as:

- Whey protein concentrate, 30-89% protein.
- Whey protein isolate, 90% or more.

Whey is essential in the bodybuilding world today because of its ability to be digested very rapidly. It can be used for making processed meats, though it faces strong competition from soy products which are less expensive.

Egg is often added to sausages to increase binding ingredients. It should be noted that only the egg white possesses binding properties and egg yolk contributes to more fat and calories. One large egg weighs about 50 grams, of which the yolk accounts for around 20 grams and white for 30 grams.

Egg (100 g serving)	Protein (g)	Fat (g)	Carbohy-drates (g)	Salt (mg)	Energy (cal)	Choles-terol (mg)
Egg Whole, raw	12.56	9.51	0.72	142	143	372
Egg White, raw	10.90	0.17	0.73	166	52	0
					Source: USDA Nutrient database	

Egg white is often added (1-3%) to frankfurters with low meat content. It increases protein content, forms stable gel and contributes to a firm texture of the sausage. Powdered egg whites are also available and you generally mix 2 teaspoons of powder with 2 tablespoons of water for each white.

Ingredient (100 g serving)	Protein (g)	Fat (g)	Carbohy-drates (g)	Salt (mg)	Energy (cal)
Egg, white, dried	81.10	0.00	7.80	1280	382
				Source: USDA Nutrient database	

Ready to use liquid egg *whites* that are packaged in convenient size containers have just recently started to appear more frequently in supermarkets.

Ingredient (46 g serving)	Protein (g)	Fat (g)	Carbohy-drates (g)	Salt (mg)	Energy (cal)
Egg, white, liquid	5	0.00	0.00	75	25
				Source: Crystal Farms, All Whites®	

46 g corresponds to 3 Tbsp which is the white of 1 ½ large eggs. 1/3 cup is whites of 2 large eggs, 3/4 cup is whites of 4 large eggs.

Gelatin

Gelatin, technically classified as an hydrocolloid, is made from by-products of the meat and leather industry (bones, hides, pig skin). When mixed with water, it forms a semi-solid colloid gel. Gelatin forms a thermoreversible gel - it melts to a liquid when heated and solidifies when cooled again. Gelatin may be used as a stabilizer, or thickener in foods such as jams, yoghurt, cream cheese, and margarine. It is used in fat-reduced foods to mimic the mouthfeel of fat and to increase volume without adding calories. Combining gelatin with various hydrocolloids has resulted in new food additives that closely mimic the mouthfeel of fats.

Ingredient (100 g serving)	Protein (g)	Fat (g)	Carbo-hydrates (g)	Salt (mg)	Energy (cal)
Gelatin, dry powder	85.60	0.10	0.00	196	335
					Source: USDA Nutrient database

Powdered gelatin added at 1-2% helps to bind de-boned meat together or stuffing individual cuts of meat which are not perfectly lean. The strength of gelatin is measured in Bloom numbers (named after inventor of the system Oscar T. Bloom). The higher the Bloom number the stiffer the gelatin will be. Gelatin used in food usually runs from 125 Bloom to 250 Bloom; the unflavored gelatin sold in supermarkets is at the higher end of this range. Gelatin is widely used in meat products for decorative jellies for pates and for the coating and glazing of ham and other cooked meat products giving these products an attractive appearance. Gelatin, also improves the slicing characteristics of meats by penetrating and filling any cavities in the meat tissue, especially where the bone has been removed. This bonds individual meat pieces together which is of crucial importance when making molded hams.

Gelatin is also used in the manufacture of canned meat products where it serves to absorb the juices that are released during the retorting process. Gelatin, being almost pure protein, also enhances the protein balance of the final product. Gelatin is first dispersed in cold water and then completely dissolved in water at 122-140° F (50-60° C).

Note: traditionally made head cheese or meat jelly can be made without commercial gelatin as long as meats rich in collagen tissue are selected.

Soy proteins are firmly established as a protein of choice for making meat products. They are described in detail in Chapter 5.

Fat-Based Fat Replacers

Fat-based substitutes are produced by large companies and provide fewer or no calories at all. Fat replacers with 0 calories mimic the sensory characteristics of fat, but *pass through the body unabsorbed*. Their production involves chemical changes to fatty acids and they are costly to produce. Then, they face a long battle with the Food and Drug Administration for approval. For example Olestra (presently called Olean), manufactured by Proctor and Gamble, Cincinnati, OH. A label statement was required saying that olestra may induce abdominal cramping, loose stools, and inhibit the absorption of fat-soluble vitamins that are important to a human body. Those vitamins (A, D, E, and K) had to be added to olestra during the manufacturing process. In 2003, the FDA decided to remove the warning requirement from the label.

Commercial fat-based fat replacers: *Caprenin, Salatrim (Benefat), Bohenin, Neobee, Captrin, Captex, Olestra, Sorbestrin.*

Commercial Brand Name Fat Replacers

The majority of fat replacers are based on natural ingredients such as starches, sea weeds, or protein as they are almost guaranteed to be approved by the Food and Drug Administration.

Any products of synthetic nature require a long and costly period of testing as some manufacturers discovered, for example Olestra. Olestra was discovered by Procter & Gamble (P&G) in 1968 but approved by the Food and Drug Administration (FDA) as a food additive only in January 1996. The FDA considered Olestra a new substance that therefore needed more intensive safety studies than a product derived more directly from natural ingredients. In addition the development of the product was plagued by complaints of abdominal cramping and loose stools. Olestra is used as an ingredient in Pringles Light and Lay's Light chips.

In 1994 the RJR Nabisco has introduced the food additive Salatrim that was added to cookies and crackers. Salatrim was not considered a synthetic compound, and the Food and Drug Administration accepted a Nabisco petition to have it included on a list of substances the federal agency considers "generally recognized as safe." In 2003 the European

Commission approved Salatrim as a food ingredient. Getting the approval was not easy as Salatrim faced very bad reports in the Danish press that the excessive consumption of the ingredient could lead to gastro-intestinal problems and stomach trouble, and that it was particularly harmful to children.

CP Kelco, *www.cpkelco.com* - manufactures a great number of fat replacers and hydrocolloids.

SIMPLESSE® - a multi-functional dairy ingredient made from whey protein used for emulsion, foam stabilization and fat mimicking.

GENU® Carrageenan - made from red seaweed (*Rhodophyceae*) and used for gelling, thickening and stabilizing.

Carboxymethyl Cellulose - made from tree pulp and cotton linters. Used for thickening, water-binding, emulsifying, film forming and tableting excipients. Many brands.

GENU® Pectins - made from citrus peels, sugar beet pulp. Used for gelling, thickening and stabilizing; excellent acid-stability, skin pH balancing. Many brands.

SLENDID® Specialty Pectin made to mimic a fat-like mouthfeel.

GENU® GUM refined locust bean gum for food application such as ready-to-consume desserts. It is made from seeds of the carob tree and used for thickening, water-binding, gel strengthening.

CP Kelco xanthan gums - made by biofermentation using a sugar source. Used for thickening and stabilizing. Many brands.

Maltrin®, maltodextrin, *Grain Processing Corporation, www.grainprocessing.com*

Pure-Gel®, modified starch, *Grain Processing Corporation, www.grainprocessing.com*

Paselli®, potato maltodextrin, *Avebe, www.avebe.com*

Citri-Fi® - specialty pectins made from pure citrus fiber. Used in a wide variety of food applications, including processed meats and sausages. *Fiberstar, Inc www.fiberstar.net*

Corn Z Trim® and **Oat Z Trim®**, *Z Trim Holdings www.ztrim.com* Both products display the superior water-holding capacity. Water Holding Capacity:

Corn Z Trim powder = 25-30 grams water per gram Z Trim

Oat Z Trim powder = 9-12 grams water per gram of Z Trim

Avicel® PH Microcrystalline Cellulose

FMC BioPolymer www.fmc.com

Z Trim® is used by food manufacturers on 6 continents, across a multitude of food categories, such as meats, sauces, soups, dressings, baked goods, fillings, toppings, prepared meals, dairy products, frozen handheld snacks, and pizza dough.

Oatrim - made from oats, **Quaker Oats Company**, *www.quakeroats. com*. It was developed by the USDA (United States Department of Agriculture). The product is unique in that it is the only fat replacer that naturally contains both a carbohydrate and a gum. Most of the natural oat cereal flavor is removed, making it suitable for a wide range of flavored food systems. The ß-glucan imparts a creaminess not present in other carbohydrate fat replacers. The product can be used as a partial or total replacement for fat.

Nutrim - made from organic oat and barley beta-glucan soluble fiber. It was developed by the USDA (United States Department of Agriculture). Nutrim acts as a healthy fat replacer in foods- replacing dairy creams, oils, butter, coconut cream at high replacement levels with minimal sensory change.

All three products, Oatrim, Nutrim and Z Trim were originally developed by the USDA (United States Department of Agriculture) by *Dr. George Inglett* from the Center for Agricultural Utilization and Research.

Orafti® Fat Replacements - Beneo Orafti, www.beneo-orafti.com Beneo - Orafti®, the Belgian company has pioneered and patented the use of inulin, a dietary fiber extracted from chicory roots, as a fat replacer. When mixed with water, it results in a creamy structure which can easily be incorporated into foods to replace fat and provide a smooth fatty mouthfeel and a well-balanced round flavor.

Orafti® inulin and **Orafti® oligofructose** come from the chicory plant and as such have been part of our diet for generations. They are not digested in the stomach or small intestine, and so reach the large intestine intact, where they stimulate the growth of our own beneficial bacteria. This means that our digestive system is healthier and our whole body benefits. Orafti® inulin and Orafti® oligofructose can also be used to replace fat in all water based products or to replace sugar in combination with intense sweeteners in most food products. In meat products mostly **Orafti®HP** is used due to the binding ability of Orafti®HP with water and its synergy with hydrocolloids, the overall concentration of hydrocolloids can be reduced. Orafti® is used as a partial fat replacer that immobilizes water in a particle gel network.

Other Useful Ingredients for Making Low Fat Sausages

Water Retention Agents play the most important role in today's methods of producing meat products. A significant part of machinery that is produced for the meat industry is related to pumping water and distributing it within the meat. To perform those operations fast and to produce a product that will be visually appealing with a long shelf life, a number of additives, some natural and some of chemical nature, are added.

Flours and Starches are often added to sausages with low meat content. Starch is added when making sauces, to trap moisture and to make the sauce heavy. In sausages starch is used for its properties to bind water and to improve the texture of the product. The most common sources are potato, wheat, corn, rice and tapioca. You can add as much as you like but around 10% (100 g per kilogram of total mass) will be the upper limit. Starch is a common additive in extended injected products like a ham. It is usually applied at 10 - 50 g/kg (1-5%) of a finished product.

Rusk is a popular baked and ground product, made from wheat flour. It can be ground to different diameters and there is a coarse, medium or fine rusk. Rusk can absorb water at 3 - 4 times its weight.

Other popular binders are: oatmeal, bread crumbs, general flour, cornflour, potatoes, rice, farina, and semolina. Rusk and oatmeal are especially popular in England. Popular extenders are: rice, potatoes, and barley or buckwheat groats.

Meat Glue - Transglutaminase (TG), better known to chefs as "Meat Glue," has the wonderful ability to bond protein-containing foods together. Raw meats bound with meat glue are strong enough to be handled as if they were whole muscles. Transglutaminase was discovered in 1959 but was not widely used as it was hard to produce and was expensive. Only in 1989 the Japanese company Ajinomoto (best known for the production of MSG) made it cost efficient. The product is safe, natural, easy to use and expensive. Meat glue is primarily used for:

- Binding smaller cuts of meat into a larger ones. Small fish fillets can be bound together and rolled to form a large diameter roll.
- Making formed hams which are produced from individual cuts of meat.

Although meat glue will glue different meats together, for example fish and chicken, it is not such a good idea as they exhibit different textures and are cooked to different temperature requirements. Meat glue can be sprinkled on like a powder, mixed in water to make a slurry, or added directly into meat mixtures. About 0.1% is all that is needed to improve cohesion between the meat pieces.

Curing Accelerators

Curing accelerators speed up color formation in cured meat products. These substances accelerate the reaction of sodium nitrite with meat's myoglobin resulting in the development of the red color. Antioxidants prolong the products shelf life by preventing fat rancidity and color changes that are caused by exposure in oxygen in the air. They also stabilize color in the finished products and act as antioxidants. Curing accelerators are of little use in air dried products as by increasing nitrite reaction they soon deplete its amount. As a result less nitrite is available for long time curing.

The best known cure accelerators are:

Ascorbic acid (vitamin C) - should not be added with sodium nitrite at the same time as they react violently creating fumes. Therefore, ascorbic acid should be added last into the sausage mass. A vitamin C tablet may be pulverized and applied to meat. It is usually applied at 0.1%.

Sodium ascorbate - sodium salt of ascorbic acid.

Sodium erythorbate (isoascorbate) - salt of erythorbic acid.

Curing accelerators are added at about 0.03-0.05% (0.3-0.5 g/kg).

Phosphates - are the most effective water holding agents. Salt forces meat proteins to swell which helps them trap and hold more water. Phosphates are able to open the structure of the protein which helps them to hold even more water. This increased water holding capacity of the protein is what prevents water losses when smoking and cooking. Phosphates directly increase the water holding capacity of meat protein by raising the pH (acidity) of the meat.

Phosphates are alkaline (pH>7.0), meats are slightly acidic (pH 6.0). Phosphates are the strongest water binders and protein extractors and all commercial producers use them. Most countries permit up to 0.5% of phosphates (5 g per kilogram of meat). Today, the whole meat industry operates on this principle, inject the maximum allowed amount of water and make sure it does not leak out.

Typical phosphates used in the meat industry are:

- Sodium tripoly-phosphate STTP (pH 9.8), better choice for brines that would be pumped into the meat.
- Sodium di-phosphate SDP (pH 7.3), good choice when added to meat batter in powdered form.

A meat processor usually obtains a prefabricated phosphate blend which has been optimized for a particular application.

Flavor Enhancers

MSG (monosodium glutamate) is a flavor enhancer that is produced by the fermentation of starch, sugar beets, sugar cane, or molasses. Although once stereotypically associated with foods in Chinese restaurants, it is now found in many common food items, particularly processed foods. MSG is commonly available in food stores.

Ribonucleotide is a much stronger flavor enhancer than MSG and is carried by commercial producers.

Preservatives

Sodium metabisulphite and **sodium sulphite** are added to keep food safe for a longer period of time by preventing the growth of spoilage and pathogenic bacteria.

Sodium lactate or **potassium lactate** are used to increase the shelf life of the product in the amount of 3% (30 g/kg).

Acetate can be added to increase shelf life at around 3%. Larger amounts may impart a vinegar-like taste to the product.

Potassium sorbate is an effective mold inhibitor.

Additives Typical Usage Amounts

Name	Common amount
Soy protein concentrate	1-3%
Soy protein isolate	1-3%
Non-fat dry milk	1-3%
Milk caseinate	2%
Whey protein concentrate	1-3%
Whey protein isolate	1-3%
Agar	0.2-3.0%
Alginate	0.5-1%
Carrageenan-Kappa	0.02-1.5%
Konjac	0.25-0.50%
Xanthan	0.02-0.03%
Locust bean gum (LBG)	0.1-1.0%
Gellan	0.4-0.7
Guar gum	0.1-0.7%
Gum Arabic	10-90%
Microcrystalline cellulose (MCC)	0.5-5%
Carbomethyl cellulose (CMC)	1.0-2.0%
Low methoxy pectin (LM Pectin)	0.5-3.0%
Gelatin	0.5-1.7%
Textured vegetable protein (TVP)	0.1-15%
Starch	1-5%
Monosodium glutamate	0.2-1.0%
Phosphate	0.1-0.5% (0.5% is the max allowed)
Ascorbate and erythorbate	0.03-0.05% (0.05% is the max)

Chapter 5

Power of Soy

Soybeans were cultivated in Asia about 3,000 years ago. Soy was first introduced to Europe in the early 18th century and to British colonies in North America in 1765, where it was first grown for hay. Benjamin Franklin wrote a letter in 1770 mentioning bringing soybeans home from England. Soybeans did not become an important crop outside of Asia until about 1910. Soy was introduced to Africa from China in the late 19th Century and is now widespread across the continent.

In America, soy was considered an industrial product only and not used as a food prior to the 1920's. The main producers of soy are the United States (35%), Brazil (27%), Argentina (19%), China (6%) and India (4%). Traditional non-fermented food uses of soybeans include soy milk, and from the latter tofu and tofu skin. Fermented foods include soy sauce, fermented bean paste, natto, and tempeh, among others. Originally, soy protein concentrates and isolates were used by the meat industry to bind fat and water in meat applications and to increase protein content in lower grade sausages. They were crudely refined and if added at above 5% amounts, they imparted a "beany" flavor to the finished product. As the technology advanced, the soy products were refined further and exhibit a neutral flavor today. Today, soy proteins are considered not just a filler material, but a "good food" and are added to processed meats all over the world. They are used by athletes in diet and muscle building drinks or as refreshing fruit smoothies.

The dramatic increase in interest in soy products is largely credited to the 1995 ruling of the Food and Drug Administration allowing health claims for foods containing 6.25 g of protein per serving. The FDA approved soy as an official cholesterol-lowering food, along with other heart and health benefits. The FDA granted the following health claim for soy: "25 grams of soy protein a day, as part of a diet low in saturated fat and cholesterol, may reduce the risk of heart disease."

Soybean Nutrient Values(100 g)					
Name	Protein (g)	Fat (g)	Carbo-hydrates (g)	Salt (g)	Energy (cal)
Soybean, raw	36.49	19.94	30.16	2	446

Soybean Fat Values (100 g)			
Name	Total Fat (g)	Saturated Fat (g)	Monounsaturated Fat (g)	Polyunsatu-rated Fat (g)
Soybean, raw	19.94	2.884	4.404	11.255
			Source: USDA Nutrient database

Soybeans are considered to be a source of complete protein. A complete protein is one that contains significant amounts of all the essential amino acids that must be provided to the human body because of the body's inability to synthesize them. For this reason, soy is a good source of protein, amongst many others, for vegetarians and vegans or for people who want to reduce the amount of meat they eat. They can replace meat with soy protein products without requiring major adjustments elsewhere in the diet. From the soybean many other products are obtained such as: soy flour, textured vegetable protein, soy oil, soy protein concentrate, soy protein isolate, soy yoghurt, soy milk and animal feed for farm raised fish, poultry and cattle.

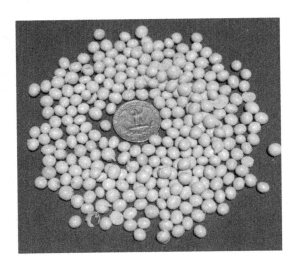

Photo 5.1 Soy beans.

In the past the soybean industry begged for acceptance, but today soybean products start to shine and become the sparkle of the food industry. Differently flavored soy milk can be found in every supermarket and roasted soybeans lie next to almonds, walnuts and peanuts.

Photo 5.2 A variety of soy products.

Soy flour is made by milling soybeans. Depending on the amount of oil extracted the flour can be full-fat or de-fatted. It can be made as fine powder or more coarse soy grits. Protein content of different soy flours:

- Full-fat soy flour - 35%.
- Low-fat soy flour - 45%.
- Defatted soy flour - 47%.

Generally, soy flour is not added to processed meats due to its flavor profile.

Textured soy flour (TSF) is obtained from regular soy flour which is processed and extruded to form products of specific texture and form, such as meat like nuggets. The formed products are crunchy in the dry form and upon hydration become moist and chewy.

Soy Proteins

Soybeans contain all three of the nutrients required for good nutrition: complete protein, carbohydrate and fat, as well as vitamins and minerals, including calcium, folic acid and iron. The composition of soy protein is nearly equivalent in quality to meat, milk and egg protein. Soybean oil is 61% polyunsaturated fat and 24% monounsaturated fat which is comparable to the total unsaturated fat content of other vegetable oils. Soybean oil contains no cholesterol.

Soy concentrates and isolates are used in sausages, burgers and other meat products. Soy proteins when mixed with ground meat will form a gel upon heating, entrapping liquid and moisture. They increase firmness and juiciness of the product, and reduce cooking loss during frying. In addition they enrich the protein content of many products and make them healthier by reducing the amount of saturated fat and cholesterol that otherwise would be present. Soy protein powders are the most commonly added protein to meat products at around 2-3% as the larger amounts may impart a "beany" flavor to the product. They bind water extremely well and cover fat particles with fine emulsion. This prevents fats from lumping together. The sausage will be juicier, plumper and have less shrivelling.

Soy protein concentrate (about 60% protein), available from most online distributors of sausage making supplies is a *natural product* that contains around 60% protein and retains most of the soybean's dietary fiber. SPC can bind 4 parts of water. However, *soy concentrates do not form the real gel* as they contain some of the insoluble fiber that prevents gel formation; they only form a paste. Before processing, soy protein concentrate is re-hydrated at a ratio of 1:3.

Soy protein isolate (80-90% protein), is a natural product that contains at least 80-90% protein and no other ingredients. It is made from de-fatted soy meal by removing most of the fats and carbohydrates. Therefore, soy protein isolate has a *very neutral flavour* compared to other soy products. As soy protein isolate is more refined, it costs slightly more than soy protein concentrate. Soy protein isolate can bind 5 parts of water. Soy isolates are excellent emulsifiers of fat and their *ability to produce the real gel* contributes to the increased firmness of the product. Isolates are added to add juiciness, cohesiveness, and viscosity to a variety of meat, seafood, and poultry products. This enhances both the nutritional quality and taste of meat products.

For making quality sausages the recommended mixing ratio is 1 part of soy protein isolate to **3.3** parts of water. SPI is chosen for delicate products that require superior flavor such as yoghurt, cheese, whole muscle foods and healthy drinks. Soy protein isolates sold by health products distributors online usually contain 92% of protein.

Textured Vegetable Protein - TVP

Textured vegetable protein (TVP), also known as textured soy protein (TSP), soy meat, or soya meat has been around for more than 50 years. It contains 50% protein, little fat, no cholesterol and is very rich in fiber. It is an excellent filler material for *ground meat and sausages.* TVP is made from defatted soy flour, a by-product of extracting soybean oil, and is relatively flavorless. Its protein content is equal to that of the meat, and it contains no fat.

Photo 5.3 Textured vegetable protein (TVP) flakes and the quarter coin. TVP must be rehydrated with water/liquid before use.

TVP flakes are the size of the finely ground meat and they have the texture and the bite of the meat. Textured vegetable protein is cheaper than meat and was used to extend meat value. It adds an unexpected bonus - the final product contains less fat and cholesterol and still retains its full nutritional value.

Textured Vegetable Protein (100 g = 1 cup)					
Name	Protein (g)	Fat (g)	Carbohydrates (g)	Salt (mg)	Energy (cal)
TVP	50	0	30	8 mg	333

Source: Bob's Red Mill

Soy TVP can also be used as a low cost/high nutrition extender in comminuted meat and poultry products. Textured vegetable protein provides substance and taste to low fat meat products by imitating lean meat. Half a cup of soy TVP provides 126 calories, 25 g protein 14 g carbohydrates and 0 g fat. TVP flakes or powder are usually soaked in water (1 part of flakes to 2 parts of water) and then mixed with minced meat to a ratio of up to 1:3 (rehydrated TVP to ground meat). TVP has no flavor of it's own and is practical to use as a meat substitute or extender. Besides, it offers the best value for the money. You don't necessarily need to add TVP to your healthy sausage which would consist of mostly lean meat, but lean meat such as pork loin is expensive. You may replace up to 30% of lean meat with re-hydrated TVP lowering the cost of the sausage and bringing down the cholesterol level. This may be less important when only a few pounds of meat are produced.

However, when ten or more pounds of sausages are made to meet the needs of a large family, the savings are substantial. TVP is a great ingredient for making *vegetarian foods*. TVP is made from high (50%) soy protein, soy flour or concentrate, but can also be made from cotton seeds, wheat and oats. It is extruded into various shapes (chunks, flakes, nuggets, grains, and strips) and sizes, and is primarily used as a meat substitute due to its very low cost. When a TVP enriched meat product is cooked, it will lose less weight as TVP absorbs meat juices and water that would normally be lost.

The small granules of TVP are easy to rehydrate but hydration rates can further be improved by using warm water. However, the mixture must be cooled down before it can be blended with minced meat. Rehydrated TVP must be refrigerated and treated like a meat. Usually 1 part of textured soy protein will absorb 2-3 parts of water. *Rehydrating TVP at a 2:1 ratio*, drops the percentage of protein to an approximation of ground meat at 16%. *TVP can be mixed with ground meat to a ratio of up to 1:3 (rehydrated TVP to meat)* without reducing the quality of the final product. Adding 3% re-hydrated TVP will result in a high quality sausage. Higher levels of TVP (3-10%) may result in sausages with a decreased meaty flavor. However, higher levels of up to 15% of TVP are accepted in burgers and patties.

Protein rich powders, 100 g serving					
Name	Protein (g)	Fat (g)	Carbo-hydrates (g)	Salt (mg)	Energy (cal)
Soy flour, full fat, raw	34.54	20.65	35.19	13	436
Soy flour, low fat	45.51	8.90	34.93	9	375
Soy flour, defatted	47.01	1.22	38.37	20	330
Soy meal, defatted, raw, crude protein	49.20	2.39	35.89	3	337
Soy protein concentrate	58.13	0.46	30.91	3	331
Soy protein isolate, potassium type	80.69	0.53	10.22	50	338
Soy protein isolate (Supro®) *	92.50	2.8	0	1,400	378

Source: USDA Nutrient database
* Data by www.nutrabio.com. Soy isolates sold by health products distributors online usually contain 92% of protein.

Emulsions

Protein is needed to mix substances such as fat and water. Proteins are released from muscles during mechanical action such as cutting or grinding. Salt and phosphates greatly advance the release of proteins. Protein and all those particles such as salt, protein, sugar, parts of fiber, muscles, and collagen create a liquid which coats each fat particle with a thin layer of soluble protein. Those coated fat particles combine with water and meat and the emulsion is created. The leaner the meat, the more protein it contains. If little or no fat is used, there will not be any real emulsion, and the proteins will simply hold the texture of the sausage together. Due to the high protein content (80-90%) soy protein isolate is a very strong emulsifying agent and will help to make quality liver and emulsified sausages (hot dog, bologna). In order to take full advantage of soy protein isolate capabilities, it should be cut in a bowl cutter. Milk protein (caseinate) is a binder that promotes a strong emulsion by interacting with water and fat particles.

For sausages that will be processed using a grinder only, it is advisable to use premixed emulsion.

Binder	Binder/fat/water ratio	Average amount	Added as
Milk caseinate	1:5:5 to 1:8:8	2% in relation to meat mass.	Dry powder or pre-mixed emulsion
Soy protein isolate	1:5:5	2% in relation to meat mass.	Dry powder or pre-mixed emulsion

In healthy sausages animal fat can be partly or completely replaced with a vegetable oil. In such a case the protein : oil : water emulsion can be made.

Binder	Binder/oil/water ratio	Average amount	Added as
Soy protein isolate	1:4:5	5-10% in relation to meat mass.	Dry powder or pre-mixed emulsion.

In the past soy protein isolate cost twice as much as soy protein concentrate and the concentrate became an obvious choice for the majority of products. Soy protein isolate it still costlier today, but not as much, so a hobbyist's decision will be based not on economics, but on the application. Soy isolates are excellent emulsifiers of fat and their ability to produce gel contributes to the increased firmness of the product. For these reasons they may be chosen over soy protein concentrate for making liver and emulsified sausages.

Soy protein concentrates do not form the real gel as they contain some of the insoluble fiber that prevents gel formation; they only form a paste. This does not create a problem as the sausage batter will never be emulsified to the extent that the yoghurt or smoothie drinks are. Soy protein concentrate is carried by all distributors of sausage making equipment and supplies online.

Commercially processed meats contain soy protein today throughout the world. Soy proteins are used in hot dogs, other sausages, whole muscle foods, salamis, pepperoni pizza toppings, meat patties, vegetarian sausages etc. Hobbyist have also discovered that adding some soy protein concentrate allowed them to add more water and improved the texture of the sausage. It eliminated shrivelling and made the sausage plumper. Soy proteins play a very crucial role in making reduced fat sausages.

Chapter 6

Making Healthy Sausages

There is nothing wrong with sausages, it is we who need to change the way we make them. We have been enjoying sausages for centuries so why make them differently now? The difference lies in a lifestyle, we have grown fat and obese, our metabolism is down, blood pressure is up, half of us will become diabetics and will develop some kind of cancer. Consumers are more educated now and are increasingly aware of the link between fat intake, excess weight and heart disease.

When a wood cutter was swinging an ax most of the day his problem was not accumulating fat, but how to get enough of it in order to remain strong. Children walked miles to school every day, their parents walked miles to the nearest church. Kids did not have video games and spent more time outside playing ball or just running around. Calories were burnt as fast as they came. Food was cooked at home and families ate together. People were slim and fit.

And today? Fast food franchises kill our children with fries, cokes, burgers, desserts and the portions get bigger. If you order a portion, the salesperson asks: supersize? Kids seldom walk to school, then they sit in front of a computer or television hours every day, nibbling on potato chips and other snacks. Families are eating out more often, the meals are bigger and contain higher amounts of fat. We cook less at home as in most cases we warm up commercially prepared foods that we bought in a local supermarket. Those foods are loaded with salt that in time may trigger hypertension even in healthy individuals. The modern Western society is getting weaker and sicker by the minute. You don't need an expert to tell you what kind of sausage you should eat, just look at yourself in the mirror.

If you are athletic, slim and leading an active live, *you can eat anything and everything is good for you*. We gain most weight by not eating sausages, but by ingesting too much sugar. Fat does contain more calories than sugar, but we don't drink vegetable oil or swallow fried bacon in front of the television, do we? We eat sweets, snacks, ice creams, lolipops and potato chips all the time. We drink plenty of beer and soda. Those calorie loaded products make us sick and not the sausages, which usually do not contain sugar. Making healthier sausages makes sense only if we also limit our exposure to carbohydrates. It is only fair to put some blame on carbohydrates for our obesity problem.

There is no such thing as bad sausages, only bad eating habits.

If you are obese and in desperate need of exercise, well, forget regular food and sausages and start eating low fat and low salt products. You may still avoid getting seriously sick and will definitely live longer. You never know, you may get fit again and be able to enjoy foods that your grandfathers once ate.

Commercial producers do not care if the sausage you buy is healthy, all they care is to make the maximum profit. They do not worry much about the taste, as long as supermarkets repeat the orders the manufacturer is happy. On the other hand, supermarkets require products with a long shelf life, and that forces manufacturer to add chemicals in order to comply with this requirement. The U.S. Food and Drug Administration does not care about the quality of the sausage as long as the ingredients are not hazardous to our health. A customer has no control over the manufacture of a commercially produced product which may contain up to 50% of fat (fresh sausages), plenty of salt and added chemicals. Only when he cooks his own food can he decide what goes inside. Making healthy sausages does not end with just lowering the amount of salt or using lean meat. *The sausage must still look like a sausage, feel like a sausage and taste like a sausage.* It should be noted that in the USA sausage choices are quite limited and hotdogs, frankfurters and bologna constitute the majority of processed sausages available. Commercial producers make some low fat sausages, notably hotdogs and frankfurters. If one wants to make low-salt, low fat versions of well known classical sausages, he has to make them himself.

Making healthy sausages constitutes only a little part of the overall strategy for staying healthy. It makes little sense to spend a significant amount of time to make a healthy sausage, only to devour a bag of potato chips in front of the television later on. However, the sausages can be made in such a way that they are healthy and tasty at the same time. There is nothing wrong when a kid orders a double cheeseburger from a fast food establishment. But, when he supplements his order with supersize fries and a supersize soda, he is on his way to become a supersize fellow himself.

Reinventing Sausage Making

For thousands of years sausages were identified with comminuted meat that was mixed with spices and stuffed into casings. There was never a question about the nutritional composition and whether it was healthy or not. The flavor was the main criteria that decided the quality of the sausage. Any sausage that contained filler material was considered to be inferior and associated with a poor man's diet. When the second world war ended, most European countries were damaged and the shortage of meat was prevalent. One could not buy meat in a store, because there were no stores. Sausages were made at home and people added fillers to increase the volume and lower the cost. In many areas of the world people still eat sausages filled with rice, flour, potatoes, bread crumbs, oats, groats etc. Well, those people are much thinner, and they are eating healthier food than us.

Fifty years ago smoking cigarettes was a thing to do, watch any older movie and you will see that ladies and men were smoking cigarettes all the time. Yet today we know that smoking kills. The time has come to realize that many food products, sausages included, are not as healthy as we have thought before. This does not mean that one can not eat a traditional product like dry salami. If you are fit, ride a bicycle, run every day, and go to the gym, you can eat everything. But, if you are like the rest of us: overweight, leading a sedentary life, driving to work, and using your phone and computer as the only exercise, well you should change your eating habits. You can still eat dry sausages, but think of it as *a treat, and not as a meal.* Eating four ounces of dry sausage will meet the daily limit for salt intake. Eat a slice on a cracker, but don't eat a regular portion. It is still better for you than consuming a cone of ice cream. More and more people eat reduced fat ice cream, and more people will eat reduced fat processed meats.

Today, an educated and health conscious consumer expects more of the sausage he eats and the definition of the sausage must be modified. The manufacturing technology remains the same, but the selection of ingredients must change. Meat must not be the main defining ingredient, but it must be thought of as one of many ingredients that will make a healthy sausage. The practice of adding back fat, or fatty trimmings should be replaced by partial replacement with vegetable oils. It is permissible to grind the whole pork in order to save cost, but it is still recommended to trim away as much outside fat as possible.

What is a Healthy Sausage

Let us assume that an average person eats three meals a day and that the amount of calories and salt he consumes is equally distributed. According to the latest recommendations an individual should eat less than 2,000 calories and 2,300 mg (2.3 g) of salt (1/3 teaspoon) per day. Individuals at health risk should limit their salt intake to 1,500 mg per day (1/4 teaspoon). The conclusion is that each meal should contain less than 666 calories and 766 mg (1/10 teaspoon) salt. Those hold true for the sausage as well, but you should take under consideration that a sausage will be served with another ingredient like a roll, potatoes, rice etc. These ingredients will contribute extra calories.

Who Needs Healthy Sausages

Sausages taste good and are a very rich source of energy, but they are not a very healthy product as they contain plenty of fat. To make the matter worse they contain the saturated fat which should be avoided as much as possible. Substitution of plant oils for animal fat considerably reduces the cholesterol content and increases the ratio of unsaturated to saturated fatty acids. The following individuals should consider eating healthy sausages:

1. People with hypertension problems, but who are otherwise healthy. In this case the solution is rather easy and requires lowering salt intake and some clever choosing of spices.

2. People who already have some type of cardiovascular disease or are at risk of developing one. Those individuals must pay a lot of attention to the meat and fat/oils selection. As cardiovascular problems go often hand in hand with hypertension, they will have to lower salt intake as well. By just replacing solid fats with oils already brings a significant benefit, although the calorie intake remains the same, nevertheless a lot of cholesterol is removed from the sausage.

3. People who are trying to lose weight. This group must minimize the amount of fat/oil that goes into the sausage, which will lower the calorie intake.

4. Healthy individuals such as body builders who are constantly looking for a source of rich protein but little fat. Body builders are very fond of chicken breasts which are one of richest sources of protein, yet contain very little fat. They drink a lot of liquids which contain soy proteins. Nothing stops them from making a chicken sausage with added soy protein concentrate, which is a common ingredient added to sausages anyhow. More water can be added to the sausage mass as it will be bound by soy protein concentrate and will create a juicy feeling even if most of the fat will be removed from the recipe.

5. For diabetics sugar control is of utmost importance and fortunately sausages rarely incorporate sugar. The tiny amount of sugar present in meat can be considered a negligible amount. Some fermented sausages such as summer sausage, pepperoni and other semi-dry products need sugar as food for lactic acid producing bacteria, but these sausages do not fit into the healthy sausage definition as they include elevated amounts of salt that is needed for safety reasons. For these reasons we are not going to cover them in this book.

It is advisable that a reader familiarizes himself with the main sausage types which are listed below. He must feel confident about making his choices and be comfortable with the basic sausage making process.

Sausage Types

Sausages come in many shapes and different combinations of meat and spices. Some sausages are better suited for lowering salt levels and fat than others and it will be helpful to be familiar with the basic types of sausages.

Not Ready to Eat sausages are fresh sausages that are made normally from pork, but sometimes also beef or veal. The meat is not cured, sausages must be refrigerated and fully cooked before serving. Polish White Sausage is a fresh sausage that is boiled before serving. Another example is German Bratwurst that is grilled. The South American version, Spanish chorizo, is a fresh sausage that is fried with eggs for breakfast. These sausages can easily be made healthier, yet fully retain their nutritional value.

Ready to Eat Sausages is the main group of sausages that covers almost every sausage. With the exception of fermented and air dried sausages, all sausages that belong to this group are *cooked* either in hot water or baked in a smokehouse or in the oven.

Fermented sausages can be classified as:

◊   Cold smoked and dried but uncooked - Hungarian salami.

◊   Cold smoked and uncooked - spreadable raw sausages (Mettwurst), very popular in Germany.

◊   Not smoked, dried and uncooked - dry salami, dry chorizo.

◊   Hot smoked partially or fully cooked semi-dry sausages (Summer Sausage, Pepperoni, Salami).

Dry fermented sausages which are traditionally made slow fermented sausages are produced at low temperatures and are smoked with cold smoke. Semi-dry sausages are smoked with hot smoke.

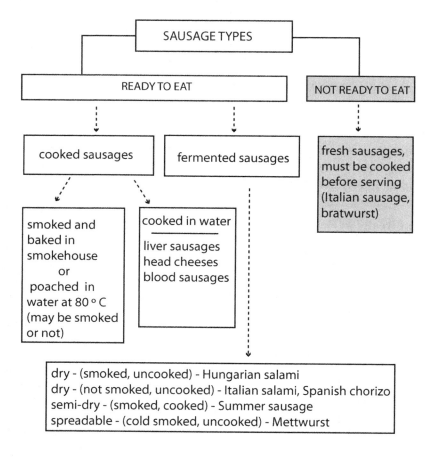

Fig. 6.1 Types of sausages.

All sausages can be smoked or not. What was once an important preservation step has become a matter of personal preference. If you like
the smoky flavor, smoke the sausage, it's that simple. After smoking,
most sausages enter the cooking process which can be an extension
of the smoking step or may be performed in a different unit such as
an oven or in a different media (hot water). There are sausages such
as spreadable fermented sausages whose manufacture ends with the
smoking step. They are cold smoked and not cooked, but stored in a
refrigerator. As a rule cold smoked products are not followed by cooking. Some sausages are more suitable for salt substitution than others:

Sausage Type	Suitable For:	
	Low Salt	Low Fat
Fresh	Yes	Yes
Cooked - course grind	Yes	Yes
Cooked - emulsified	No	Yes
Cold Smoked - Not Cooked	No	Yes
Liver	No	Yes
Headcheese	Yes	Yes
Blood Sausages	Yes	Yes
Dry Fermented - Not Cooked	No	Yes
Semi-Dry Fermented (Cooked)	No	Yes

Fermented sausages and cold smoked products should not be made
with less salt. Although it is possible to make a low salt semi-dry
fermented sausage by rapidly increasing acidity (lowering pH) of the
meat, such procedures should be left to experienced sausage makers.

Emulsified Sausages

Emulsified sausages such as hot dog, frankfurter or bologna are well
suited for making reduced fat sausages as long as the amount of salt
is not lowered too much. Salt is needed for protein extraction and
emulsification. They are finely comminuted in a bowl cutter or food
processor using about 30% of flaked ice, and contain binders (soy
protein isolate or milk caseinate), and phosphates. They can be easily
extended by using flours and starches and the product would still be
of high quality.

Special Sausages: Liver, Head Cheese And Blood Sausages

There is a special group of sausages that consists of *liver sausages, blood sausages, and head cheeses.* They are normally made from pork only although on occasion lean beef is added to liver sausages. Head cheeses and liver sausages are usually prepared from fresh uncured meats, although occasionally meats are cured for the development of a pink color and not for safety reasons. Head cheese made with tongues looks much better when the meat is red and not grey. Meats used in these sausages are first precooked in hot water, then stuffed into casings and then they are cooked in hot water until the safe internal meat temperature is obtained. In simple words the cooking is performed twice. These sausages are usually not smoked although cooked liver sausages are occasionally briefly treated with cold smoke. Those products are fully cooked and kept under refrigeration.

What makes them unique is that meats are pre-cooked in water, then *stuffed into a casing and cooked again.* Their production is more time consuming as it requires additional cooking. This secondary cooking is not performed for the safety of the product as the meats were already cooked. *The secondary heating of the sausage creates a proper bond between meat and gelatin.* Take head cheese as an example: cold meats were stuffed into the casing and the gelatin was already starting to solidify. As a result, there was little binding between meat pieces and gelatin. The secondary heating melts the gelatin again and creates a strong bond with meat pieces.

Strategies for Making Healthier Sausages

Originally USDA regulations permitted only 10% added water and this requirement did not entice the production of low fat sausages where added water makes up for the absence of fat. Then, the regulations were modified to allow up to 40% fat and added water, with fat restricted to a maximum of 30% of the finished product. This modification allowed to solubilize meat protein with fat and water, creating in effect the emulsion. When government regulations finally allowed the production of low fat and fat free sausages, the new methods of production followed. Most fat replacers such as starches, pectin and gums are able to absorb a significant amount of water and are mixed together in a bowl cutter of a food processor. Then they are chopped finely and mixed with meat and other ingredients. The resulting paste is the emulsified sausage which can be a hot dog, frankfurter or bologna.

Any sausage recipe can be converted to a healthy sausage recipe by:
- Taking the bad stuff out (animal fat).
- Putting the good stuff in (non-meat materials).

Once you know what is the good stuff and what is the bad stuff, you will be able to make any kind of sausage, be it low salt, reduced fat or no fat at all. An additional step will be making up for the lost flavor, due to fat removal, and may be improving the color, although the latter is not necessary.

The healthier sausages can be made by:
- Decreasing the amount of salt.
- Decreasing the amount of animal fat and replacing it with a vegetable oil.
- Introducing filler material.
- Lowering calories.
- Eliminating chemicals.

Replacing fat with vegetable oil makes the sausage healthier because:
- Bad fat (saturated) is removed.
- More good fats (polyunsaturated and monounsaturated) are introduced into the batter.
- A significant amount of cholesterol is eliminated.

Replacing fat with protein is an excellent exchange as it reduces the percentage of calories derived from fat. One gram of protein is equivalent to 4 calories vs. one gram of fat which is equivalent to 9 calories. Low fat sausages are healthier because they contain less calories, less saturated fat and less cholesterol. Lowering calories can be accomplished by the following methods:
- Decreasing amount of fat.
- Increasing the amount of lean meat.
- Adding filler material.
- Downsizing the portion size.
- Not frying them in oil.

When adding filler material think in terms of "diluting" the sausage. Although the original amount of fat and meat remains the same, there is more sausage now. This sausage contains low calorie filling material and consequently the same size serving portion will contain less calories. Think in terms of preparing a meal with rice, vegetables and chunks of sausage. If you stuffed all this mixture into a casing, you will get a healthy sausage. This is how most healthy sausage recipes are listed on the Internet. Technically speaking, they are meals, but if they were stuffed, they may qualify to be called sausages.

The biggest challenge that a manufacturer faces when lowering the amount of fat in a sausage is that the customer *will not like it.* The supermarket will not renew orders and such a scenario looks like the manufacturer's nightmare. Not surprisingly, manufacturers are not rushing into doing costly research and market evaluations as the risks are so high. A hobbyist making sausages at home faces none of these problems and can experiment with countless numbers of recipes and different ingredients. When he finds his sausage not salty or hot enough, it is easy to spice it up, if it tastes to dry, he can pour barbecue sauce over it. There are no risks for him and he only gets wiser.

Downsizing the portion size is easily accomplished by stuffing sausages into shorter links. It is wiser to make 4" long sausages than let's say a 10" or 12" one. A child with a healthy appetite will easily eat a 10" long sausage, but will be content with two 4" links as well. Then, you may stuff sausages into smaller diameter casings which will result in less calories as well. Keep in mind that the way you serve the sausage can impact your calorie count. If the sausage is fried in oil, you will increase the calories, but that will not occur when the sausage is boiled or grilled. Home made sausage do not need to contain unnecessary chemicals, which are usually added to increase the shelf life of the product and preserve its color.

There many ways to make a healthy sausage.

In the lat 30 years the advances in technology have brought a variety of wonderful natural ingredients which are used for making reduced fat products such as ice creams, cheeses, yoghurts, spreads, dressings sauces and other items. The trend was followed by the professional cooks who started to use gums and meat glues to create very innovative products such as shrimp spaghetti, imitation crab meat or imitation caviar. There is no reason why an educated hobbyist could not adapt those new ingredients for making products at home.

Fat Replacement Strategies

The major challenge in making low fat sausages is to achieve fat reduction while preserving as closely as possible its eating qualities. The basic methods are:

1. Fat removal.
2. Water substitution.

1. The simplest method is to remove fat from the meat without any attempt to replace it. This method has worked well with making low-fat or no-fat milk and the products were eventually accepted by the consumer. Direct fat removal without any compensation is better suited for general cooking, for example when making burritos or meat balls where more ingredients are introduced such as bean paste, cheese, sour cream or tomato sauce. Those ingredients tend to mask the removed fat and the product tastes fine. Such methods can also be applied to sausage making, as the process always begins with trimming of the meat. However, this approach has its shortcomings as it adversely affects the texture and the mouthfeel of the product. In addition it will make the sausage more expensive as the fat will have to be discarded.

Commercially produced sausages are made from little meat trimmings, pieces of fat, machine removed meat from bones and it will be impractical to discard fat. Then a fat replacer, which costs more than fat, would have to be added. This makes the process costlier and more labor intensive. Such an idea will never catch on with commercial producers unless a customer agrees to pay a high premium for such a product. A hobbyist is in a different situation as he is making sausages for himself and he can be more choosey. He can select a lean, noble meat cut at the local supermarket and make a great healthy sausage. As he is making sausage for himself, the extra cost of lean meat plays a secondary role for him. The advice is to start with a lean meat so less fatty trimmings will be discarded. They may be added to other sausage types, for example to value added sausages or liver sausages.

Fat Removal Problems

When processed meats were made in a traditional way, there was a correct balance between lean meats and fats. There were thousands of years of experimentation behind making hams and sausages. However, the latest scientific research, government regulations and the ever growing pressure from our doctors and nutritionists, have forced the food industry to come up with healthier meat products. The fat does not supply just energy, it provides a smooth feeling to the palate, known as "good mouthfeel" and it carries the flavor. Remove the fat, and the customer refuses to buy the product. "It does not taste right" is the answer. Hydrocolloids mimic the fat feeling, they provide this "good mouthfeel" without employing fat. They cheat our senses and try to convince us that a low fat product is really not such a bad item. We have been using many hydrocolloids for general cooking before without much thinking: flours and cornstarch to thick sauces and gravies, egg for making mayonnaise, pectin for jams and jellies, soy proteins and maltodextrins for making energy drinks. The same hydrocolloids can be added to meat products in order to make up for the removal of fat. In addition, there are many recently created products which display an enormous water holding and gelling properties.

In order to cover the subject thoroughly many fat replacers are mentioned. Some of them are used on a commercial scale. A big challenge that a hobbyist faces is that commercial fat replacers are available in large quantities only, for example 50 lb bags. That makes those products of lesser value for home production. The manufacturer will not deal with individual customers. They want to sell products by truckloads.

Many of us have used fat replacers such as soy proteins, non fat dry milk, potato flour, starch, egg, gelatin, pectin and other hydrocolloids before. They were used for making soups, gravies, jams, jellies, meat jellies, head cheeses, liver sausages and more. In most cases these ingredients were added because the recipe called for them and the author of the recipe discovered through his experience, that they make a better sausage. We have never thought that we were adding hydrocolloids, all we knew was the correct way to make those products. This way is still correct today, and although the in-laboratory created products may be more cost effective, nevertheless we can obtain the same results with commonly available ingredients as long as we understand how to apply them.

Discarding *all* visible fat makes sense for people suffering from chronic heart disease, as saturated animal fat is the last thing they need. It is relatively easy to remove surface and intermuscular fat, but intramuscular fat will remain. This is the fat inside of the muscle, which is easily noticeable when meat is cut across. This fat is called "marbling" and a good steak contains plenty of it. A very lean cut of meat still contains about 2.5% fat though it can not be seen with the naked eye. It should be noted that ground meat is available with a fat content as low as 5 percent. The amount of fat can be lowered by the following procedures:

*   Trimming off and discarding all visible fat.
*   Replacing fat with vegetable oil. The amount of calories remains the same, but the vegetable oil is much healthier and does not contain cholesterol.
*   Replacing fat with premixed oil emulsion (soy protein isolate, oil and water). This solution significantly lowers calories and cholesterol.

2. The second method introduces a water binding fat replacer. The majority of fat replacers can hold significant amounts of water. This extra water results in increased "juiciness" that mimics the sensory characteristics that fat normally provides. Adding extra water offers many advantages as it is:

*   Label friendly - not subject to regulations.
*   Cheap and available everywhere.
*   Does not add calories.

On the negative side adding water shortens shelf life by facilitating growth of bacteria. This should be of lesser concern for a hobbyist whose product will have a short span between manufacture and consumption cycles.

There is only a certain amount of water that meat proteins can hold. An excessive amount of water will not be bound by the meat or water holding agents and will leak out. This purge is of great concern in retail packaged processed meats. Lean meat has the strongest capacity for holding water and beef can bind water more effectively than pork. To bind water better, meats are finely comminuted to obtain the maximum protein extraction. Adding salt and phosphates improves the results. We add water during mixing or emulsifying, but some of it

will evaporate during smoking and cooking. The solution is to introduce ingredients that will trap more water and prevent it from escap-
ing during the cooking process. This results in higher profits for the
manufacturer. Increasing the juiciness of the product by adding water
is important as it makes up for the "smooth" feeling of fat, which has
been eliminated from the sausage. The ingredients which are known to
accomplish that goal are: *flours and starches, soy proteins, non-fat dry
milk, caseinate, gums, maltodextrins, pectins and cellulose fat replacers.* It would be confusing to create sausage recipes that will include
all of those ingredients. Instead our recipes include ingredients which
are commonly available and simple to use such as potato flour, non-fat
dry milk or soy protein concentrate. Distributors of sausage making
equipment and supplies start to carry premixed blends of fat replacers
such as Konjac flour, xanthan gum and microcrystaline cellulose. For
those who want to experiment further, the section Links of Interest
provides sources where one can obtain ingredients that can be used for
making low fat sausages.

The addition of water has become an accepted procedure for making reduced fat emulsified products and the lower the fat content of
the sausage, the more water is added. Commercial producers generally
add 50-80% of water to emulsified sausages. However, it must be noted that water does not possess any properties of fat like carrying the
flavor and providing pleasant mouthfeel. This must be compensated
by adding fat replacers, replacing water with chicken or beef broth, or
using any other means that would enhance the flavor of the sausage.

Application of Non-Meat Ingredients

Non-meat ingredients allow us to create very healthy sausages. Fat
can be trimmed away as much as possible, most extenders and fillers
are good binders and strong water holders. The oil does not have to be
used at all and the hardest part is to bind all those ingredients together.
Non-meat ingredients can be added directly to meat materials prior to
grinding. This can be followed by manual mixing. In emulsified sausages, non-meat ingredients are added directly to a bowl chopper or
food processor. Coarse fillers such as bread crumbs, rusk or granulated Textured Vegetable Protein are usually re-hydrated. Fine powders
such as soy protein isolate, milk caseinate, non-fat milk powder, flour,
and starch can be added in dry form. Commercial producers may have
those ingredients prepared in emulsion form and stored in a cooler.

Dietary Fiber

As people around the world eat more processed convenience foods, their consumption of healthy dietary fiber typically falls far short of recommended minimums. The average American consumes just 14-15 grams of fiber a day, well below the recommended 20-35 grams. Fortefiber soluble dietary fiber is derived from cellulose and is suitable for many food and nutritional supplement formulations. It has been shown in clinical trials to provide several health benefits related to promoting a healthy lifestyle, such as maintaining normal levels of blood glucose, cholesterol and insulin in healthy people. Applications range from liquids to hard-formed products. The vendor's proprietary process makes it water soluble. Fortefiber does not cause allergic reactions, bloating or gas, and does not have a bad taste or texture when used at typical product formulation levels.

Vegetables and Fruits

Three reasons support the recommendation for Americans to eat more vegetables and fruits:

1. Most vegetables and fruits are major contributors of a number of nutrients that are under consumed in the United States, including folate, magnesium, potassium, dietary fiber, and vitamins Q, C, and K.

2. Consumption of vegetables and fruits is associated with reduced risk of many chronic diseases. Specifically, moderate evidence indicates that intake of at least 2-1/2 cups of vegetables and fruits per day is associated with reduced risk of cardiovascular disease, including heart attack and stroke. Some vegetables and fruits may be protective against certain types of cancer.

3. Most vegetables and fruits, when prepared without adding fats and sugars, are relatively low in calories. Eating them instead of higher calorie foods can help adults and children achieve and maintain a healthy diet.

Potato, tomato, banana, plantain, apples, plums, mango, dried fruits and nuts go well with many types of sausages.

Low Salt Sausages

Removing animal fat and decreasing calories makes a healthier sausage for most people, but the large amounts of salt still create a problem for many. If we want to conform to the USDA recommendations for daily salt intake, the sausage recipes must still be further modified. The amount of salt added to all commercial products (not just sausages) is huge and will in time increase blood pressure in even healthy individuals.

A large percentage of the western population will develop high blood pressure in later years. Once when we get this problem, it is hard to reverse it, and at best we can only try to control it. We control it by suddenly paying attention to the amount of salt a particular food contains. Salt increases blood pressure, that is a fact. Some people are more tolerant to salt, but about 20% of the population will become salt sensitive, especially later in life. Eating a good dinner with a salty pickle can increase blood pressure in a person with hypertension even 50 points and as long as he keeps on eating salty foods, his pressure will continue to be dangerously high. When such a person lowers consumption of salty foods his blood pressure returns to an acceptable level.

We do not develop high blood pressure by eating sausages, but by consuming ready to eat products which we warm up at home. Just look at the amount of salt a canned soup, canned vegetable, or fish contains. Look at an healthy vegetarian sausage. The amount of salt those items contain *is simply scary.* Salt is added in such a high amount to prevent the growth of bacteria and to prolong the shelf life of the product. We have no control over manufactured products, but we can prepare our own meals ourselves. *By cooking at home we can add only as much salt as is needed for good flavor.* This amount will be well below what is added by commercial producers.

The problem is that we lead such a hurried life that we have no time to cook, besides less and less people even know how. Our canned products and easy to prepare meals are to blame for the high blood pressure we develop. If you look at the labels, you will see that the amount of salt they contain is staggering. The salt is added to everything, meat products and sausages, canned fish, peanut butter, canned vegetables, nuts, soups, milk, cheese, butter, vegetable spreads – the list is endless.

Our salt intake Percent Daily Values is based on a 2,000 calorie diet. This is the amount of calories that the average person needs to function daily. The recommended daily salt intake corresponds to no more than 2,400 mg (2.4 g) which is about 1/3 of a teaspoon as 1 teaspoon usually accommodates around 6 g of salt. If you eat one 18.8 oz (533 g) can of soup you consume 790 mg salt and you use 33% of your daily salt quota. Add to it a few more meals, maybe French fries with a hamburger for lunch, then a ready to eat microwave dinner and you are well over the limit. An average person consumes much more salt than is needed, which makes his kidneys work harder and puts him at risk of developing high blood pressure. Most of us are leading such a busy life than we are left at the mercy of commercially prepared and packed foods. This leaves us with no control over what goes into the food.

There is no way to eliminate salt all together but at best we can read the labels, pay more attention to what we buy and minimize the damage which might affect us later in life. You can reduce the amount of sodium in your diet by following these guidelines:

- Read labels carefully and choose foods that have less salt. All commercially prepared foods such as fast food, canned vegetables, soups, commercially prepared meats, and other packaged convenience foods contain very large amounts of salt.
- Cook your own meals.
- Use salt substitutes.

Different Salt Types

There are different types of salt and people often speculate which kind is the best. Well, probably the cheapest salt that is known as rock or canning salt might be the best as it is very pure. Salt was originally mined and transported in huge slabs to different areas. It was a valuable commodity and was named after the mine which had produced it. Different mines produced salt with different impurities content. If a particular salt contained more Nitrate, it induced a pink color to the meat and improved its keeping qualities. Such salt of course, became popular for meat preservation. Cleaner salt will produce cleaner gelatin in a head cheese. Some salts are finely ground and some are flaked. A finely ground salt will be more suitable for curing fish in brine. Due to a short time involved finely pulverized salt will penetrate fish flesh faster. On the other hand dry cured products such as ham or bacon which cure for weeks at the time, might benefit from a coarsely ground salt.

Table salt that we use for general cooking contains many added ingredients such as iodine (there is a non-iodized salt, too) and anti-caking agents such as sodium silicoaluminate or magnesium carbonate that prevent salt from acquiring moisture.

Rock salt, also called pickling or canning salt is the cleanest of all salts, its price is lower and it is a great choice for making any products. Pure rock salt will lump together and will not sift from a salt shaker. Salt lumping is of a minor inconvenience as the hardened salt can be reversed to its original powdery form by shaking the container.

Sea salt is made by evaporating sea water, includes traces of different minerals which were diluted in water and were too heavy to evaporate. Those impurities include different minerals and chemicals such as magnesium, calcium or nitrate. Due to impurities sea salt may taste a bit bitter. Sea salt is occasionally added to dry cured and air dried products which are made without Nitrates. It is often used in making dry cured hams which are made without sodium nitrite/nitrate. Each gallon of sea water (8.33 lb) produces more than 1/4 pound of salt.

Kosher salts are very pure and for general cooking purposes both table salt and kosher salt will work equally well, though kosher salt, and in particular Diamond® Crystal kosher salt dissolves more readily. What is important to remember is that kosher salts are less dense than ordinary table salts and measure quite differently from a volume standpoint.

Kosher salt has larger crystals and is bulkier. A given weight of Diamond® Crystal takes up nearly twice the volume as the same weight of table salt. One teaspoon of table salt weighs 6 g but 1 teaspoon of Kosher salt weighs 4.8 g. Five tablespoons of Diamond® Kosher Salt (72 g) or five tablespoons of Morton® Table Salt (90 g) will add a different percentage of salt to your product as the former salt is much lighter. Yet when you weigh 90 g of salt on a scale it makes no difference what kind of salt you choose. Ninety grams of table salt equals to 90 g of flaked salt regardless of the volume they might occupy. The table below shows approximate equivalent amounts of different salts:

Table Salt	1 cup	292 g (10.3 oz)
Morton® Kosher Salt	1⅓ to 1½ cup	218 g (7.7 oz)
Diamond® Crystal Kosher Salt	1 cup	142 g (5 oz)

As the table demonstrates it is *always advisable to weigh out your salt*. The above table proves how misleading a recipe can be if listed ingredients are measured in volume units only (cups, spoons, etc). To make matters worse, American, English or Australian spoons are not the same.

Whether you eat table salt, sea salt, Kosher or rock salt it does not really matter. Each salt is sodium chloride (NaCl) and each contains sodium (Na) which is associated with increasing blood pressure. The only difference is the amount of impurities each salt contains.

Potassium Chloride vs. Sodium Chloride

The salt we use for cooking is Sodium Chloride (NaCl) and *sodium* is what increases our blood pressure. Potassium chloride *does not contain sodium* and is used by commercial manufacturers to make low sodium salts. It has a bitter metalic taste so it is mixed in varying proportions with regular sodium chloride salt. Salt substitutes vary in their composition, but their main ingredient is always potassium chloride. For example, the listed contents of the **NuSalt** are: potassium chloride, cream of tartar and natural flavor derived from yeast. It contains less than 20 mg of sodium per 100 grams. The contents of the **NoSalt** are: potassium chloride, potassium bitartrate, adipic acid, mineral oil, fumaric acid and silicon dioxide. A salt substitute does not taste exactly like sodium chloride, but it is close enough, and it contains less or none of the sodium that some people are trying to avoid.

Here comes to our rescue another salt, KCl, known as potassium chloride. You can see that does not contain Na (sodium), the part that is responsible for increasing blood pressure. When used alone, it has a salty bitter flavor, so the preferred choice is to mix it with a common salt. A good combination is to mix one part of KCl with one part NaCl. What we get is the new salt: NaCl + KCl, which contains only 50% of Na (sodium) of the common table salt. Our biggest salt producer Morton makes such a salt called "Lite Salt" which is available in every supermarket. Morton produces another salt under the name "Salt Substitute" which contains 0 sodium (Na). You may call it *the salt without salt* as it has salty/bitter flavor, yet it does not contain any sodium.

The following table compares all three salts:

Name	% Daily Value based on 2,000 calorie diet		Serving size
	Sodium	Potassium	
Morton Salt	590 mg, 25%	0	¼ tsp (1.5g)
Morton Lite Salt	290 mg, 12%	350 mg, 10%	¼ tsp (1.4g)
Morton Salt Substitute	0	610 mg, 17%	¼ tsp (1.2g)

It can be seen in the table above that with Lite Salt, we immediately cut sodium consumption in half, and Salt Substitute allows us to make a sodium free product. People with kidney failure, heart failure or diabetes should not use salt substitutes without medical advice.

Salt Perception is an Acquired Taste

If you decide to go on a low sodium diet and start decreasing the amount of salt you consume, after about three weeks you may reach a point when your food tastes enjoyable, though you use less salt than before. This is fine as long as you prepare those meals for yourself. When making sausages for your friends, try to adhere to the amount of salt the original recipe calls for, as other people might like a different amount of salt. When smoking large amounts of meat that will be kept for a week or longer, remember that *it will keep on drying out* (losing moisture), even when kept in a refrigerator. *Salt will, however, remain inside and your sausage will now taste saltier though its diameter will be smaller.* The meat flavor will also be stronger now. In such a case you may use less salt than originally planned for as the saltiness and meat flavor will be more pronounced in time. And if you find your sausage not salty enough use the salt shaker, that is what they are for.

Choosing salt substitute. The number one step is to pick up a salt substitute which will be used and become familiar with it. Let's assume that a sausage will contain 1% of salt and that calls for adding 10 g of salt to 1 kg (1000 g) of meat. Mix 10 g of salt substitute (about 1½ teaspoon) with 1 kg of meat, make a tiny hamburger, cook it and see how you like it. Let your palate be the judge. Read the label carefully to see how much regular salt (sodium chloride) a particular salt substitute contains and you will know exactly how much salt your sausage contains. There are different brands of salt substitutes in supermarkets and online so do your own research.

Curing. Best quality smoked products incorporate meat which is cured with salt and sodium nitrite (Cure #1 in the USA or Peklosol in Europe). To cure 1 kg of meat, introducing 150 parts per million of sodium nitrite, only 2.4 g of Cure #1 is required (about 1/3 teaspoon). As Cure #1 contains 6.25% sodium nitrite and 93.75% of sodium chloride, 2.25 g of salt will be introduced. This comes to 0.2% salt, which is of little concern even for people on low sodium diets.

Salt and Sausages

Buying commercially prepared meats and sausages does not leave us much choice, we end up eating a lot of salt. It is added to protect meat against bacteria and to extend the life of the product. Some products such as traditionally made dry salami or dry hams must be made with large amounts of salt, otherwise the product will spoil and/or become unsafe to consume. Home made sausages can easily be made with much less salt than their commercial counterparts. First of all one should familiarize oneself with different types of sausages that can be made safely at home using lesser amounts of salt. Contrary to a popular belief, the sausages do not contain as much salt as we normally like to think. A typical range is from 1.5% to 2% salt in relation to the weight of the sausage mass. An average figure will be around 1.8%.

When the second World War ended in 1945, there was no refrigeration in heavily damaged countries like Poland, Germany or Russia. Sausages were produced with food preservation in mind and they contained about 2-2.3% of salt. Those countries lay at a similar latitude like Quebec in Canada, which provides good conditions for keeping food at room temperatures most of the year. Everybody had a storage unit in the common basement of a building or a designated pantry in the apartment. Those conditions plus the right amount of salt, Nitrate and manufacturing procedures such as curing and cold smoking allowed the creation of meat products with a very long shelf life. We don't need to go over 2% salt today as everybody owns a refrigerator. If a person is on a low sodium diet, 1-1.5% salt will be fine too. The only exception are slow fermented dry sausages (salami type) or cold smoked spreadable fermented sausages, which are not submitted to heat treatment and must contain larger amounts of salt. Those sausages need 3% salt to protect meat from bacteria and there is no room for compromise here. However, it should be expected that the overall quality of the sausage may suffer once the level of salt drops below 1.5%.

Emulsified sausages such as hot dogs, frankfurter or bologna require good emulsification which is dependent on protein extraction. Those proteins are needed to coat fat particles with a protein film which prevents fat separation by creating strong emulsion. Salt contributes largely to this process as many proteins are salt soluble, this means they mix with salt solutions. Using less salt will inhibit protein extraction and it will be harder to produce a good emulsified sausage. To make up for this, it is recommended to select very lean meat which contains more protein. Adding phosphate helps to extract more protein. Soy protein isolate is another source of extra protein. Lastly a sharp knife, a small grinder plate 1/8" (3 mm) and a good food processor will aid in protein extraction.

Liver sausages are usually made with less salt to begin with and aromatic spices they usually contain will mask the absence of salt. A proper amount of salt is needed for protein extraction and strong emulsification.

Head cheese can be made with little salt or even without it. Meat binding is accomplished by the bonding properties of gelatin, not by protein extraction due to the action of salt. Head cheese is usually served with vinegar or has vinegar added during production (souse) and it further masks the absence of salt.

Herbal Salt Substitutes

Selecting a right and generous combination of spices is a very effective tool for covering up the lack of salt. In many instances there is no need for salt at all. Some spice combinations, for example mixing equal amounts of ground cumin and pepper, can effectively mask the lower dosage of salt. Lemon juice activates the same taste receptors as sodium, so adding some lemon juice, or grated lemon zest makes a lot of sense. The Internet is full of recipes for herb and spice mixtures and many ready to use mixtures, such as Mrs. Dash or Salt-free Spike, can be purchased in most supermarkets.

Herb Salt Substitute 1

1 teaspoon ground cayenne pepper
1 tablespoon garlic powder
1 tablespoon onion powder
1 teaspoon dried basil
1 teaspoon dried oregano
1 teaspoon dried thyme
1 teaspoon dried savory
1 teaspoon dried parsley flakes
1 teaspoon ground mace
1 teaspoon fresh ground black pepper
1 teaspoon dried sage
1 teaspoon dried marjoram
1 teaspoon lemon, rind of, ground, dried, grated

Herb Salt Substitute 2

1 tablespoon dried basil
1 tablespoon dried thyme
1 tablespoon ground coriander
2 teaspoons onion powder
2 teaspoons dried parsley flakes
2 teaspoons ground cumin
1 teaspoon garlic powder
1 teaspoon ground mustard
1 teaspoon cayenne pepper
1 teaspoon paprika
1 teaspoon lemon, rind of, ground, dried, grated

Some people may object to garlic or lemon zest so those ingredients can be removed from the recipe without harming it in any way. You may consider other classical herb combinations and incorporate them into your own mixtures:

French Quatre Epices

black pepper, ground	2 Tbsp.
cloves, ground	2 Tbsp.
nutmeg, ground	2 Tbsp.
cinnamon, ground	2 tsp.
ginger, ground (optional)	1/2 tsp.

Highly aromatic mixture that can be added to liver sausages.

Chinese Five Spices

cloves, ground	1 tsp.
black pepper, ground,	2 tsp.
anise star, ground	1 tsp.
cinnamon, ground	2 tsp.
fennel, ground	1 tsp.
ginger, ground (optional)	1/2 tsp.

Highly aromatic mixture that can be added to liver sausages.

Italian Herb Mix

marjoram, dried	3 Tbsp.
thyme, dried	1 tsp.
rosemary, dried	1 tsp.
sage, dried	1 tsp.
savory	1 tsp.
oregano, dried	3 Tbsp.
basil, dried	3 tbsp.

This is a typical Italian seasoning mix. All it needs is cayenne pepper and some onion powder and it becomes a herb salt substitute.

Useful Additives

There are many additives that can be used to make a reduced fat sausage. We have performed many tests and experiments and positive results were obtained with the oil emulsion, carrageenan, konjac flour, starches or commercial fat replacer blend. In our opinion the additives that are of most value for making reduced fat sausages are:

- Soy protein isolate.
- Carrageenan.
- Konjac flour.
- Potato starch/other starches.
- Potato flour/other flours.
- Non fat dry milk.
- Gelatin.
- Textured vegetable protein.

There are two ingredients which are not absolutely necessary, although recommended:

- Phosphate - for maximum protein extractability.
- Sodium erythorbate, sodium ascorbate or ascorbate acid (vitamin C) - for the faster development of the curing (pink) color.

Oil emulsion described in detail in Chapter 8 consists of soy protein isolate, vegetable oil and water and is a great replacement for animal fats.

The Sausage Maker Fat Replacer

The Sausage Maker Inc., Buffalo, NY, has been the first distributor to offer fat replacers for making reduced fat sausages. The company carries a premixed fat replacer blend that consists of natural products:

- Konjac flour - binds water, mimics fat.
- Xanthan - synergistically increases the power of konjac.
- Microcrystalline cellulose - provides the better mouthfeel by mimicking the sensation of fat.

The properties of each ingredient are described in Chapter 4. It is a premixed blend so we can only speculate about the proportion of each ingredient but the following composition should work: konjac flour 0.5%, xanthan gum 0.75%, microcrystalline cellulose 1%.

This is free flowing fine white powder that does not dissolve fully in water. Konjac flour dissolves readily but, microcrystalline cellulose particles do not. For this reason add fat replacer in dry form into ground meat. Once the fat replacer becomes wet it becomes very slippery and since the sensation of fat in the mouth. This fat replacer blend works very well and is easy to apply.

Suggested use: 2 teaspoons (7.5 g) for each 1 lb. of very lean meat. 3/4 of a cup for 25 lb. of meat.
This corresponds to around 0.8%.

Photo 6.1 Sausage Maker Fat Replacer.

Chapter 7

Sausage Making Process

Making Sausages - Basic Tutorial

Making sausage is like making hamburger - the meat is ground, salt, pepper and the required spices are added, and then it is cooked until it is safe for consumption. If this prepared meat were stuffed into casings, it would become a sausage. The proper amount of salt in meat (tastes pleasant) is between 1.5-2%, and 3.5-5% will be the upper limit of acceptability; anything more and the product will be too salty. There is less room for compromise when making fermented sausages where salt is used as a safety hurdle to prevent the growth of bacteria in the first stage of processing. Dry sausages require about 3% of salt and semi-dry around 2.5%.

The sausage making process:

- Meat selection.
- Curing.
- Grinding.
- Mixing.
- Stuffing.
- Drying.
- Smoking.
- Cooking.
- Cooling.
- Storing.

There are some exceptions to the above process:

- Fresh sausages-manufacture ends with stuffing.
- Liver, head cheese and blood sausages - meats are precooked, the sausage is stuffed and then cooked.
- Fermented sausages - cooking step is often eliminated.
- Smoking process may be employed or not.

Meat Selection

All cuts of good meat make good sausages. Trim out all gristle, sinew, blood clots, and excess fat but save suitable trimmings. They can be used for making emulsified sausages or head cheeses. Those lower quality trimmings are hard to grind through a grinder but a food processor will chop them fine. If you choose only lean cuts, your sausage will definitely be healthier, but you will miss out on the taste.

Sausages can be made from all kinds of meats, some of them quite exotic, but we limit our choices to meats that are common. Chicken is the most popular meat which is consumed worldwide as it is easy to raise and can be eaten by the average family at one sitting. Other meats of value are fish, venison and wild game. However, it is still recommended to mix these lean meats with pork to achieve better texture and flavor. Most sausages are made of either pure pork, or a combination with other meats, most often beef. Sausages made entirely from beef will be drier with a harder texture. Veal makes a light colored sausage and has excellent binding properties. Mutton can also be used in sausage. It has poor water holding properties and its distinctive flavor is not appreciated by many. For this reason it should be limited to around 15% in any recipe.

When it comes to selecting pork meat for sausages, the majority of books and recipes mention the same magical word: "use a pork butt". Sure, it has the right lean meat to fat ratio of 70/30 and pork butts lend themselves as excellent choices. A beginner might think that only butt can be used for making sausages. Keep in mind that a pig has only two pork butts weighing together about 15 pounds but the farmer is left with an additional 250 pounds of meat that must be used. Without a doubt pork butt is a lovely cut for making sausages and the best choice for someone living in a large city as it is widely available and is economically priced. Its little blade bone is easy to remove and we are left with six pounds of lean meat, meat with some fat, meat with a lot of fat, some pure fat and the skin.

Imagine a butcher cutting pork into pieces until nothing is left on the table. Before he can carve out a ham from the leg he has to separate it from the body, then cut off the lower leg, remove the bones, tendons, gristle, sinews, skin, pieces of fat etc. To get a clean piece of meat like a ham, butt or pork loin a lot of work has to be performed first that leaves scraps of meat which can not be sold in one piece. All those trimmings go into sausages. The point is that any scrap of meat is suitable for making sausages, not just a butt. Pork but is actually a poor choice for making non-fat sausages - you have to discard about 25-30% of the meat (fat). You may as well buy pork loin and save yourself a lot of work.

Fat. There are different types of fat and they will all be used for different purposes. There are hard, medium and soft fats and they have a different texture and different melting point. Some head cheese and emulsified sausage recipes call for dewlap or jowl fat that may be hard to obtain. Bacon looks similar and it seems like a good replacement, but it is not. Bacon is a soft belly fat and dewlap/jowl is a hard fat.

Pork fat is preferred for making sausages as it is hard, white and tastes the best. It exhibits different degrees of hardness depending from which animal part it comes from. Back fat, jowl fat, or butt fat (surface area) have a very hard texture and higher melting point. They are the best choice for making products in which we expect to see the individual specks of fat in a finished product such as dry salami. Soft fat such as bacon fat is fine for making fermented spreadable sausages such as mettwurst or teewurst. *For most sausages any fat pork trimmings are fine* providing they were partially frozen when submitted to the grinding process. This prevents fat smearing when temperature increases due to the mechanical action of knives and delivery worm on fat particles.

Beef fat has a higher melting temperature than pork but is yellowish in color which affects the appearance of the product where discrete particles of fat should be visible. Besides, beef fat does not taste as good as pork fat. If no back fat is available, use fat pork trimmings or meats which contain more fat and grind them together. Instead of struggling with fat smearing when processing meats at higher than recommended temperatures, it is better to use cuts that contain a higher proportion of fat. It will help to overcome the problem of smearing as long as the materials are partially frozen. Partially frozen back fat may be manually diced with ease into 3/16" (5 mm) pieces.

Chicken fat is neutral in flavor and is suited for making chicken sausages although it presents some problems. It is soft and melts at such low temperatures that it is hard to work with. Softer fats can be used for making emulsified or liver sausages where it will become a part of emulsified paste. For instance, vegetable oil can be successfully mixed with liver and fat when producing liver sausage.

Curing Meat For Sausages

Let's make something absolutely clear, you don't need to cure meat to make your sausage. Curing is an extra process that requires more time, designated containers and space in a refrigerator. Curing imparts a certain peculiar flavor which is in demand by the consumer and if we cure hams, bacon, chops, butts, and fish because they taste better, so why not cure meat for sausages? The fact that we grind meat makes it only easier on our teeth to chew - it does not improve the color, texture or the flavor of the sausage. The dry method of curing is used to cure meat for sausages. Meat should be cut into smaller pieces, about 2 inches (5-6 cm) and not heavier than 0. 5 lb (250 g).

The curing time depends on:

- Diameter of the meat - making cuts smaller or grinding them in a grinder increases the meat's surface area and speeds up curing.
- Temperature - usually set by the refrigerator setting. In the past when Nitrates were used, curing temperatures were higher (42-46° F, 6-8° C) which allowed curing bacteria to react with Nitrate. As a result nitrite was released which would then cure meat.
- Additives - adding ascorbates speeds up curing. More important for commercial producers.

Meat should be thoroughly mixed with salt, Cure #1 (salt, nitrite), sugar (if used) and packed tightly in a container, not higher than 8 inches (20 cm). Then the meat is covered with a clean cloth and stored in a refrigerator. There are chemical reactions taking place inside meat and the cloth allows the gases to evaporate through. It also prevents the surface of the meat from reacting with oxygen which sometimes creates gray color areas on the surface. The curing times at 40° F (4° C) (refrigerator temperature) are as follows:

- Meat pieces size 2" - 72 hours.
- Ground meat - 24 - 36 hours, depending on plate size.

What will happen to smoked sausages if the meat is not cured? Basically nothing as long as you add salt and Cure #1 (sodium nitrite) to the ground meat during mixing (you are still curing meat). The final color might not be as good as the properly cured sausage but it will still be a great sausage. If you don't want to cure meat using the traditional method, use the alternative curing method described below.

Alternative curing methods

Method 1. Grind each meat through a proper plate (as dictated by the recipe). The reason that we grind now and not cut meat into pieces for curing is that salt and sodium nitrite will penetrate a tiny piece of ground meat much faster than a 5 cm (2") cube. Mix meat with salt and Cure #1. Pack tightly (to remove air) and separately, place each type of ground meat in a container and cover with a cloth to allow breathing. Let it "set" for 3-4 hours at room temperature 20-22°C (68-71°F). Chemical reactions proceed much faster at higher temperatures and so does curing. Add spices, mix all together and stuff casings.

Method 2. Grind each meat through a proper plate (as dictated by the recipe). Mix meat with salt, Cure #1 and other ingredients. Stuff sausages and place in a cooler for 12-24 hours before smoking. When removed from the cooler they have to be conditioned at room temperature for a few hours to remove moisture from the surface.

Method 3. Grind each meat through a proper plate (as dictated by the recipe). Mix meat with salt, Cure #1 and other ingredients. Stuff sausages and hang at room temperature for 2 hours. Transfer to a smokehouse.

As you can see in all instances we are buying extra time to allow curing inside the meat. A commercial producer will not perform curing at higher than cooler temperature as this will affect the shelf life of the product. Commercial processors cure meat faster and at lower temperatures by using ascorbic acid (vitamin C), erythorbic acid, or their derivatives, sodium ascorbate and/or sodium erythorbate. These additives speed up the chemical conversion of nitrite to nitric oxide which in turn will react with meat myoglobin to create a pink color. They also deplete levels of meat oxygen which prevents the fading of the cured meat color in the presence of light and oxygen.

Curing With Nitrates/Nitrites

Meat cured only with salt, will have a better flavor but will also develop an objectionable dark color. Adding nitrites to meat will improve flavor, prevent food poisoning, tenderize the meat, and develop the pink color widely known and associated with smoked meats.

We had been and still are using Nitrates because:

- Nitrates can preserve meat's natural color. The same piece of ham when roasted will have a light brown color and is known as roasted leg of pork. Add some nitrates to it, cook it and it becomes ham with its characteristic flavor and pink color.

- Nitrates impart a characteristic cured flavor to meat.
- Nitrates prevent the transformation of botulinum spores into toxins thus eliminating the possibility of food poisoning.
- Nitrates prevent rancidity of fats.

Cure #1 (also known as Instacure #1, Prague Powder #1 or Pink Cure #1). For any aspiring sausage maker it is a necessity to understand and know how to apply Cure #1 and Cure #2, as these two cures are used worldwide though under different names and with different proportions of nitrates and salt. Cure #1 is a mixture of 1 oz of sodium nitrite (6.25%) to 1 lb of salt. It must be used to cure all meats that will require smoking at low temperatures. It may be used to cure meats for fresh sausages (optional).

Cure #2 (also known as Instacure #2, Prague Powder #2 or Pink Cure #2). Cure #2 is a mixture of 1 oz of sodium nitrite (6.25%) along with 0.64 oz of sodium Nitrate (4%) to 1 lb of salt. It can be compared to the time-releasing capsules used for treating colds. It must be used with any products that do not require cooking, smoking or refrigeration and is mainly used for products that will be air cured for a long time like country ham, salami, pepperoni, and other dry sausages. Both Cure #1 and Cure #2 contain a small amount of FDA approved red coloring agent that gives them a slight pink color thus eliminating any possible confusion with common salt and that is why they are sometimes called "pink" curing salts. Cure #1 is not interchangeable with Cure #2 and vice versa.

Comminuted products - small meat pieces, *meat for sausages*, ground meat, poultry etc. Cure #1 was developed in such a way that if we add 4 ounces of Cure #1 to 100 pounds of meat, the quantity of nitrite added to meat will comfort to the legal limits (156 ppm) permitted by the Meat Division of the United States Department of Agriculture.

If we stay within Food and Drug Administration guidelines (1 oz. Cure #1 per 25 lbs of meat - about 1 level teaspoon of Cure #1 for 5 lbs of meat) we are applying 156 ppm of nitrite *which is enough and safe* at the same time.

Comminuted Meat (Sausages)	Cure #1 in ounces	Cure #1 in grams	Cure #1 in teaspoons
25 lbs.	1	28.35	5
5 lbs.	0.2	5.66	1
1 lb.	0.04	1.1	1/5
1 kg	0.08	2.5	1/2

Usually, most home sausage makers omit the curing step. This can be attributed to the lack of information available on curing meats for sausages as many recipes on the Internet are very amateurish at best.

A commercial plant might avoid the traditional way of curing meats in order to save time and space but they make up for it by injecting larger cuts with curing solution or adding salt, nitrite, and curing accelerators during meat chopping and mixing. As a result the meat is still cured although using different methods. For example, a frankfurter which is a smoked sausage, is cured, smoked, peeled and packed in about 30-45 minutes.

Grinding

The lean meat should be separated from the fat. As a rule, lean meat is ground coarsely while fatty cuts are ground very finely. This way our sausage is lean-looking and the fat is less visible. It is much easier to grind cold meat taken directly out of the refrigerator. The fat is usually ground through a plate with very small holes and if it is not partially frozen a smeared paste will be produced. The locking ring on a grinder head should be tight and the knife must be sharp, otherwise the meat will smear. Otherwise we would have meat smearing and the sausage will look greasy even when lean meat was used. Ideally, meat should always be chilled between 32-35°F (0-2° C) for a clean cut. Since refrigerator temperatures are roughly 38-40°F (3-4° C), we should place the meat in a freezer for about 30 min just before grinding. In domestic conditions, we could choose to cut the meat either during the early hours of the morning, or during late evenings when temperatures are not higher than 70°F (21°C). After we are done cutting the meat, we should separate it into different groups: lean, semi - fat, and fat. Then they should be placed back into the refrigerator.

It is possible to purchase minced meat in a supermarket, just make sure it has been minced the day of the purchase. Such minced meat should be processed not later than the following day.

Emulsions. Understanding emulsions is important for making emulsified products such as hot dogs, frankfurters, bologna or liver sausages. During the comminution process fat cells become ruptured and the free fat is released. Fat does not dissolve in water or mix with it well. *The purpose of emulsion is to bond free fat, meat and water together so they will not become separated.*

Emulsions types:

1. Natural meat emulsion. This is a natural emulsion where meat must form a matrix to hold the fat. *The leaner the meat the stronger matrix* will be created. This matrix will hold water as well and will give a sausage its proper texture. Meat proteins are needed not only for their nutritional value but for their contribution towards emulsification and binding of meat products.

- Pork rind emulsion. Pork skins are precooked for about 1.5 hours in hot simmering water and then chopped in a bowl cutter or food processor *when still warm*. About 1/3 of water, 1/3 pork skins and 1/3 back fat are combined to create emulsion. Such emulsion must be used quickly or cooled down and frozen for later use.

- Liver emulsion. Liver contains the natural emulsifying agent and around 30% is added when making liver sausages.

2. Caseinate (type of milk protein) and soy-based emulsion. A typical caseinate based emulsion: 5 parts water : 5 parts fat : 1 part caseinate.
3. Soy isolate based emulsion: 5 parts water : 5 parts fat : 1 part soy-protein isolate. When less than lean meats are used, the binding will still take place providing enough exudate has formed. It may be further enhanced by lightly sprinkling meat surfaces with powdered gelatin.

A variety of materials may be used to enhance binding: soy protein isolate, soy protein concentrate, non-fat milk powder, caseinate, carrageenan, egg white.

A food processor is an invaluable tool for making reduced fat sausages. Without fat it is hard to obtain a good sausage texture and a food processor can cut and mix ingredients very well. Protein extraction depends to a great degree on the size of comminuted meat. The smaller meat particles the more protein is extracted and more "meat glue" is produced. This becomes very important when making emulsified and liver sausages.

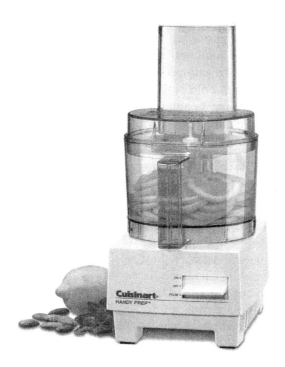

Photo 7.1 Cuisinart® Food Processors can chop a variety of foods, meat included.

Photo courtesy Cuisinart®

Mixing

Mixing meat raises its temperature and should be done as quickly. It takes roughly about 5 minutes to thoroughly mix 10 lbs. of meat. The time is important because fat specks start to melt at 95-104° F (35-40° C). We want to prevent this smearing to keep the sausage texture looking great. The ingredients may be premixed with cold water in a blender, and then poured over the minced meat. The water helps to evenly distribute the ingredients and it also helps soften the mass during stuffing. We can easily add 1 cup of cold water to 5 lbs. of meat because it is going to evaporate during smoking any how. A rule of thumb calls for about 8% of water in relation to the weight of the meat.

Apply some force when mixing, kneading might be a good word for it. *This will help to extract proteins* which will combine with salt and water and will create a sticky exudate. This "glue" holds meat particles together and contributes towards a good texture. Cold water is often added during mixing and is absorbed by extracted proteins. The finer degree of comminution the more water can be absorbed by the meat. Reduced fat sausages are often made with additives that do not readily mix with cold water and may create clumps. Those will gelatinize during heat treatment but will chop up in slices. Flours, carrageenan, xanthan gum, and soy powders should be added to meat in dry form and mixed well. When a food processor is used, the ingredients are added during the chopping process, which results in uniform distribution.

Stuffing

Taste the sausage before it's stuffed as there is still time for last minute corrections. People make mistakes when reading recipes, they get confused with ounces and grams, they use different size spoons to measure ingredients, etc. Make a miniature hamburger, fry it for a a minute and you can taste your sausage. After the meat is ground and mixed it has to be stuffed into a casing, preferably as soon as possible. Allowing the meat to sit overnight causes it to set up and absorb all this moisture that we have added during mixing and stuffing. The ample amount of salt inside will perform this trick and we'll be struggling with stuffing the casings the next day. Such sausage masses should be remixed.

Conditioning

This is the drying/setting step which at first look seems to be insignificant but in reality it is very important. Stuffed sausages may contain meat that was not cured at all or only partially cured. Leaving sausages for 12 hours at 2-6° C (35-42° F) or for 2-3 hours at temperatures below 30° C (86° F) will provide extra time to fully cure the meat, though it complicates the process. It is more practical to leave stuffed sausages for 1-2 hours at room temperature. The time will depend on the diameter of the sausage and the amount of moisture it contains. This simple process dries out the surface of the casing so it can acquire smoke better and develop the proper smoking color. This drying process is often performed inside the smoker and lasts about 1 hr (no smoke applied) at 40-54°C (104-130°F) until the casings feel dry. The conditioning may be eliminated altogether by adding cure accelerators such as sodium erythorbate or ascorbic acid (vitamin C) to ground meat.

Smoking

Nothing improves the flavor of a sausage in a such a rapid and inexpensive way as submitting it to a smoking process. Smoking meat is exactly what the name implies: *flavoring meat with smoke. Using any kind of improvised device* will do the job as long as the smokehouse is made from environmentally safe material. As long as smoke contacts the meat surface it will impart its flavor to the meat. The strength of the flavor depends mainly on the time and density of the smoke. *Smoking may or may not be followed by cooking.* Generally we may say that smoking in consists of two steps:

1. Smoking.

2. Cooking - this step determines the design and quality of your smokehouse as it needs temperature controls, a reliable heat supply and good insulation to hold the temperature when the weather gets cold. *If cooking is performed outside the smokehouse, the unit can be incredibly simple,* for example an empty cardboard box.

After smoking is done we increase the temperature to about 170° F (76° C) to start cooking. The smoked meats must be cooked to 154° F (68° C) internal temperature and here the quality and insulation of the smoker plays an important role. Nevertheless, the main smoking process is performed below 160° F (71° C). Smoked meats are usually eaten cold at a later date. Many great recipes require that smoked products hang for a designated time to lose more weight to become drier. It is only then that they are ready for consumption.

We now know that the smoked meat must be cooked, but *does that mean that it must be cooked inside of the smokehouse?* Don't we have wonderfully designed and factory built electrical or gas stoves inside every kitchen? They are insulated, have built-in temperature controls and are almost begging for these smoked sausages to be baked inside. How about putting your smoked meats into a pot full of hot water and cooking these products on top of the stove?

Cold Smoking

Continuous smoking at 52-71° F (12-22° C), from 1-14 days, applying *thin smoke* with occasional breaks in between, is one of the oldest preservation methods. We cannot produce cold smoke if the outside temperature is 90° F (32° C), unless we can cool it down, which is what some industrial smokers do. *Cold smoking is a drying process* whose purpose is to remove moisture thus preserving a product. You will find that different sources provide different temperatures for cold smoking. In European countries where most of the cold smoking is done, the upper temperature is accepted as 86° F (30° C). The majority of Russian, Polish and German meat technology books call for 71° F (22° C), some books ask for 77° F (25° C). Fish starts to cook at 85° F (29.4° C) and if you want to make delicious cold smoked salmon that is smoked for a long time, obviously you can not exceed 86° F (30° C). Cold smoking is not a continuous process, it is stopped (no smoke) a few times to allow fresh air into the smoker. In XVIII century brick built smokehouses a fire was started every morning. It smoldered as long as it could and if it stopped, it would be restarted again the following morning. *Cold smoked products are not submitted to the cooking process and they should not be made with lower amounts of salt.*

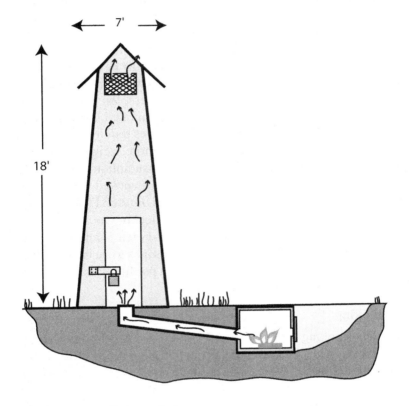

Fig. 7.1 Old Polish smokehouse.

Fig. 7.2 American XVIII century smokehouse.

Photo 7.2 Cold smoking at its best.

Photo courtesy Waldemar Kozik

In the photo below, at the Catskill Mountains of New York, Walde-mar Kozik is making meat products of the highest quality. There is no room for chemicals, binders or colorants here, just quality meats, Mother Nature and the art of smoking of Mr. Waldemar. The same way it has been done for centuries, the right way.

Photo 7.3 Cold smoked sausages.

Hot Smoking

Hot smoking needs little introduction, all meats and sausages are hot smoked today. Smoke is often generated during barbecuing to flavor the meat with smoky flavor. Hot smoking is continuous smoking at 105-140° F (41-60° C), 0.5-2 hours, 5-12% weight loss, *heavy smoke*. After the product acquires a desired color it is often baked in a smoke-house at 167-194° F (75-90° C) until the inside of the meat reaches 154° F (68° C). The above smoking times apply to a regular size sausage (32-36 mm) and smoking times for a thin meat stick or a large diameter sausage have to be adjusted accordingly.

Wood For Smoking

Any hardwood is fine, but evergreen trees like fir, spruce, pine, or others cause problems. They contain too much resin and the finished product has a turpentine flavor to it. It also develops a black color due to the extra soot from the smoke, which in turn makes the smoker dirtier, too. This wood will burn quickly and cleanly, but will not be suitable for smoking. The type of wood used is responsible for the final color of the smoked product and it can also influence its taste. All fruit and citrus trees have a light to medium sweet flavor and are excellent with poultry and ham. Many say that cherry wood is the best. *Oak, available all over the world, is probably the most commonly used wood for smoking.* It produces a brown color. If hickory is used, the color will have a more vivid red tint in it.

Smoked Sausages Cured with Nitrite

The step which differentiates smoked sausages from others is the addition of sodium nitrite (Cure #1). This is a must procedure when smoking meats below 170° F (77° C) smoke temperature. Although cases of food poisoning by *Clostridium botulinum* are very rare, they have one thing in common: they are fatal. If every manufacturer adds nitrite to naturally smoked meats to protect the consumer, a hobbyist should do the same to protect his loved ones. Smoking is done at temperatures from 50° F (10° C) to 140° F (60 °C) and depending on a particular smoker, the humidity levels and the amount of fresh air varies too. The combination of low temperature with evaporating moisture from the sausages and the absence of oxygen creates the right conditions for the growth of the *Clostridium botulinum* pathogen, the strongest poison known to man.

Many people say they don't use nitrites when smoking meats. Most of them barbecue or grill meats at high temperatures which kill all bacteria, including *Clostridium botulinum*. They cook meats with smoke which is not the same as the classical meat smoking method. Adding nitrite not only protects against pathogenic bacteria, it provides us with such benefits as a characteristic cured meat flavor, pink color that is liked and expected by the consumer, delays the rancidity of fats, delays meat color change due to light and oxygen.

Smoking Sausages Without Nitrite

A common question is: can I smoke meats without nitrite? Of course you can. As we have explained above you have to smoke your sausage at above 170° F (77° C) which will affect its texture and will produce an inferior color. The sausage will be most likely greasy on the outside. You may like it, but a commercial plant can not produce inferior products which will not be purchased by the consumer.

The Length of Smoking

In most cases smoking is finished *when the desired color is obtained.* Preservation is accomplished by cooking and keeping the product in a refrigerator, and smoking today is just a flavoring step. In the past, cold smoking/drying continued for weeks as it was the preservation method.

Hot smoking is performed with a dense smoke and smoke deposition is more intense at higher temperatures. About one hour of smoking time for 1" (25 mm) of sausage diameter is plenty. If your sausage is stuffed into 36 mm casing 1½ hours is fine. Nothing will happen if it is smoked for 2 or 3 hours, the smoky flavor will be more intense. Smoking much longer with a heavy smoke might create a bitter flavor. There isn't one universal time, use your own judgement and keep records.

Smoking Temperatures

Smoking temperature is one of the most important factors in deciding quality. There is no steadfast rule that dictates exact temperature ranges for different types of smoking. A few degrees one way or the other should not create any problem as long as the hot smoking upper temperature limit is not crossed. Crossing this limit will significantly affect the look and the taste of the product. When smoking, the inside temperature of the smoker cannot exceed 170° F (78° C) for any extended time. At this temperature, fat starts to melt quickly. Once it melts, the sausage inside will be a mass of bread crumbs, have a greasy outside, will lose its shine, and will have an inferior taste. If your sausage:

- Is greasy on the outside.
- Contains spots of grease under the sausage.
- Is too shriveled and wrinkled.
- Has lost its shine and looks opaque.
- Is crumbly inside with little empty pockets.

- it means that the internal temperature of the sausage was too high during smoking or cooking. The fats start to melt at very low temperatures and we don't want them to boil and leak through the casings. When faced with excessive temperatures, they begin to melt, and there is no way to undo the damage.

Smokehouses

Any design will do as long as it supplies smoke. Things get more complicated if you want to cook meats inside the smokehouse. There are books about building smokers that offer plans and detailed information, for example our own "Meat Smoking and Smokehouse Design." All distributors of sausage making equipment and supplies offer smokers designed for home use.

Cooking Sausages

Fats start to melt at 95-104° F (35-40° C) and going over 170° F (76° C) internal meat temperature will decrease the quality of the sausage. Staying within 154-160° F (68-72° C) will produce the highest quality product. Special sausages such as blood sausage, liver sausage and head cheese have their ingredients pre-cooked before being minced, mixed and stuffed. As different cuts like skins, tongues, or jowls for example, will call for different cooking times it may seem that many pots might be needed. The solution is to use one pot but place the meats in separate bags made of netting. Each bag is removed as soon as the meat in it is cooked sufficiently. The leftover stock should be saved and used as a cooking medium as these sausages are cooked in water. If not enough stock remains, add more water. After sausages are cooked the remaining stock may be used for a soup.

Methods of Cooking

It is important that meat reaches the safe internal temperature. There are basically two methods of cooking sausages:

- Cooking in a smoker or an oven.
- Cooking in water. A large pot plus thermometer is needed. The process can be simplified by using an electric water cooker, soup cooker or turkey fryer as these devices come with an automatic temperature control.

The fact to remember is that fat melts down at quite low temperatures and although it solidifies again, its looks are already gone. Fry a piece of solid fat on a frying pan and see what happens when it solidifies, it doesn't look the same. We can't avoid it altogether (unless we make cold smoked and air dried products), but there is no reason to intensify the problem by creating unnecessarily high temperatures.

When the source of heat is switched off, the product's internal temperature will still increase by a few degrees. This is due to the heat transfer from the surface into the inside of the meat. The temperature of the surface of the cooked product is higher than the temperature inside of it.

Sausages, hams and other pieces of meat are considered raw products and must be cooked after smoking. A sausage smoked at 100° F (38° C) for 6 hrs, will have a great smoky taste, flavor and color but it will still be a raw sausage like a fresh sausage that was only ground, mixed with spices, and stuffed into casings. Both of them must be cooked to safe temperatures before consumption. The U.S. Department of Agriculture recommends cooking fresh pork to an internal temperature of 160° F (71° C) and The National Pork Producers Council recommends an internal cooking temperature of 155° F (68° C) for maximum juiciness and flavor. Those extra 6° F (between 154° and 160° F) might kill a few more microbes and as a result the sausage might have a few hours longer shelf life, which is more important from a commercial point of view.

For a home sausage maker the inside temperature of the meat should fall between 154-160° F (68-72° C). We can stop cooking at 154° F (68° C) as most products will be of smoked variety and thus previously cured with salt and nitrite which gives us considerably more safety. Meats, which were not previously cured, will not be smoked, just cooked before consumption and the recommended temperature of 160° F should be observed. The lower the cooking temperature, the juicier and tastier the product is and the weight loss is also smaller.

Meats that were not cured and smoked should be cooked to the following temperatures:

- Fish should reach 145° F (63° C) as measured with a food thermometer.
- All cuts of pork to 160° F (72° C).
- Ground beef, veal and lamb to 160° F.
- All poultry should reach a safe minimum internal temperature of 165° F (74° C).
- Leftovers to 165° F.

Cooking in a Smokehouse

It makes a lot of sense to cook smoked meat in the smoker as it is already there. Besides, it will have a slightly better taste than by using the poaching method and it will shine more. Negatively, it will lose more weight than by other methods. It is also the slowest and the most difficult method that largely depends on the technical possibilities of the smoker. A slowly increasing temperature inside the smoker will achieve the best effects. The smoking process is relatively fast and a typical 36 mm sausage will be smoked in about 1.5-2 hours. Depending on the temperature when the smoking process has ended, such a sausage may be cooked to the safe internal temperature of 68° C (154° F) in 30 minutes or three hours.

While it takes 1-2 hours to smoke a sausage, it may take an additional 3 hours to cook it inside the smoker. It will largely depend on the inside temperature of the meat when smoking was stopped. That shows a need for some intelligent planning and it is advisable to slowly *increase the smoking temperature* to about 160° F. When smoking is done, the temperature should be increased to 170° F (77° C) and maintained at that level until the inside temperature of the smoked meat reaches 154° F (68° C).

It is a good idea to start raising the smoking temperature within the last hour of smoking in order to finish smoking at a high temperature. Actually cooking may become part of the smoking process itself and the smoking may end at 68° C (154° F) making the product *both smoked and cooked.* A lot will depend on *outside conditions and how well the smoker is insulated.* That may be difficult to achieve sometimes and we will have to increase the temperature of a smoker to about 185° F (85° C) to bring the internal temperature of the meat to the required level. Cooking can also be accomplished in the kitchen oven although in the electric type the lowest thermostat setting may be as high as 88° C (190° F). This way the process will be relatively short.

The other easier method is to set the temperature of the smoker to 77-80° C (170-176° F) and wait until the meat's inside temperature reaches 154° F (68° C). Keep in mind that the smokehouse temperature is around 25 degrees higher than the temperature inside of the meat, but that largely depends on the meat's diameter.

Cooking in Water

People seldom realize that most sausages, including smoked ones, are cooked in hot water (around 80° C, 176° F), which on average takes 15-60 minutes, depending on the diameter of the product. It is also easier and faster to apply than cooking in a smoker and the meat weight loss is smaller. This is due to the fact that *water conducts heat more efficiently than air*. Water is brought to the temperature of 158-194° F (70-90° C) and the meats or sausages are immersed in it. For instance, home made hams are poached at 176° F (80° C) and this temperature is maintained until the meat's inside temperature reaches 154° F (68° C).

A rule of thumb calls for about 30 minutes per pound, depending of course on the cooking temperature. Some recipes call for preheating the water before adding the sausages and some call for adding the sausages to cold water. Most people prefer the latter method. The poaching water should be heated rapidly to 175-185° F (80-85° C). At 176° F (80° C) the sausages are poached from 10-120 minutes, depending on the type and size of the product. It is generally accepted that 10 minutes are needed for each 1 cm of the width (diameter) of the sausage.

Poaching times for products up to 60 mm in diameter:
- Typical sausage - 10 min per 1 cm. Sausage 30 mm in diameter is cooked 30 minutes.
- Liver sausage - 12 min per 1 cm. Sausage 50 mm in diameter is cooked 60 minutes.
- Blood sausage - 15 min per 1 cm. Sausage 40 mm in diameter is cooked 60 minutes.

Once the diameter of the sausage is larger than 60 mm, the above times are less accurate and should be increased. Double up the time, it is better to be safe than sorry. For example pork stomach may be cooked for 2-3 hours. *The best solution is to use a meat thermometer.* The poaching method is a good method for sausages that are smoked with hot smoke. The short hot smoking process creates a dry layer on the outside of the sausage, similar to a second skin, that prevents the migration of moisture and juices from inside of the sausage to the water in the pot. A cooking pot remains uncovered during poaching. Cooking meats and sausages in hot water is more convenient than baking in hot air. Water in an open container at sea level will always boil at 212° F (100° C) and no higher. This precisely controls the maximum temperature that can be obtained using the simplest equipment. When baking we depend more on the technical capabilities of the smoker or the oven and more supervision is required.

Baking in the Oven

You can bake your meat or sausages in the oven as long as your unit can maintain temperatures of 190° F or lower (preferably 170° F) and home ovens are normally capable of delivering such low temperatures. If the oven's lowest temperature will be higher than 190° F (88° C) switch to the poaching method. Baking sausages in a smokehouse is less efficient that poaching them in water, but they look better having a glossy look on the outside. This is due to the fat that has melted under the surface of the casing and moved to the surface where it resides as a thin coat of grease. It is like putting grease on a pair of boots, they are going to shine and look better. Besides the looks, the flavor of a baked sausage is also slightly better as there was no loss of meat juices which in the case of poached sausages will migrate to the water. The disadvantage is that the baked sausage loses more weight than the same sausage poached in water.

Cooling Sausages

Immediately after cooking the sausages should be showered with cold water. However, showering with hot water cleans the surface from any soot or grease accumulation better. A hot spray is applied by commercial producers and very seldom by the hobbyist. At home a cold shower is normally practiced. As most smokehouses are located outside of the house the common method employs the use of a garden hose. Sausages cooked in water should be placed in another vessel filled with cold water (50-60° F, 10-15° C). Cooling sausages with water offers the following advantages:

*   Cleans the surface from grease.
*   Extends product's shelf life.
*   Decreases time of air cooling which subsequently follows.

Sausages should remain at temperatures between 130° - 50° F (55° - 10° C) for the shortest time possible as this temperature range facilitates the growth of bacteria. Although bacteria have been killed during the cooking process, new bacteria is anxious to jump back into the sausages surface.

Cooling time depends on the diameter of the product but it may be estimated as:

- Small diameter sausages such as frankfurters - 5-10 min.
- Large diameter sausages - 15-20 minutes.

When the sausages have cooled down it is recommended to rinse them briefly with hot water to wash down any grease that might have accumulated on the surface. Then they should be wiped off with a moistened cloth until they are clean and dry. Once the temperature drops below 68° F (20° C) it is safe to hang sausages for air cooling. The sausages will develop a darker color and better looks but may also become more shriveled, though some shriveling is normal. The solution is to poach it again for 30-60 seconds with hot water (194° F, 90° C) and then cool as before.

During this cooling/drying process a smoked sausage will further improve its shine, color, and will develop a darker shade of brown. Some call it "blooming" but this is the air drying we are writing about. Sausages should be hung in a dark place with a newspaper on the floor to catch any grease dripping down. After that, the sausage can be refrigerated.

Storing

Meats and sausages can be kept in a refrigerator for a few days only. For longer storage they must be frozen. After months of storage they are still microbiologically safe and safe to consume, but the flavor starts to deteriorate due to the "rancidity" of fats. Those chemical changes known as "rancidity" occur spontaneously and are triggered by light or oxygen.

There are dry meats and sausages such as dry hams, salamis, and chorizos that can be kept at room temperatures. as long as humidity remains low. However, in order to be safe, these products are made with a significant amount of salt and do not qualify to be covered in this book.

Chapter 8

Creating Your Own Recipes

It is mind boggling to see people clicking for hours and hours on a computer keyboard to find magic recipes on the Internet. Searching for the Holy Grail of a sausage. Then when they find something they like, they mess it up by applying too high smoking or cooking temperatures. The recipe of course, gets the blame. Then they look for another magic recipe again.

A recipe is what the word says: "the recipe", it does not imply that one will produce an outstanding sausage. Making quality sausages has little to do with recipes, *it is all about the meat science and the rules that govern it.* All sausage making steps, especially temperature control, are like little building blocks that would erect a house. It is like the strength of the chain, which is only as strong as its weakest link. *Each step in sausage making influences the step that follows, and all those steps when performed correctly will, as a final result, create the quality product.* Let us quote Madame Benoit, the famous Canadian cookery expert and author who once said:

"I feel a recipe is only a theme, which an intelligent cook can play each time with a variation."

A good chef is not looking at his notes when making chicken soup and an experienced sausage maker knows how to make a good sausage. We could fill this book with hundreds of recipes but that won't make you more knowledgeable. *There isn't one standardized recipe for any of the sausages.* The best meat science books, written by the foremost experts in this field list different ingredients for the same sausage. Salami Milano and Salami Genoa are basically the same sausage, the difference lies mainly in meat particle size. Replacing mace with nutmeg, using white or black pepper, adding/removing a particular spice will have little final effect on a sausage.

Grinding cold meat or frozen fat is more important for making a quality sausage than a pretty arrangement of expensive spices. It's all about the technology. By all means look at different recipes but be flexible and not afraid to experiment. Use ingredients that you personally like as in most cases you will make a sausage for yourself, so why not like it? When making a large amount of the product, a wise precaution is to taste the meat by frying a tiny piece. After mixing meat with all ingredients there is still time for last minute changes to the recipe. There is not much we can do after a sausage is stuffed. Tasting should always be performed when mixing ground meat with spices to make a sausage. *A recipe is just a recipe and let your palate be the final judge.*

General Guidelines

Use spices that you and your kids like, after all you will end up eating it. Keep in mind that increasing the amount of spices will make up for using less salt too. Basically a sausage is meat, salt and pepper. I will never forget when I made my first Polish smoked sausage that turned out very well and I proudly gave it to my friend - professional sausage maker Waldemar to try. I have included salt, pepper, garlic, and added optional marjoram. I also added nutmeg and other spices that I liked. Well my friend's judgement was as follows:

"Great sausage, but why all those perfumes?"

For him it was supposed to be the classical Polish Smoked Sausage and all it needed was salt, pepper and garlic. The moral of the story is that putting dozens of spices into the meat does not guarantee the best product. Another real example is when the owner of a popular Texas barbecue restaurant was asked this question: "what do you put inside your sausages that they taste so great?" The answer was: *"it is not what I put into them, but what I don't put is what makes them so good."* Keep it simple. Combining meat with salt and pepper already makes a great sausage providing that you will follow the basic rules of sausage making. It's that simple. Like roasting a chicken, it only needs salt and pepper and it always comes out perfect. If you don't cure your meats properly, grind warm fat or screw up your smoking and cooking temperatures, all the spices in the world will not save your sausage. There is one rule though which is obeyed by professionals who keep on winning barbecue contests: *cook it low and slow.* The same principle applies to traditional methods of smoking meats and sausages. It is all about temperatures and patience, other factors such as marinades, sauces, and different woods for smoking are just a dressing.

Sausage Recipe Secrets - Traditional Sausage Making

1. Fat. The meat for a sausage should contain about 25 - 30% fat in it. This will make the sausage tender and juicy, without fat it will feel dry. This is not as big an amount as it may seem so at first. Fresh sausages made in the USA can legally contain 50% fat and this is what you get in a supermarket. The fat is cheap and the manufacturer is not going to replace it with a higher priced lean meat. This is where the main advantage of making products at home comes to play: you are in control and you may skip fat all together.

2. Salt. *The sausage needs salt.* Salt contributes to flavor, curing and firmness, water holding and juiciness, binding and texture, safety and it prevents water cooking loss. In general sausages contain 1.5-2% salt. About 3.5-5% will be the upper limit of acceptability, anything more and the product will be too salty.

Low salt sausages present some technical problems as salt is instrumental in extracting proteins. Extracted proteins solubilize in salt and water and become the sticky substance called exudate that contributes to water and fat binding and proper texture of meat products. Protein extraction is of most importance in finely comminuted products such as hot dog, frankfurter, bologna and in liver sausages. Phosphates help to extract proteins even more than salt alone, and should be added to emulsified meat products. Lower salt amount is of lesser distraction in fresh sausages, which are characterized by a coarser grind and can be made with many fillers (flour, starch, potato, oats, rusk).

3. Pepper. "Black or white, that is the question." The dividing line is *whether you want to see the pepper in your product or not.* Otherwise it makes no difference and you can replace black pepper with the same amount of white pepper, although the black pepper is a bit hotter. Then there is the Capsicums family of peppers which includes hot **Red pepper, Cayenne** pepper, Chili pepper and paprika. Chili powder is a combination of chili pepper, cumin, oregano and garlic. Interestingly, the smaller the fruit of the pepper is, the stronger the pepper. California produces most peppers by variety and volume except tabasco peppers which are grown in Louisiana and made into Tabasco sauce.

4. Sugar. As a flavoring ingredient, sugar plays a little role in making sausages and is added for other reasons:

- To offset the harshness of salt. Adding some sugar can correct the problem but only to a some degree. Anyhow sugar should not be detectable. Chinese sausages may be an exception as Chinese recipes contain a lot of sugar. No more than 3 g of sugar is added to 1 kg of meat otherwise it can be noticeable. Process of making semi-dry fermented sausages depends on adding sugar. Adding sugar to traditionally made slow fermented salamis (Hungarian salami) is less crucial as their manufacture does not depend on lactic acid production.

- Adding 1 - 2 g sugar per 1 kg of meat helps to preserve the color of the sausage.

- A small quantity of sugar is said to brighten the color of a sausage.

Often dextrose is used, but keep in mind that it is only 70% as sweet as sugar. Dextrose is the sugar of choice for making fermented sausages as it can be immediately consumed by lactic acid bacteria and other sugars must be broken down to glucose first. Brown sugar carries more flavor than a regular sugar due to the addition of molasses.

5. Spices and Herbs. Throughout history spices were known to possess antibacterial properties and cinnamon, cumin, and thyme were used in the mummification of bodies in ancient Egypt. It is hard to imagine anything that is being cooked in India without curry powder (coriander, turmeric, cumin, fenugreek and other spices). *Spices alone can not be used as a hurdle against meat spoilage* as the average amount added to meat is only about 0.1% (1 g/1 kg). To inhibit bacteria, the amounts of spices will have to be very large and that will alter the taste of the sausage. Rosemary, mace, oregano and sage have antioxidant properties that can delay the rancidity of fat. Marjoram is a pro-oxidant and will speed up the rancidity of fats. Black pepper, white pepper, garlic, mustard, nutmeg, allspice, ginger, mace, cinnamon, and red pepper are known to stimulate *Lactobacillus* bacteria to produce lactic acid. Curcumin has been shown to be active against *Staphlococcus aureus* (pus-producing infections). An ointment based on turmeric is used as an antiseptic in Malaysia.

In reduced-fat sausages, a greater quantity of spices are used compared to the regular versions. Spices are very volatile and lose their aroma rapidly which is more pronounced in slow-fermented sausages that take three months or longer to make. Dark spices such as nutmeg, caraway, cloves, and allspice can darken the color of the sausage. To weigh spices, gums and starter cultures accurately, specialized digital scales are necessary. They are inexpensive and highly accurate.

AWS Compact Digital Scale v2.0 by *American Weigh Systems.*

www.awscales.com
Capacity: 100 g
Accuracy: 0.01 g (0.001 oz).
Units: grams, ounces, carats, grains.
Size: 5.6 x 4.9 x 0.5."
Warranty: 10 years.

Photo 8.1 Weighing whole cloves. We have been using this scale for 5 years and it's as good today as on the first day.

Guidelines for Spice Usage

The following is a very valuable table which will help you create your own recipes. This is how much spices the professional sausage maker adds to 1 kilogram (2.2 lbs) of meat.

Spice in grams per 1 kg of meat	
Allspice	2.0
Bay Leaf	2 leaves
Cardamom	1.0 - 2.0
Caraway seeds	2.0
Caraway powder	0.5
Celery salt	1.0
Chillies	0.5
Cinnamon	0.5 - 1.0
Cloves	1.0 - 2.0
Coriander	1.0 - 2.0
Cumin	1.0
Curry powder	1.0
Fennel	2.0
Fenugreek	1.0
Garlic paste	3.0 - 5.0
Garlic powder	1.5
Ginger	0.5
Juniper	2.0
Mace	0.5
Marjoram	3.0
Mustard	2.0
Nutmeg	1.0
Onion (fresh)	10.0
Onion powder	2.0 - 10.0
Paprika	2.0
Pepper-white	2.0 - 3.0
Pepper-black	2.0 - 3.0
Thyme	1.0
Turmeric	2.0 - 4.0

Useful Information

1 US Tablespoon (Tbs) = ½ US fl. oz. = 14.8 ml
1 metric tablespoon = 15 ml (Canada, UK, New Zealand)
1 metric tablespoon = 20 ml (Australia)
1 Tablespoon = 3 teaspoons in both the US and the UK.
1 tsp salt = 6 g
1 tsp Cure#1 or Cure #2 = 6 g
1 tsp sugar (granulated) = 4.1 g
1 tsp sugar (brown) = 4.6 g
1 Tbs water = 15 ml (15 g)
1 cup oil = 215 g
1 Tablespoon of oil = 13.6 g
1 Tbs of butter = 14.19 g
1 cup of all purpose flour = 120 g (4.2 oz).
1 Tbs of flour = 9.45 g
1 cup ground bread crumbs = 120 g
1 small onion = 60 g
1 large egg = 50 g
1 egg yolk = 18 g
1 egg white = 32 g
16 tablespoons = 1 cup
1 dry ounce = 28.3495 grams.
1 cup of water weighs 8.3454 ounces.
There are 236.588 ml in one cup so 1 cup of water weighs 236.588 g.
1 liter = 1.0567 US quart
1 ml water = 1 g

How many grams of spice or ingredient in one flat teaspoon			
Allspice, ground	1.90	Marjoram, dried	0.60
Aniseed	2.10	Marjoram, ground	1.50
Basil	1.50	Milk powder	2.50
Bay leaf, crumbled	0.60	Mustard seed, yellow	3.20
Basil, ground	1.40	Mustard, ground	2.30
Caraway, seed	2.10	Nutmeg, ground	2.03
Cardamom, ground	1.99	Onion powder	2.50
Cayenne pepper, ground	2.50	Oregano, ground	1.50
Celery seed	2.50	Paprika, ground	2.10
Cilantro, dry	1.30	Parsley, dry	0.50
Cinnamon, ground	2.30	Pepper-black, ground	2.10
Cloves, ground	2.10	Pepper-white, ground	2.40
Coriander, ground	2.00	Pepper, flakes, red	2.30
Coriander, seed	1.80	Pepper, whole	6.00
Cumin, ground	2.00	Poppy seed	2.84
Cumin seed	2.10	Rosemary, leaf	1.20
Cure #1 or Cure #2	6.00	Saffron	0.70
Curry powder	2.50	Sage, ground	0.70
Dill, whole	2.42	Savory	1.72
Fennel, whole	2.00	Tarragon, dry	1.00
Fenugreek, ground	3.70	Thyme, crumbled	0.60
Garlic powder	2.80	Turmeric, ground	3.00
Ginger, ground	1.80	**Additives**	
Juniper berries	1.53	Sodium erythorbate	5.0
Mace, ground	1.69	Phosphate	5.0
Soy protein isolate	2.5	Gelatin	4.0
Soy protein concentrate	2.5	Carrageenan	4.0
Textured vegetable protein	2.5	Konjac flour	3.0
Flour	5.0	Salt	6.0
Starch	5.0	Cure#1	6.0
Non fat dry milk	3.0	Sugar, granulated	4.1
Bread crumbs	3.0	Sugar, brown	4.6

General rule: *1 tsp of dried ground spice weighs about 2 grams and provides around 5-6 calories.*

Do Your Own Math

By the time you are done with this chapter you will be able to not only create a professional recipe, but to control how much fat, protein, calories and salt it will contain. And the math is so embarrassingly simple, that even a child can do it. All you need to know is listed below:

Source of Calories (Calories per 1 g of material)		
Animal Fat	9 cal	Bad fat, a significant amount of cholesterol
Vegetable Oils	9 cal	Good fat, no cholesterol. The same calories as solid fats, but safer food for people with cardiovascular problems.
Protein	4 cal	Body needs protein to stay healthy and to build muscles.
Carbohydrates	4 cal	Sugars are the main culprit for our weight problems. Not present in sausages in any significant numbers.

Let's see how many calories are in 1 kg (2.2 lb) sausage. A typical ratio of 70% meat and 30% fat is used for the calculation. Different meats contain different amount of protein, the average being around 16-18%. For all our calculations we choose that protein accounts for 20% of meat total. One kilogram of meat now contains 700 g lean meat and 140 g protein (700 x 20%). In addition to lean meat, the sausage contains 300 g of fat.

1 kg (1000 g) sausage		Calories
Meat, 70%	700 g (20% Protein = 140 g)	140 x 4 = 560 cal
Fat, 30%	300 g	300 x 9 = 2700
	Total calories:	3260 cal

A typical serving size is 100 g (3.5 oz) which is 1/10 of 1 kg (100 g) of the whole sausage. If 1 kg sausage provides 3260 calories, the 100 g serving must supply 326 calories. It is conclusive that *fat is responsible for the bulk of calories* which in our case comes to a whopping 82 percent. Let's see now how our calculations compare with some commercially produced sausages. Looking at the table it can be seen that a hot dog supplies the smallest amount of fat and calories. This is due to the fact that a hot dog contains 53% of water. We usually don't think that we are paying so much for water as for the meat itself.

Sausage Composition - Serving Size 100 g (3.5 oz)				
Name	Protein (g)	Fat (g)	Sodium (mg)	Energy (cal)
Polish sausage, pork	14.10	28.72	876	326
Italian sausage, pork, raw	14.25	31.33	731	346
Pork and beef, fresh, cooked	13.80	36.25	805	396
Liver sausage, liverwurst, pork	14.10	28.50	860	326
Pork and turkey, pre-cooked	12.05	30.64	876	342
Chicken and beef, smoked	18.50	24.00	1020	295
Beef sausage, fresh, cooked	18.21	27.98	652	332
Hotdog, plain	10.60	14.84	684	247
Oscar Meyer, Wieners (beef franks)	11.35	30.26	1025	327
McDonald's Sausage Biscuit	9.62	25.49	875	376
Thuringer, cervelat, summer sausage, beef, pork	17.45	30.43	1300	362
Salami, dry or hard, pork	22.58	33.72	2260	407

The above data obtained from the USDA National Nutrient Database

Looking at the table, one can understand why sausages are not considered a healthy food. The above example demonstrates how much effect fat has over our calorie intake. The only problem that remains is that the fat tastes so good to our palate that most customers reject a sausage which is devoid of fat. We have to replace fat with ingredients that would mimic the sensation of fat - *we have to cheat our senses.* And this is the basis of successful production of low fat sausages. An intelligent manipulation of ingredients is what making healthy sausages is about.

Although fat and protein account for most of the calories, other ingredients must be considered too. Even 1 teaspoon of ground spice that weighs on average around 2 g provides about 3 calories. Keep in mind that it is impossible to select 100% lean meat. There will always be about 2.5% of fat that is buried deep in the meat muscles so at best we can get 97% lean meat. Of course fish such as cod will have almost no fat (oil) at all.

Adding filler material is encouraged, after all there are many classical sausages which are made with potatoes, rice, groats, bread crumbs, oats and other materials. A sausage becomes a "package of health ingredients" and meat is just one of them. The nutritional value of the sausage will be decided by the ingredients that you will select. It can be said that a healthy sausage is the sausage that is made "smartly." To make a "better sausage" one has to understand the sausage making process and the ingredients that may be added. Actually, he must be a better sausage maker than someone who only stuffs hamburger meat into a casing.

About Recipes in this Book

Serving size. All recipes are based on 1 kg (2.2 lb) weight of a raw sausage. This includes meat and all other ingredients. The calories are calculated for the 100 g (3.5 oz) serving portion, which should accommodate the needs of most individuals. For example most sliced meats are packed in 1 lb. packages and there are 16 slices to a pound. This means that each slice weighs one ounce, and 100 g serving corresponds to 3.5 slices.

Salt. All recommendations and recipe calculations are based on the latest recommendations which ask that: Americans should reduce their sodium intake to less than 2,300 mg or 1,500 mg per day depending on age and other individual characteristics. *African Americans, individuals with hypertension, diabetes, or chronic kidney disease and individuals ages 51 and older*, comprise of about half of the U.S. population ages 2 and older. While nearly everyone benefits from reducing their sodium intake, *the blood pressure of these individuals tends to be even more responsive to the blood pressure-raising effects of sodium than others*; therefore, *they should reduce their intake* to 1,500 mg per day.

    You have to do some tweaking with salt. Some sausage recipes call for 1.8% salt, some ask for less. Keep in mind that lowering the salt level may influence the texture and the mouthfeel of the sausage. Salt promotes extraction of proteins which are needed for binding meat, fat and water together. Each 1.8 g of salt (3 tsp) in 100 g serving portion corresponds to 1800 mg of salt which is a lot for people with a hypertension problems. People at risk should respect the 1,500 mg daily salt limit and this is still too close as they are going to eat two or 3 meals more. For them, the best solution is to use Morton's Low Salt which contains 50% sodium chloride and 50% potassium chloride. Now, adding 18 g of salt results in 900 mg of salt per 100 g serving. This comes to 39% of the daily salt limit for healthy individuals and 60% of the daily limit for people at risk. Keep in mind that salt is an acquired taste and after a few weeks of eating less salty foods our body does not feel much difference.

% of Salt in Sausages per **100 g** serving		
% Salt	**Common Salt** - Sodium in milligrams	**Morton Low Salt** - Sodium in milligrams
2.0	2,000 mg	1,000 mg
1.8	1,800 mg	900 mg
1.5	1,500 mg	750 mg
1.2	1,200 mg	600 mg
1.0	1,000 mg	500 mg
Daily Limit for Healthy Individuals - 2,300 mg. Daily Limit for People at Risk - 1,500 mg.		

Meat selection

Do you intend to make a low fat or fat free sausage? This largely defines how healthy your sausage will be. This step starts when you choose meat in a supermarket. Select lean meat such as loin, ham, pork butt and lean beef. Don't buy other cuts such as picnic or fat trimmings, unless you plan on making different types of sausages. Keep in mind that prime cuts such as loins or hams cost more and will not be selected by commercial processors in order to keep the cost down. Trimming *all fat* from meat cuts is an inefficient and expensive option. A hobbyist can afford himself such a luxury as he creates a specialty product and in most cases the cost plays for him a secondary role. Commercially produced low-fat sausages often contain different types of meat such as pork, beef, turkey or chicken. This is not done to create better flavor, but to lower the costs and helps to manipulate ingredients on the nutrition label.

The choice of the sausage that will be made, also affects the manufacturing process:

- The reduced fat sausage requires a finer particle size, the meat has to be finely cut in order to extract proteins, salt should not be lowered too much as it is needed to solubilize those proteins. Phosphate should be added as well. As there is less fat in reduced fat sausage, less fat particles must be coated with protein film. When fat is removed and replaced with vegetable oil, the protein is still needed to coat the oil particles. Adding soy protein isolate will aid in the process. A food processor is needed to accomplish this task.

The Importance of Fat

Fat is instrumental in providing a pleasant mouth feel in meat products. This feeling will decrease in a low fat sausage, but it can be compensated by adding ingredients such as *potato starch*, soy proteins, gums or pectins. A home based sausage maker can easily lower the fat percentage to 10% and still produce a good sausage. Using very lean meats limits our choices to pork loins, lean hams and lean trimmings. Those cuts are expensive and when economics are important, other methods may be employed. Most traditional recipes call for about 70-75% lean meat and 35-30% fat. The fat portion was usually added as pork back fat or fatty pork trimmings. Beef tallow (suet) was seldom added as it did not taste as good as pork fat. In addition, its color is yellowish, unlike the white color of pork fat. The fat portion of the recipe should be eliminated or decreased as much as possible. Only lean meat should be chosen without adding fat or fatty trimmings. This removes a lot of saturated fat, cholesterol and calories. Although calories don't affect our health directly, they contribute to the weight gain. About 10% vegetable oil can be added for better mouthfeel. Vegetable oils bring very little saturated fat into the sausage mass and none of the cholesterol. Not adding oil at all is the best option as it results in the lowest calorie count of the sausage. The USA government permits our processors to use a lot of fat, for example, a fresh sausage may contain 50% of fat. Italian fresh sausage is healthier as it can have only 35% fat.

The fat carries the flavor around and with reduced fat, the flavor suffers, even though the amount of spice remains the same. To offset this problem we can either introduce a flavor enhancer, for example monosodium glutamate (MSG) at around 1%, or increase the amount of spices. The table that follows below breaks down different meats by protein, fat and calories content. Red meat such as beef and pork will never lose its dominant position, but a part of it can be substituted with soy proteins and that will make the sausage healthier. A new way of thinking is that the meat is just one of many ingredients of the sausage and not the only one. You may consult the table when choosing materials for your sausages.

Materials, 100 g portion				
Name	Protein (g)	Fat (g)	Energy (cal)	Choles-terol (mg)
Pork back fat, fresh, raw	2.92	88.69	812	57
Pork belly, fresh raw	9.34	53.01	518	72
Pork shoulder (Boston butt), fresh raw	17.42	12.36	186	62
Pork shoulder, arm picnic, fresh, raw	16.69	20.19	253	71
Pork loin, center rib, boneless, lean only, raw	21.80	6.48	152	55
Pork leg (ham), whole, fresh, lean only	20.48	5.48	136	68
Pork ground, 72% lean, 28% fat, raw	14.87	28.00	314	76
Pork, ground, 84% lean, 16% fat, raw	17.99	16.00	218	68
Pork ground, 96% lean, 4% fat, raw	21.10	4.00	121	59
Beef fat, tallow	0.00	100.00	902	109
Beef brisket, flat half, boneless, trimmed to 0", fresh	20.32	9.29	165	67
Beef chuck, shoulder clod, top blade, trimmed to 0", raw	18.75	11.32	182	65
Beef, ground, 70% lean, 30% fat, raw	14.35	30.00	332	78
Beef ground, 85% lean, 15% fat, raw	18.59	15.00	215	68
Beef, ground, 95% lean, 5% fat, raw	21.41	5.00	137	62
Veal breast, whole, boneless, raw	17.47	14.75	208	71
Veal, ground, raw	19.35	6.77	144	82
Chicken, fat	0.00	99.80	900	85
Chicken breast, meat only, raw	21.23	2.59	114	64
Chicken, ground, raw	17.44	8.10	143	86
Turkey, all classes, dark meat, raw	20.07	4.38	125	69
Turkey, all classes, light meat, raw	23.56	1.56	115	60
Turkey fat	0.00	99.80	900	102
Turkey, ground, 93% lean, 7% fat	18.73	8.34	150	74
Fish, bass, freshwater. raw	18.86	3.69	114	68
Fish, catfish, farmed, raw	15.23	5.94	119	55
Fish, cod, Atlantic, raw	17.81	**0.67**	82	43
Fish, salmon, pink, raw	20.50	4.40	127	46
Fish, tuna, yellowfin, raw	24.20	0.49	109	39
				Source: USDA Nutrient database

The data in the table clearly demonstrates that the healthiest meats are: 1. Fish, 2. Poultry, 3. Pork, 4. Beef.

Your meat selection process should be based as much as possible on technical data and not on educated guesses. By using the table you can estimate the caloric value of materials and that will enable you to make decisions that could ultimately influence your health. The data in the table comes *the United States Department of Agriculture Nutrient Data Laboratory http://www.nal.usda.gov/fnic/foodcomp/search.* The information is available online and the database contains detailed data on thousands of food products. The evidence of benefits of eating of fish and poultry over other meats is overwhelming. Keep in mind that poultry is lean meat, but much of the fat is located next to the skin and *the skin should be discarded.*

Fat acts as flavor intensifier and with reduced fat, the flavor suffers. Secondly, fat provides a juicy feeling and with reduced fat this mouthfeel suffers and is compensated in low fat products by adding extra amounts of water. This dilutes the flavor as well, and the amount of spices and flavorings *have to be increased.* Another point to make is that our flavor sensitivity diminishes with age.

Particle Size

Fat, acting like a lubricant, is instrumental in providing the feeling of creaminess, often described as mouthfeel. This smooth feeling will start to disappear when we start to decrease the percentage of fat. The mouthfeel will become rougher and it will correspond to the size of the meat particles. A bigger particle will be more easily noticeable than a small one. The sausage might feel powdery, gritty or sandy. This can be somewhat offset, but only to a small degree, by grinding meat through a small grinder plate or processing it in a food processor.

Proteins

Proteins are the main components in meat muscle that hold water. They play an important role for binding smaller meat cuts during the making of formed hams, as well as making strong emulsion in liver sausages. On many occasions it is required to add more water into meat batter than the proteins can retain and ingredients such as soy proteins, starches and gums are added to bind more water within the meat structure. In order for the meat to release proteins, the meat must be comminuted. *The finer the cut, or the smaller grinder plate, the more protein will be released.*

Salt greatly contributes in this process, which is even stronger when phosphate is added. Most of the water holding proteins are salt soluble and decreasing the amount of salt will adversely affect the water binding properties of the meat batter. This negative effect can be offset by adding soy proteins or starches. Low fat emulsified sausages do not need to have as much protein (myosin) as is needed to coat fat particles and create strong emulsion. However, more proteins improve meat's ability to hold water.

Safety Considerations

A reduction in fat content is usually associated with an increase in moisture content of the sausage. This in turn affects the safety and shelf life of the product as extra water becomes a nutrient for bacteria. This becomes even more pronounced when less salt is added to the sausage as salt inhibits the growth of bacteria. For those reasons fresh sausages must be consumed in a day or two, unless they are frozen.

Cold smoked and dry sausages should not be made at all as their manufacturing process calls for larger than usual amounts of salt and prompt removal of moisture, the latter will make little sense if extra water is added in the first place.

You should not decrease the amount of salt and nitrite in traditionally made dry and fermented sausages. In those sausages salt and nitrite provide the only protection during the initial stages of the process against spoilage and pathogenic bacteria, and they should be applied at the maximum allowed limits.

The oil should be cooled down in a refrigerator before adding to the sausage mass.

Non-Meat Materials Used for Making Sausages

In the past sausage was meat, fat, salt and spices and this is still the best way to make a high quality product. Those who stay fit and healthy may as well eat the best, but for the majority sausage making has been re-designed. There are countless numbers of new ingredients, both natural and lab-produced that are introduced to food and they all can be called the *additives*. They are not food, but when added they provide all kinds of new characteristics, they allow us to manipulate food. The sausage becomes just a container which holds ingredients and additives together, and we decide how much (if any) meat, fat and salt are needed.

Additives used in sausage production can be classified as:

1. Meat extenders - extend expensive meat proteins with cheaper plant proteins, like soy beans. Non-fat dry milk, sodium caseinate (milk protein) and egg white fit into this category, too. The main purpose of using meat extenders has been to lower the cost of a product. Extenders are usually added at 1-3%. They are capable of holding water and bind fats as well. The most cost effective meat extender is textured vegetable protein. The most commonly used meat extenders are:

- Soy protein isolate (SPI).
- Soy protein concentrate (SPC).
- Textured vegetable protein (TVP).
- Vegetable oil can be considered a meat extender as it replaces the animal tissue (fat).

2. Fillers - increase volume of the sausage. The result is a lower cost yet still nutritive product. Fillers are usually added at 2-15%. By using meat extenders and fillers together, the cost of the extended product can be lowered significantly.

Oats (steel cut type, not the instant type), buckwheat groats and rice should be pre-soaked. Buckwheat groats should be pre-cooked. Buckwheat or barley groats are added to Polish blood sausages.

Rice should be pre-cooked. Keep in mind that rice might swell inside stuffed casings and increase in volume. Because of that the casings should be stuffed loosely. Rice grains have strong cohesive properties. Rice can be added as flour.

Rusk is a popular filler in England. It is made from flour mixed with water, baked and crushed. It is a good binder and can absorb water at **3 - 4** times its weight.

Flours and starches make great fillers, water absorbers and binders. Flours such as corn, potato, wheat, soy and rice are in common use in the Western world. However there are tubers such as cassava that grow in very hot climates in Africa, South America or the Caribbean region. The Caribbean and the nations with populations of West African origin, such as Cuba, the Dominican Republic and Puerto Rico often use mashed plantains or yams which are then combined with other ingredients. Popular products are gari and tufu flour.

Potato flour and potato starch are well suited for making reduced-fat sausages. Potato flour's flavor agrees quite well with reduced-fat sausages, and improves their mouthfeel. Both flour and starch absorb water well. Potato starch has no taste, dissolves in cold water very well but does not thicken unless heated. Potato starch produces a very clear gel.

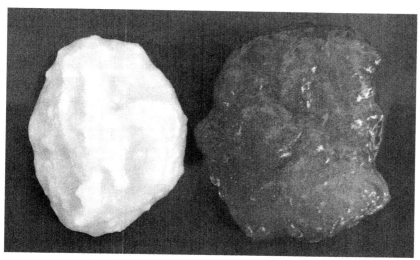

Photo 8.2 Potato flour on the left, starch on the right. Both were mixed with 4 parts of water, then heated.

Photo 8.3 Potato starch produces a very clear gel.

Processed meats are usually cooked to 160-170° F (72-77° C). Cured and smoked sausages are often cooked to only 154° F (68° C).

Unmodified potato starch gelatinizes at 147° F (64° C) which is below the recommended meat internal temperature for cooked meats and a strong gel is assured. Other starches gelatinize at temperatures from 165° F (73° C) to 178° F (81° C).

Potatoes are usually precooked and added at around 20% to meat barter. Dry flake potatoes can be re-hydrated and used as well.

Bread crumbs are ground and roasted bread particles absorb water very well, similarly to rusk. After World War II ended in Europe, people would save and dry bread rolls. Then they would be soaked in water or milk and used as a filler in meat products. Bread crumbs can absorb water at 2 times their weight.

Beans other than soybeans make a good filler too. Everybody likes burritos, which is ground meat mixed with bean paste. Beans can be soaked in water for a few hours, then simmered in a little water. The resulting bean paste can be used as a filler.

Banana is a good filler for chicken and pork sausages.

Textured Vegetable Protein (TVP) can be used in amounts up to 15% and can be considered a filler.

3. Binders - are used to improve water and fat binding. They can be of animal or plant origin (soy, wheat and milk, egg white). Carbohydrate based binders such as flour and starch contain little protein but are able to bind fat and water. They also fit into the filler category. Binders are not used for volume increase, but to improve texture and are usually added at 1-3%. Popular binders are soy protein isolate and milk caseinate.

4. Hydrocolloids - can be characterized as binders and fat replacers. Hydrocolloids are described in Chapter 4.

5. Fat replacers. A hobbyist generally has no access to commercial products, but can achieve *the same results* with commonly available products such as soy protein, non fat dry milk, carrageenan, potato starch or maltodextrin, gums or even the white of an egg. Any single or combinations of these additives will do a great job as long as it is properly administered and correctly chosen for the right sausage type.

All additives presented in the book are natural and classified as (GRAS-Generally Recognized As Safe) by the U.S. FDA, so there aren't any risks to the safety of the product. The safety will also not be jeopardized by adding too little or too much of any particular additive, in the worst case the taste and flavor of the product might suffer.

Recipe Modification

A recipe has to be somewhat modified as in most cases the reduction of fat is associated with an increase in water content. This extra water makes the sausage juicier and results in a better mouthfeel. Increases in water content can be achieved by adding natural water binders such as soy protein concentrate, potato starch, non-fat dry milk or by commercially produced fat replacers. These fat replacers bind not only large amounts of water, but mimic the sensory characteristics of fat. Adding non fat dry milk (1-2%) into low fat sausage formulations results in improved flavor, texture, overall mouthfeel and cooking yield. There may be a slight increase in whiteness of the sausage due to the addition of white milk powder. Reducing fat and increasing the protein content results in a less juicy, fatty, adhesive sausage, but with a harder texture. Adding a soy protein/carrageenan mix can compensate for that.

The recipes in this book should be considered as typical formulas for sausages, but not as the only possible way of making a particular sausage. *The healthy sausage is a "package" of different ingredients and the meat is just a one of them.* A recipe is not the secret, but how well the "package" is assembled together will make the difference between an average sausage and an outstanding one. By taking the undesired ingredients out (fat) we create a better sausage, but by putting beneficial ingredients in (protein, fiber, omega 3 oil), we can make an excellent one. Sausages with protein content up to 40% and vegetable fat between 3-5% result in an acceptable quality product.

The government guidelines ask that no more that 30% of calories should be derived from fat. This is impossible to meet when making sausages. Even meats which are 95% fat free (ground meat) would still account for over 50% calories and will go over the limit. It will be futile to try to reduce all fat which meat contains as some fat is inside of the muscle. Replacing fat with oil does not change the total calorie amount as both solid fat and oils provide 9 cal/g. Though it is fair to say that replacing saturated fat from solid fat with monounsaturated/polyunsaturated oil makes a sausage much healthier for people who may have cardiovascular problems. The government guidelines ask that no more that 30% of calories should be derived from fat. This is impossible to meet when making sausages. Even meats which are 95% fat free (ground meat) would still account for over 50% calories and will go over the limit. It will be futile to try to reduce all fat which meat contains as some fat is inside of the muscle.

Reduced-Fat Sausages

Replacing animal fat with vegetable oil delivers good results, eliminates much cholesterol and lowers calories. It is not easy to manually
mix oil with meat, and some extra water. It often results in poor binding and the texture may crumble. *Using pre-mixed oil emulsion provides the best texture and is strongly recommended.* Such an emulsion
is easily made from soy protein **isolate**, vegetable oil and water. It has
a consistency of a soft cream cheese, it is a white gel that looks and
tastes like fat. Oil emulsion is easy and fast to make and can be stored
in a refrigerator for up to 5 days.

Photo 8.4 Oil emulsion.

Sausage, 100 g (3.5 oz) serving		
Type and the amount of fat added	Meat	Total calories
Animal fat - 30% (30 g), 270 cal	lean pork, 70 g, 98 cal	368 cal
Oil - 4% (4 g), 36 cal	lean pork, 70 g, 98 cal	134 cal
Oil emulsion, 10% (10 g), 40 cal	lean pork, 70 g, 98 cal	138 cal
Oil emulsion is the mixture of soy protein isolate, oil and water.		

Replacing Fat with Protein/Oil/Water Emulsion

Preparing protein/fat/water emulsion is practiced by commercial producers. Such emulsion is kept in a cooler until needed. It is a very practical solution for making reduced fat sausages. Think of it as a fat replacer solution that offers many advantages:

- It can be prepared in advance.
- Making emulsion is a clean and simple process.
- Its calorie content is well defined.
- It does not provide any cholesterol.
- It preserves the original texture and mouthfeel of the sausage.

Oil emulsion is easy to administer and its calorie content is precisely defined. A 100 g chunk of emulsion provides 398 calories. One hundred grams of fat provides 900 calories.

soy protein isolate/oil/water emulsion 1 : 4 : 5			
	100 g	200 g	300 g
SPI (92% protein)	10 g	20 g	30 g
Vegetable Oil	40 g	80 g	120 g
Water	50 g	100 g	150 g
Calories	398 cal	796 cal	1194 cal

As all recipes are calculated for 1000 g material (100%), and it is extremely easy to calculate the amount of emulsion. Ten percent emulsion is 100 g, twenty percent is 200 g and so on. Let's assume that a recipe calls for 70% lean meat and 20% fat, the rest being water and other ingredients. Use 700 g of lean meat and 200 g emulsion, that simple. You don't need add more water, as 1/2 of the emulsion is the water. All 200 g of fat is replaced with 200 g emulsion. No animal fat was used and 80 g of oil was introduced. The original animal fat supplied 1800 calories (200 x 9 = 1800), but the 200 g of oil emulsion provides only 796 calories. The net result is elimination of 1004 calories and most of the cholesterol from the sausage.

Soy protein concentrate (SPC, 70% protein) is commonly added to home made sausages, but will not produce an emulsion. Soy protein isolate (SPI, 90% protein) produces the real gel: a white, soft, cream cheese-like substance that tastes like fat. Soy protein concentrate (SPC) produces a yellowish paste at best. In addition SPC will not even make a paste when used at 1:4:5 (SPC : oil : water) ratio. The amount of SPC has to be increased and the final product is still a paste. Soy protein isolate is pure protein with a very few impurities and that is why it makes such a great emulsion. Although SPI is slightly more expensive than SPC, it is used in such a small amount that the price should not be the decisive factor.

Making emulsion

1. Using a food processor start cutting cold water with *soy protein isolate* until a shiny paste is obtained. This takes about one minute.
2. Add chilled oil and cut at high speed until a stable emulsion is obtained. It should take about 2 minutes.
3. Place the emulsion in a shallow container and store in a refrigerator. It can be stored for up to 5 days.

Photo 8.5 Oil emulsion.

A number of sausages were made using oil emulsion and the following combinations were most satisfactory:

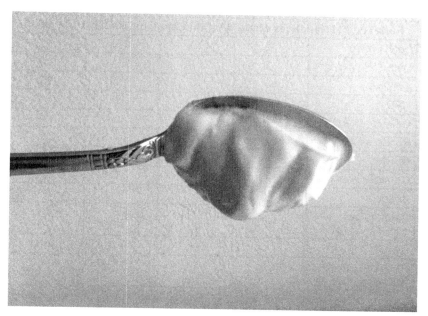

Photo 8.6 Oil emulsion sticks to the spoon.

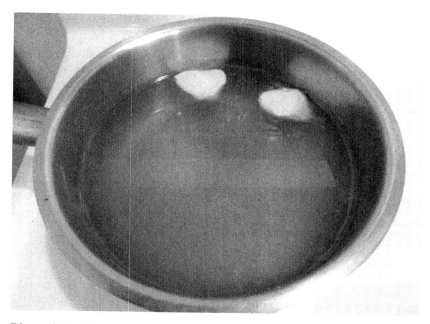

Photo 8.7 Oil emulsion after being heated for 10 min at 176° F.

Reduced Fat Sausages Made With Oil Emulsion. Values in percent.			
Lean pork	70	70	70	70
Salt	1.8	1.8	1.8	1.8
Emulsion	10	10	10	10
SPC	-	-	-	2.0
Gelatin	-	1.0	1.0	1.0
Potato starch	-	2.0	-	2.0
NFDM	-	-	2.0	-
Carrageenan	-	-	0.5	-
Water	-	-	-	-
Calories per 100 g serving	138	148	149	154
Result	Good	Good	Best	Good
SPC-soy protein concentrate NFDM-non-fat dry milk.				

Discussion:

- The texture of sausages was adversely affected when 10-15% water was added. There is plenty of water present in the oil emulsion.
- Carrageenan made sausages firmer with great sliceability. Adding more than 0.5% carrageenan has resulted in a tough gummy texture.
- Using prepared oil emulsion produced not only better sausages than mixing ground meat with oil and water, but made the process simpler and faster.
- 100 g serving of a typical commercially produced sausage contains about 330 calories which are mainly derived from fat. Using emulsion cuts down calories by almost half and eliminates a lot of cholesterol by replacing animal fat with vegetable oil (emulsion).
- Adding 1% of powdered gelatin greatly improves texture of reduced-fat and non-fat sausages.

The data in the table are in percent and are easy to convert into weight. For example, the sausage in the first column can contain 700 g lean pork, 18 g salt and 100 g emulsion. Then, of course ingredients such as curing salt, pepper and other spices may be added.

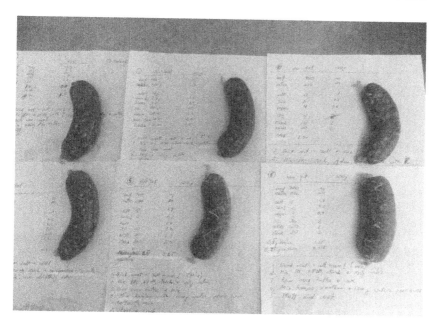

Photo 8.8 Test sausages.

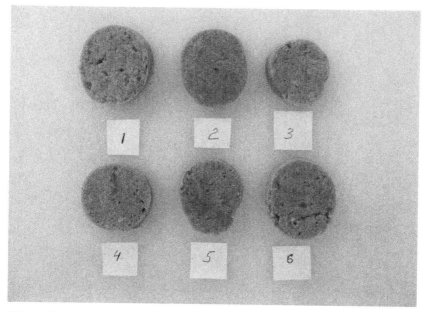

Photo 8.9 Test sausages-cross sections.

Photo 8.10 Reduced-fat sausages made with oil emulsion.

Photo 8.11 Reduced-fat sausages made with oil emulsion. Meat was ground through a 3/16" (5 mm) plate.

Non-Fat Sausages

It is more difficult to produce non-fat sausage with a good texture. If too much water is added, the texture will crumble even if binders such as starch, SPC, NFDM and gelatin are used.

Non Fat Sausages Made Without Fat or Oil. Values in percent.			
Lean pork	70	70	70	70
Salt	1.8	1.8	1.8	1.8
Emulsion	-	-	-	-
SPC	-	2.0	2	2.0
Gelatin	-	1.0	1.0	1.0
Potato starch	-	2.0	-	2.0
NFDM	-	-	2.0	-
Carrageenan	-	-	0.5	-
Water	-	15	15	15
Fat replacer	1.5	1.5	-	-
Calories per 100 g serving	98	114	107	114
Result	Good	Very good	Best	Good

SPC-soy protein concentrate
NFDM-non-fat dry milk.
Fat replacer - blend of konjac gum, xanthan gum and microcrystalline cellulose distributed by the Sausage Maker Inc, Buffalo, NY.

Discussion:

- The water content should stay below 15%.
- When 10% emulsion was added to the sausages with more than 15% water, the texture visibly suffered.
- Adding a fat replacer improves mouthfeel in non-fat sausages.
- Adding 1% of powdered gelatin greatly improves the texture of reduced-fat and non-fat sausages.

The data in the table are in percent and are easy to convert into weight. For example, the sausage in the first column can contain 700 g lean pork, 18 g salt and 100 g emulsion. Then of course ingredients such as curing salt, pepper and other spices may be added. The sausages contained only about 1/3 of the calories of the commercially produced sausages and little cholesterol.

Hydrocolloids Reference

In Chapter 4, there is a vast amount of technical information about hydrocolloids which at times may be intimidating to a reader. The names themselves sound very technical and one may think that these food additives are synthetic products made in a laboratory. On the contrary, they are all natural products which are derived from plants, seaweeds, milk or animal parts. The table below lists hydrocolloids which are added to processed meats. They are available on the Internet and may be used by a hobbyist as well.

Origin	Name	Use
Animal	Gelatin	Gelling
	Caseinate	Gelling
	Whey protein	Gelling
Vegetable	Konjac	Gelling, Thickening, Stabilizing
	Soy protein isolate	Gelling
	Locust bean gum	Thickening, Gelling**
	Guar gum	Thickening
	Gum arabic	Thickening
	LMA pectin	Gelling
	Microcrystalline cellulose	Stabilizing
	Carbomethyl cellulose	Thickening
Seaweed	Carrageenan	Gelling, Stabilizing
	Agar	Gelling
	Alginate	Gelling, Thickening, Stabilizing
Microbial	Xanthan	Gelling*, Thickening, Stabilizing
	Gellan	Gelling

* In order to gel xanthan gum must be mixed with konjac or locust bean gum.
** Will gel only when mixed with agar, kappa carrageenan or xanthan.
Sodium alginate can form thermoirreversible gel in presence of calcium ions.
Low acyl gellan (LA) forms thermoirreversible gel in presence of sodium/potassium ions.
High acyl gellan (KA) forms thermoreversible gel.
All other above gums form thermoreversible gels.

Most of the gums are thermoreversible and become semi-liquid when heated. On cooling they become gums again. Hydrocolloids became the necessary ingredients when the food industry started to produce reduced fat products.

Soy protein, milk caseinate and gelatin have always been used in processed meats. Gums such as carrageenan, konjac, xanthan, locust bean
gum and others are added to whole muscle products to improve the
texture and to reduced fat sausages to mimic the properties of fat.

Improving Mouthfeel with Gums

In reduced-fat sausages the mouthfeel can be preserved by using oil
emulsion which looks, behaves and feels like animal fat. However, it
still contains vegetable oil, which supplies unwanted calories. Eliminating all fat/oil from the sausage adversely affects its texture. Such
a sausage, if made from very lean meat, will become a pile of bread
crumbs.

The solution is to imitate the manufacturing process for making
emulsified sausages without adding any fat. These sausages usually
contain plenty of fat, so manufacturers do not face the problem of
poor mouthfeel. The challenge is to make emulsified sausages without
fat. For the hobbyist the best solution is to add extra water and hold it
inside of the sausage.

Summary of crucial points:

- Meat must be cut as fine as possible. This extracts most protein which holds water and sausage ingredients together. It is
  harder for our tongue to feel small meat particles individually.
  Lean meat must be chosen as only lean meat contains significant amounts of those proteins.
- Salt promotes the extraction of those proteins and the proper
  salt amount (about 1.8-2.0%) should be applied.
- Phosphate is the most effective component that extracts meat
  proteins. Together, phosphate with salt create a powerful synergistic combination. This means that a combined power of
  those two ingredients is by far greater as if they were used
  alone.

The following additives will make the process of manufacturing non-
fat sausages much easier:

- soy protein isolate, soy protein concentrate.
- phosphate.
- gums: konjac, xanthan, carrageenan
- microcrystalline cellulose can mimic the sensation of fat.

Konjac flour works like magic. Take 1 g of konjac, add 100 g of water, stir and within seconds a gel is formed. Unlike gelatin, carrageenan or starch, konjac does not need to be heated in order to gel. It is transparent and almost feels like fat. A good starting point is to mix 1 g of konjac with 1/2 cup (120 g) of water. Add the mixture into the ground meat, mix with spices and you get a much better non-fat sausage. Konjac reacts synergistically with starches which makes such a combination especially useful for making reduced-fat products.

Konjac is used by people trying to lose weight as it provides the feeling of fullness. One teaspoon of konjac is mixed with 8 ounces of liquid and is drunk immediately as it will gel. For those reasons konjac gum should not be swallowed on its own, as it may draw saliva and moisture in our food tract, create gel and stoppage. It is safe when taken with large amounts of water. People on diets take konjac drinks three times a day.

Xanthan gum does not gel by itself but a combination of 2 parts of konjac with 3 parts of xanthan creates a very strong gel. One gram of konjac plus 1.5 grams of xanthan will gel within seconds in one cup of water (236 g). Xanthan gum does not need to be heated, it gels with cold liquid. Xanthan can be mixed with an equal amount of guar gum which is less expensive.

Carrageenan does not disperse easily in cold water, but will create a gel when the liquid is heated. It is the gum of choice for making brine solutions that are pumped into whole meats. It binds water well and improves sliceability of processed meats. The sausages with added carrageenan are firmer and the casing peels off much easier.

The Sausage Maker Inc., Buffalo, NY, carries a very good premixed blend of a fat replacer that consists of konjac flour, xanthan gum and microcrystalline cellulose. Konjac flour and xanthan gum can be easily obtained online, but microcrystalline cellulose is harder to find. Fat replacer powder becomes slippery when wet. It is known as Avicel FM microcrystalline cellulose and is manufactured by FMC BioPolymer.

Mixing fat replacers with lean meat without any water results in a product with a hard texture. Konjac flour is water hungry and will bind all available free water for forming gel. The texture will be fine but hard. Adding 10-15% water to manually ground and mixed meat will create a better product. Even more water can be added when making emulsified sausages in a food processor.

Photo 8.12 Reduced-fat sausage made with carrageenan.

Dry Plums

Dry plums are rich:

- Sorbitol (up to 25%), a sugar alcohol that the human body metabolizes slowly. Sorbitol is often used in modern cosmetics as a humectant and thickener. Sorbitol is a sugar substitute. Sorbitol is referred to as a nutritive sweetener because it provides only 2.6 cal per gram. It is often used in diet foods (including diet drinks and ice cream), mints, cough syrups, and sugar-free chewing gum.

- Malic Acid is known for its innumerable health benefits: Treating Fibromyalgia, Chronic Fatigue Syndrome, Skin Care - tightens the pores of the skin to result in smoother and firmer skin tone.

Dry prunes are a significant source of dietary fiber (9 g per 100 g serving) and provide plenty of potassium (1058 mg).

Dry Prunes, 100 g serving						
Name	Protein (g)	Fat (g)	Carbohydrates (g)	Salt (mg)	Energy (cal)	Choles-terol
Dry prunes, 4 % moisture	3.70	0.73	89.07	5	339	0
Source: USDA Nutrient database						

Dry Plum Powder

Dry plum powder is an unique product whose nutritional power has only in recent years been discovered. It exhibits strong moisture retention and is the strongest natural antioxidant that is known. Dry plum powder inhibits fat oxidation and extends the shelf life of the product. In industry it is used in:

*   Meat processing.
*   Baking.

Latest studies demonstrate that eating plenty of high-ORAC fruits and vegetables may help slow the processes associated with aging in both body and brain. Reprinted from USDA study of top antioxidant foods:

Top Antioxidant Foods (ORAC * units per 100 grams **)			
Fruits		**Vegetables**	
Prunes	**5770**	Kale	1770
Raisins	2830	Spinach	1260
Blueberries	2400	Brussels sprouts	980
Blackberries	2036	Alfalfa sprouts	960
Strawberries	1540	Broccoli florets	890
Raspberries	1220	Beets	840
Plums	949	Red bell peppers	710
Oranges	750	Onions	450
Red Grapes	739	Corn	400
Cherries	670	Eggplant	390

* Oxygen Radical Absorbance Capacity,   **About 3.5 ounces

Dried Plum Powder in Meat Applications

Poultry recipes often called for adding prunes or apples which were often placed inside of the bird. This allowed to retain moisture and provided a pleasant flavor. Prunes were also added to wild game and pork recipes, as well as hunter's stews which were made with sauerkraut. Not surprisingly, dry plum powder fits perfectly into any poultry recipe. It will provide flavor, retain moisture and increase the percentage of beneficial antioxidant in our body. Dried plum powder is added at 3-5%.

Dry Apple Powder or Dry Apples

Dry Apples, 100 g serving						
Name	Pro-tein (g)	Fat (g)	Carbo-hydrates (g)	Salt (mg)	Energy (cal)	Cho-les-terol
Apples, dried, sul-fured, uncooked	0.96	0.32	65.89	87	243	0
						Source: USDA Nutrient database

Apple Sauce or powder help to retain moisture in a sausage. About 10-15% of applesauce can be added to low fat sausages. Dry apple powder is added at 3-5%.

Creating Your Own Recipe

1. Choose the sausage type you want to make (fresh, smoked, cooked, uncooked etc). This step will influence the amount of salt and nitrite (if any) added and the processing steps that will follow. In case a specialty sausage such as liver sausage, head cheese or blood sausage is chosen, different meats and fillers will be selected. Choose whether you want to make a classical sausage such as Italian Sausage, Polish Smoked Sausage, Swedish Potato Sausage or others. If you decide on a known sausage, add spices which are typical for this sausage.

2. Choose the amount and the type of fat. You may use some animal fat or completely replace it with vegetable oil. Using oil instead of solid fat already makes a healthier sausage by decreasing the cholesterol level. To further lower calories use less oil. Using oil emulsion is a very practical approach.

3. Choose additives. Once you know how much fat the sausage will contain, you can choose ingredients such as: meat extenders (protein concentrate, textured vegetable protein), fillers (flour, rice, potatoes) and meat binders (protein isolates, gums, gelatin).

4. Estimate calories. You don't need to do this, but it is relatively easy. Most ingredients in this book are listed with nutritional information per 100 g serving and you can do your own math. Remember that each gram of fat/oil supplies 9 calories, but each gram of protein supplies 4 calories. Protein accounts at best for 20% in lean meat. This means that 10 g of meat contains only 2 g of protein and 2 x 4 = 8 calories.

5. Choose the amount of salt and spices. Consult the spice guidelines table. You are in command so *decide how much salt you want to add.* All you need is a calculator. For example you have 11 pounds (5 kg) of meat and you would like to have 1.2% of salt in your sausage.

0.012 x 11 pounds = 0.132 lb
OR make it simple and use metric system:
0.012 x 5000 g = 60 g (3.3 Tbsp)
One tablespoon is equivalent to 3 teaspoons so
1 tablespoon of regular table salt weighs around 18 g.
1 teaspoon of regular table salt weighs around 6 g.

If you decide to decrease the amount of salt to 1% or lower, less protein will be extracted from meat and less exudate (glue) will be obtained. This will affect the texture of the sausage, especially the emulsified types such as hot dog, frankfurter, bologna or liver sausages. Add extra protein such as soy protein isolate, soy protein concentrate, whey concentrate or textured vegetable protein. Adding gums or gelatin will be of great help too.

6. Add Cure #1 when making a smoked sausage. You can be flexible with sodium nitrite (Cure #1). Although the maximum limit allowed by law for comminuted meats is 156 ppm (parts per million), there is no established lower limit. The European limit is 150 ppm. Denmark has won a concession from the European Common Market and their max nitrite limit is only 100 ppm. You want at least 50 ppm for any meaningful curing to take place but whether the amount is 150 ppm, 120 ppm or 100 ppm you will be fine. Let's assume that you need 6 g (1 tsp) of Cure #1 to cure 5 lbs of meat. One flat teaspoon will provide the right amount but if it is only 3/4 full the meat will be equally cured, although the pink color might be less intense. If you make a mistake and apply a full teaspoon instead of a flat teaspoon of cure there is no need to despair and don't throw away your sausage. Just don't make it a habit. Nitrite dissipates quite rapidly and after cooking and a brief period of storing, there will be little of it left in a sausage.

Adding 2.5 g of Cure #1 (½ tsp) to 1 kg of ground meat results in 156 ppm of sodium nitrite. This corresponds to adding 1 teaspoon of Cure #1 to 5 pounds of meat. This is still the safe amount and you may make it your standard formula. For those who like to be perfect, it must be noted that adding Cure #1 brings an extra salt into the sausage mass as Cure #1 contains 93.75% salt. This amount can be subtracted from the salt that is added to the recipe. On the other hand this amount is so small that it makes little sense to compensate for. By now you should be aware that you don't need nitrite for sausages which will not be smoked. Nevertheless, some products such as head cheese or blood sausage, although not smoked, might incorporate cured meats such as tongues in order to develop the red color expected by the consumer. Keep in mind that *nitrite does not cure fat* and if your sausage is on the fat side, *less nitrite will do the job*. The reason we deal with nitrite and cures in this book in such detail is that many people are unnecessarily afraid of them.

U.S. Cure #1 (6.25% sodium nitrite) for 1 kg (2.2 lbs) of meat			
75 ppm	100 ppm	120 ppm	156 ppm - max
1.2 g	1.6 g	1.9 g	2.5 g

European Peklosol (0.6% sodium nitrite) for 1 kg (2.2 lbs) of meat			
75 ppm	100 ppm	120 ppm	150 ppm - max
12.5 g	16.6 g	20 g	25 g

Some recipes call for soy protein isolate and some for soy protein concentrate. You can replace soy protein isolate with soy protein concentrate which costs half as much. Soy protein isolate creates the real gel, soy protein concentrate creates paste. The real gel will provide a better texture in emulsified and liver sausages. In all other types, the paste and soy protein concentrate are fine.

The Recipes in This Book

Salt. Some recipes call for 1.8% which is needed to extract proteins when making emulsified type sausages, others call for 1.2% when coarser grind sausages are made. As explained in Chapter 6, you can cut the amount of sodium in half by replacing common salt with Low Salt brand.

Fat. A concept of replacing animal fat with vegetable oil is introduced. This eliminates cholesterol and *bad fats*, but does not reduce calories if fat is replaced with the same amount of oil. Lesser amounts of oil must be added without changing the texture and flavor of the sausage.

In our experiments it has been determined that the best quality re-duced-fat sausages are made with oil emulsion. You could manually mix SPI, oil and water with ground meat, but it does not create the same texture as oil emulsion does. The emulsion can be prepared a few days earlier and stored in a refrigerator until needed. Replacing fat with an equal amount of emulsion cuts calories in half without af-fecting the characteristics of the sausage.

Notes:

- Non-fat dry milk and potato flour/starch provide better mouth-feel in reduced fat sausages.
- Dry apples and dry plums (prunes) absorb moisture and pro-vide better mouthfeel.
- When stuffing sausages make shorter links as smaller portions contain less calories.
- Don't fry sausages in oil. Vegetable oils don't contain choles-terol, but they still provide plenty of calories. Grill them or boil instead.
- The higher the protein content in comminuted scalded sau-sages, the higher the hardness of the sausage, regardless of the fat and starch level.
- Extended value sausages result in a much paler color.
- Non-fat dry milk and vegetable oil make sausages lighter.
- For unusual flavor, instead of water add chicken or beef bouillon, tomato juice, or wine into sausages.
- For best quality sausage cure meats in a refrigerator.
- You can add 20-25% of water into beef as it has a strong water holding capacity.
- When mixing meats by hand, don't just mix but knead the mass with some force. You want to extract proteins which were cut during the grinding/cutting process. You will know when it happens as the mixture will become sticky.
- You can emulsify meat using a manual grinder.
- Cold water should be added when asked for.
- Add diced back fat, olives, nuts etc., for this special look in emulsified or liver sausages.

- Smoked sausage recipes call for holding sausages at room temperature for 1-2 hours after stuffing. The purpose of this conditioning step is twofold: to dry the surface of the casing in order to develop a nice color and to provide more time for sodium nitrite (Cure 1) to develop a pink curing color. This process can be greatly accelerated by using 0.03 % (0.3 g per 1 kg of meat) cure accelerator such as sodium erythorbate. If the meat was pre-cured in a refrigerator (see Chapter 7) the color would be well developed.
- Sliced commercial products are usually packed as 1 lb, 16 slices (each slice-1 oz). Thus 100 g (3.5 oz) serving size contains 3.5 slices which is big enough for most of us.
- Without a doubt, soy products are the best suited for a hobbyist to make sausages at home. They can be used with other inexpensive ingredients such as starches, maltodextrins and milk proteins to further improve the water holding capacity of the sausage. To enhance the juiciness and the maouthfeel of the sausage, around 1-2% of powdered gelatin may be added.
- Chicken leg meat is juicier than breast.
- It is up to you whether you want to make a fresh sausage (the process ends with stuffing) which has to be fully cooked before serving or a ready to eat cooked sausage (stuffed sausage is cooked). Cook sausages in water at 80° C (176° F) until internal meat temperature reaches 160° F (72° C). It is about 1 minute per 1 mm of diameter casing eg: cook 30 mm sausage for 30 minutes.
- To cook sausage in a smokehouse increase the temperature to 170° F (76° C) until internal temperature of 160° F (78° C) is obtained. This could be the last stage of the smoking process with smoke still applied.

There are 80 recipes in the book and all of them contain less than 200 calories per 100 g serving.

Let's examine different ways of making reduced fat sausages. The meat total in each case is 1 kg (2.2 lb.).

Sausage type	Meat	Oil or emulsion	SPC	Water	Dry milk	Energy (100 g)
Regular	ground-pork* 1000 g	0	0	0	0	314 cal
Reduced fat	lean pork 700 g	8% oil 80 g	20 g	160 g	20 g	183 cal
Reduced fat (emulsion)	lean pork 700 g	20% emulsion 200 g	0	60 g	20 g	184 cal
Non-fat	lean pork 700 g	0	20 g	240 g	20 g	111 cal
Salt, pepper, spices, gums etc., will account for about 20 g total.						

* ground pork, 72% lean, 28% fat.
The weight of each sausage - 1 kg (2.2 lb.).
Energy (calories) per 100 g (3.5 oz) serving.
SPC-soy protein concentrate.
Emulsion (200 g) = 20 g soy protein isolate (SPI), 80 g vegetable oil, 100 g water.
Emulsion energy value (200 g) = 796 calories.
One cup of water = 236 g.

The data in the table demonstrates *how easy it is to lower calories by reducing the amount of fa*t. The easiest approach is to make oil emulsion and add as much as is needed: 10%, 20%, etc., in relation to the weight of the sausage. One hundred grams of oil emulsion provides 398 calories, which is significantly less than 900 calories that 100 g of fat supplies. An additional bonus is a large reduction in cholesterol. The oil emulsion is white, with a cream cheese like spreadability and it tastes like fat. You don't need to use oil emulsion. You can mix 4-10% of vegetable oil with ground meat and add little water if needed. The fact that oil does not mix readily with water is known to everybody, however, emulsion solves the problem. The advantage of pre-made oil emulsion is that it contains 50% of water, though it cannot be seen. This increases the volume of the sausage and lowers the amount of calories per serving.

It should be noted that there is also *soy protein isolate: fatty meat particles: water emulsions,* which are applied at the ratio of 1:5:5 or 1:6:6. They are not covered here as the purpose of the book is to minimize the usage of animal fat.

Chapter 9

Fresh Sausages

Fresh sausages are considerably simple to make and the procedure resembles making a meal. A fresh sausage is not cooked nor smoked and that explains the ease of its production. Everybody knows how to make a hamburger and if you stuff ground and spiced hamburger meat into a casing it becomes a sausage. Once the sausage is finished it goes into the refrigerator where it will remain a day or two. Then it will be fried, barbecued, boiled in water, steamed or whatever. Providing that fresh meat was selected and basic safety rules were obeyed, the sausage will turn out great. Of course it has to be fully cooked before consumption.

Fresh sausages can be made with very little salt or none at all by adding a mixture of herbs and spices. Low salt sausages need more spices than regular sausages in order to mask the absence of salt. Cayenne pepper is usually added to the mix as it is a very hot spice that makes up well for the lack of salt.

The taste of the sausage will depend on meats that were selected and spices which were added to the mix. If you want to make Italian sausage use fennel which is the dominant spice in the recipe. To create a medium hot or hot version of the sausage add more or less of red pepper or cayenne. Polish white sausage requires garlic and marjoram (optional), other sausages call for different dominant spice combinations. The best advice is to use spices that you like, after all you are the one that will eat the sausage. The Internet is loaded with millions of recipes which were invented by creative cooks. You will find sausages with apples, arugula, pineapples, and other ingredients. Many large recipe oriented web sites must provide new content on a continuous basis to stay alive. They employ people with writing skills on a paid by article or recipe basis and those creative persons look everywhere to find an original or rather unusual recipe. In our opinion this has little in common with serious sausage making and rather fits into the general cooking category, which makes sense as many recipes are written by restaurant chefs who always think in terms of cooking a meal. Such an approach can only be encouraged for making healthy sausages, as any non-meat filler or ingredient will lower calories and cholesterol. A fresh sausage will end up on a breakfast plate with fries and ketchup or on a grill in the back yard.

Providing that fresh meat is obtained and safety practices are implemented, there is little to worry about *Salmonella, E.coli* or *Clostridium botulinum* as high heat during cooking takes care of those pathogens. Fresh sausages have the shortest life because:

* All original bacteria remain inside
* No moisture was removed during processing.

Fresh sausages contain much fat which is shown in the table that follows. The data comes from U.S. CFR 319. 140.

Name	Max Fat in %
Fresh Pork	50
Fresh Beef	30
Breakfast	50
Italian	35

Looking at the amount of fat that goes into those sausages, it is quite obvious that anybody can make a healthier sausage at home.

Manufacturing Process

Fresh sausages are usually not smoked so there is no need to cure meat, unless a pink color in the finished product is desired. Technically speaking, a fresh sausage, for example Italian sausage, can be smoked as well, but is a highly perishable product and must be stored in a refrigerator. Although it was smoked, nevertheless the fact remains that it is still a raw sausage that must be fully cooked before consumption. *Store fresh sausages in a refrigerator for 2-3 days or up to 2-3 months in the freezer. They must be fully cooked before serving.*

Andouille
(Reduced-fat)

Andouille sausage is a classical Louisiana smoked sausage which is used in meals like gumbo or jambalaya.

Materials	Reduced-fat	Non-fat
Lean pork	850 g	850 g
Oil emulsion*	100 g	-
Soy protein concentrate	-	20 g (2½ Tbsp.)
Gelatin	-	10 g (2 tsp.)
Potato starch*	-	20 g (2 Tbsp.)
Water	50 g	100 g (1/2 cup)
Calories per 100 g serving	160 cal	165 cal
* Potato starch can be replaced with 15 g non-fat dry milk and 5 g carrageenan for even better results.		

Ingredients per ~1000 g materials:

salt	15 g	2½ tsp.
Cure #1	2.5 g	⅓ tsp.
cracked black pepper	4.0 g	2 tsp.
chopped garlic	10.0 g	3 cloves
dried thyme	2.0 g	1½ tsp.
cayenne pepper	2.0 g	1 tsp.

Instructions:
1. Grind all meat with 1/4" (6 mm) plate.
2. Mix meat with all ingredients, including water.
3. Stuff into 38 - 40 mm hog casings.
4. Dry for two hours at room temperature or preheat smoker to 130° F (54° C) and hold without smoke for one hour.
5. Apply hot smoke (140 -160° F, 60-70° C) for 1-2 hours.
6. Shower or rinse for 5 minutes with cold water.
7. Store in refrigerator and cook before serving.

Notes:
* oil emulsion: soy protein isolate/oil/water at 1:4:5.
To make a ready to eat sausage bake the sausage in a smokehouse or cook it in water.

Bockwurst
(Reduced-fat)

173 calories per
100 g serving

Bockwurst is a German white sausage made of pork and veal.

Materials	Metric	US
lean pork	500 g	1.10 lb.
veal	300 g	0.66 lb.
oil emulsion*	100 g	0.22 lb
non-fat dry milk	20 g	2 Tbsp.
water	80 g	⅓ cup

Ingredients per ~ 1000 g materials:

salt	15 g	2 ½ tsp.
white pepper	3.0 g	1½ tsp.
ginger, ground	0.5 g	⅓ tsp.
fresh parsley, chopped	10 g	1 bunch
onion powder	6 g	2 ½ tsp.
grated lemon peel	¼ lemon	¼ lemon
large egg, white only	50 g	1 egg white
carrageenan	5 g	1 tsp.
gelatin	10 g	2 tsp.

Instructions:
1. Grind meat through 3/16" plate (5 mm).
2. Beat egg white in a food processor.
3. Add to the processor ground meats, milk and all ingredients and emulsify.
4. Stuff into 28-32 mm hog casings forming 4" (10 cm) links.
5. Keep in a refrigerator (very perishable product) or freeze for later.
OR to have a ready to eat sausage:
6. Cook in water. Store in refrigerator.

Notes:
* oil emulsion: soy protein isolate/oil/water at 1:4:5.
Egg is used as a binder. You can use the whole egg, but remember that yolk contains plenty of cholesterol
Non fat dry milk has good binding properties.
One piece of chopped scallions or chives may be added.
Grate the outside of the lemon only, not the inner white skin.

Boudin
(Reduced-fat)

126 calories per
100 g serving

Boudin is a Cajun sausage (not to be mistaken with French Boudoin Blanc) stuffed with pork and rice and it needs pork liver to be really good. Boudin is the most popular sausage in southwest Louisiana and can be purchased from just about every supermarket, convenience store and restaurant.

Materials	Metric	US
lean pork	500 g	1.1 lb.
pork liver	300 g	0.66 lb.
rice	100 g	¾ cup
small onion, diced	20 g	½ onion
water	80 g	⅓ cup

Ingredients per ~ 1000 g (1 kg) materials:

salt	12 g	2 tsp.
cracked black pepper	4.0 g	2 tsp.
dried thyme	2.0 g	1½ tsp.
cayenne pepper	1.0 g	½ tsp.
parsley, finely chopped		1 Tbsp.
green onions, chopped		½ stalk
celery, cut up		½ rib
bay leaf, crushed		½ bay leaf

Instructions:

1. Place pork meat, liver, chopped onion, chopped celery, bay leaf and black peppercorns in 1 quart (950 ml) of water and bring to a boil. Reduce heat, skim as necessary and simmer for 1 hour until meat separates from the bone.
a. Remove the meat, discard the vegetables, strain the stock and save for cooking rice and for mixing.
b. Bring stock to boil and add rice. Simmer until rice is very tender.
2. Grind all meat through 1/4" (6 mm) plate.
3. Mix ground meat with chopped green onions, chopped parsley, salt, white pepper, cayenne and rice. Add stock until mixture does not stick to your fingers. Taste it and add more salt or cayenne if necessary.
4. Stuff into casings.

Notes:

A good stock plays a very important role in making this sausage. You can use chicken parts like leg quarters along pork meat and liver. When thoroughly cooked remove the skin, dice the meat off the bones, grind it and mix it with the rest of the ingredients.
Boudin is served hot.

Bratwurst
(Reduced-fat)

143 calories per
100 g serving

Bratwurst is a German sausage which is usually fried or grilled. It can be made from pork and beef, though most bratwursts are made from pork and veal. Depending on the region where the sausage was made and the combination of spices which were added, we may find bratwursts with many names, such as: Thuringer Bratwurst, Nurnberger Bratwurst, Rheinishe Bratwurst and many others.

Materials	**Metric**	**US**
pork	650 g	1.43 lbs.
veal	300 g	0.66 lbs.
water	50 g	⅓ cup

Ingredients per ~ 1000 g (1 kg) of materials:

salt	15 g	1 Tbs.
white pepper	3.0 g	1½ tsp.
marjoram, dry	1.0 g	1 tsp.
caraway	1.0 g	½ tsp.
nutmeg	1.0 g	½ tsp.
ginger, ground	0.5 g	⅓ tsp.
large egg, white only	1 (50 g)	1 egg

Instructions:
1. Grind meat through 3/16" plate (5 mm).
2. Whisk the egg.
3. Mix meats and all ingredients together.
4. Stuff into 32-36 mm hog casings forming 4" (10 cm) links.
5. Keep in a refrigerator or freeze for later use.
6. Cook before serving.

Notes: adding the white of an egg is optional. It is common in Germany to add eggs into fresh sausages to increase the binding of ingredients.

Breakfast Sausage
(Reduced-fat)

Breakfast sausage is without a doubt the most popular sausage in the world. Served by fast food restaurants, given in the form of sausage links to patients in hospitals, and sold at supermarkets. Made like most sausages of pork, salt and pepper with *sage being the dominant spice.*

Materials	Reduced-fat	Non-fat
Lean pork	800 g	800 g
Oil emulsion*	150 g	-
Soy protein concentrate	-	20 g
Non-fat dry milk	-	25 g
Carrageenan	-	5 g
Gelatin	-	10 g
Potato starch*	-	20 g (2 Tbsp.)
Water	50 g	120 g (1/2 cup)
Calories per 100 g serving	175 cal	138 cal
* Potato starch can be replaced with 15 g non-fat dry milk and 5 g carrageenan for even better results.		

Ingredients per ~1000 g materials:

salt	15 g	2½ tsp.
pepper	2.0 g	1 tsp.
sage (rubbed)	2.0 g	2 tsp.
nutmeg	0.5 g	¼ tsp.
ginger	0.5 g	⅔ tsp.
thyme (dried)	1.0 g	1 tsp.
cayenne pepper	0.5 g	¼ tsp.

Instructions:
1. Grind meat with 1/4" (6 mm) plate.
2. Mix meat with all ingredients, including water.
3. Stuff into 22-26 mm sheep or 28-30 mm hog casings. Tie into 4" links.
4. Cook before serving. Recommended for frying or grilling.

Notes:
* oil emulsion: soy protein isolate/oil/water at 1:4:5.

Chaurice
(Reduced-fat)

Chaurice is a pork sausage that is Creole Cajun in origin and has a hot and spicy flavor. Chaurice sausage is popular in Creole Cajun cooking both as a main dish and as an ingredient in dishes such as gumbo and jambalaya. It came originally to Louisiana as the Spanish chorizo but was adapted to local customs and ingredients. Chaurice sausage is popular as a main dish but it also goes well with beans or as an ingredient in dishes like gumbo, jambalaya or even potatoes with sauerkraut.

Materials	Reduced-fat	Non-fat
Lean pork	850 g	850 g
Oil emulsion*	100 g	-
Soy protein concentrate	-	20 g
Gelatin	-	10 g
Potato starch*	-	20 g (2 Tbsp.)
Water	50 g (4 Tbsp.)	100 g (3/8 cup)
Calories per 100 g serving	162 cal	175 cal
* Potato starch can be replaced with 15 g non-fat dry milk and 5 g carrageenan for even better results.		

Ingredients per 1000 g (1 kg) of meat:

salt	15 g	2½ tsp.
dried thyme	2.0 g	1½ tsp.
cayenne pepper	2.0 g	1 tsp.
red pepper flakes	1.0 g	1 tsp.
bay leaf, crushed	½ leaf	½ leaf
garlic	7 g	2 cloves
parsley, finely chopped		2 Tbs.
onions, finely diced		1 cup

Instructions:
1. Grind all meat through the 3/8" (10 mm) plate.
2. Mix meat with all ingredients, including water.
3. Stuff into 32 - 36 mm hog casings and make 8" long links.
4. Keep in a refrigerator.
5. Cook before serving.

Notes:
* oil emulsion: soy protein isolate/oil/water at 1:4:5.

Chorizo - Mexican
(Reduced-fat)

169 calories per 100 g serving

Original Spanish chorizo is made from coarsely chopped pork and seasoned with paprika and garlic. It is a dry cured and air dried sausage. Most South American chorizos are of a fresh type which is fried for breakfast or grilled on a fire. Mexican Chorizo Sausage is made from pork that is ground and seasoned with chile peppers, garlic and vinegar. It is moister and much hotter than the Spanish chorizo.

Meat	Metric	US
lean pork	900 g	1.98 lb.
oil emulsion*	100 g	0.22 lb.

***Ingredients** per 1000 g (1 kg) of materials:*

salt	15 g	2½ tsp
pepper	4.0 g	2 tsp.
cayenne pepper	4.0 g	2 tsp.
oregano, dry	1.0 g	1 tsp.
garlic	7 g	2 cloves
white vinegar	50 ml	1/5 cup
Sausage Maker fat replacer	5.0 g	2 tsp.

Instructions:
1. Grind meat through large plate (1/2", 12 mm).
2. Smash garlic cloves and mix with a little amount of water.
3. Mix meat, all ingredients and vinegar together.
4. Stuff into 32 - 36 mm hog casings and make 8" long links.
5. Keep in a refrigerator.
6. Cook before serving.

Chorizo with eggs is often served for breakfast: put pieces of chorizo into scrambled eggs and blend them together.

Notes:
* oil emulsion: soy protein isolate/oil/water at 1:4:5.

Greek Sausage
(Reduced-fat)

176 calories per
100 g serving

Greek sausage made from lamb, pork fat and cheese.

Meat	Metric	US
lamb	800 g	1.76 lb.
olive oil	40 g	3 Tbsp.
goat or sheep cheese	50 g	0.11 lb.
cornstarch	10 g	1 Tbs.
red wine	100 ml	⅜ cup

Ingredients *per 1000 g (1 kg) of materials:*

salt	15 g	2½ tsp.
pepper	2.0 g	1 tsp.
cayenne pepper	2.0 g	1 tsp.
coriander, ground	2.0 g	1 tsp.
thyme, dry leaf	2.0 g	1½ tsp.
mint, dry leaf	2.0 g	1½ tsp.

Instructions:

1. Grind meat and fat through 3/8" plate (10 mm).
2. Cut cheese into little cubes.
3. Mix cheese with all spices. Mix salt with wine and then pour over meat. Add cheese and spices and mix. Add cornstarch and mix everything together.
4. Stuff into 32-36 mm hog casings forming 4" (10 cm) links.
5. Keep in a refrigerator or freeze for later use.
6. Cook before use.

Hurka Hungarian Sausage
(Reduced-fat)

185 calories per
100 g serving

Hurka is a well known Hungarian water cooked sausage made originally from organ meats such as pork liver, lungs, head meat, rice and onions. Blood is sometimes added.

Meat	Metric	US
lean pork	600 g	1.32 lbs.
pork liver	300 g	0.66 lbs.
oil emulsion*	100 g	0.22 lbs.

Ingredients per 1000 g (1 kg) of materials:

salt	12 g	2 tsp.
pepper	2.5 g	1 tsp.
garlic	3.5 g	1 clove
½ small onion	30 g	2 Tbs.
cooked rice	150 g	1 cup
cold water	80 g	1/3 cup
gelatin	10 g	2 tsp.

Instructions:
1. Boil all meats (except liver) for about 2 hours. Poach liver in hot water until no traces of blood are visible (cut the liver to test). Cool meats and remove the skin from tongues.
2. Grind meats through 3/16" plate (5 mm). Grind liver through a smaller plate.
3. Cook rice for about 15 minutes. Place some bacon fat or lard on a frying pan and fry onions until light brown.
4. Mix everything together, adding 80 g (1/3 cup) water. You may substitute some water with white wine.
5. Stuff loosely into large hog or synthetic casings.
6. Cook for 4 minutes in boiled water or poach in water for 8 minutes at 85° C (185° F).
Frozen Hurka sausage can be baked at 180° C (350° F) for about 50 minutes (leave the lid on or cover with aluminum foil). Then uncover the sausage and continue baking for 5 more minutes until brown. Fresh Hurka sausage can be pan fried or grilled. Goes well with pickles.

Notes:
* oil emulsion: soy protein isolate/oil/water at 1:4:5.
Hurka was originally made with 30% pork liver, 30% pork tongues and 10% pork back fat, bacon or lard.

Italian Sausage (Sweet)
(Reduced-fat)

169 calories per
100 g serving

Italian Sausage is a wonderful sausage for frying or grilling and can be found in every supermarket in the USA. The dominant flavor in fresh Italian sausage is fennel and by adding (or not) cayenne pepper we can create a sweet, medium or hot variety. Fried on a hot plate with green bell peppers and onions, it is sold by street vendors everywhere in New York City. Don't confuse it with cheap poached hot dogs on a bun, Italian sausage is bigger and served on a long subway type roll. It is leaner than other fresh sausages and the US regulations permit no more than 35% fat in the recipe. *Fennel, sometimes added with anise, is the dominant spice in this sausage.*

Meat	Metric	US
lean pork	900 g	1.98 lbs.
oil emulsion*	100 g	0.22 lbs.

Ingredients per 1000 g (1 kg) of materials:

salt	15 g	2½ tsp.
sugar	2 g	½ tsp.
coarse black pepper	2.0 g	1 tsp.
cracked fennel seed	3 g	2 tsp.
coriander	1 g	½ tsp.
caraway	1 g	¼ tsp.
Sausage Maker fat replacer	8 g	2 tsp.

Instructions:
1. Grind meat with ⅜" (10 mm) plate.
2. Mix meat with all ingredients.
3. Stuff into 32 - 36 mm hog casings.
4. Keep in a refrigerator (perishable product) or freeze for later use.
5. Cook before serving. Recommended for frying or grilling.

Notes:
* oil emulsion: soy protein isolate/oil/water at 1:4:5.
For Medium Hot Italian Sausage add 2 g (1 tsp) cayenne pepper.
For Hot Italian Sausage add 4 g (2 tsp) cayenne pepper.
Italian spices such as basil, thyme and oregano are often added.

Jalapeño Sausage
(Reduced-fat)

175 calories per
100 g serving

Meat	Metric	US
lean beef	800 g	1.76 lb.
oil emulsion*	150 g	0.33 lb.
white wine	50 ml	1/5 cup

Ingredients per 1000 g (1 kg) of materials:

salt	15 g	2 ½ tsp.
white pepper	2.5 g	1 tsp.
carrageenan	5.0 g	1 tsp.
cilantro, crumbled	0.6 g	1 tsp.
cumin, ground	1.0 g	½ tsp.
garlic,	3.5 g	1 clove
½ onion,	30 g	2 Tbs.
jalapeño, green, diced	20 g	1

Instructions:
1. Grind meat through 3/16" plate (5 mm).
2. Mix meat with all ingredients.
3. Stuff into 32-36 mm hog casings.
4. Keep in a refrigerator (perishable product) or freeze for later use.
5. Cook before serving.

Notes:
* oil emulsion: soy protein isolate/oil/water at 1:4:5.

Longanisa

(Reduced-fat)

183 calories per
100 g serving

Longanisa is a Philippine version of the Spanish Longaniza sausage. Longaniza is also popular in Argentina, Chile, Mexico and all other Spanish speaking countries, including the Caribbean Islands like Cuba and the Dominican Republic. And of course there are different varieties of Longaniza.

Meat	Metric	US
lean pork	800 g	1.76 lb.
oil emulsion*	150 g	0.33 lb.
white vinegar	50 g	1/5 cup

Ingredients per 1000 g (1 kg) of materials:

salt	15 g	2 ½ tsp.
black pepper	2.5 g	1 tsp.
gelatin	10 g	2 tsp.
sugar	2.5 g	½ tsp.
paprika	6.0 g	3 tsp.
garlic,	7.0 g	2 cloves
½ onion,	30 g	2 Tbs.
oregano, dry leaf	2 g	2 tsp.

Instructions:

1. Cut pork into small cubes or grind through a coarse plate, 3/8" (10 mm).
2. Mix meat with all ingredients.
3. Stuff into 32 mm or smaller casings.
4. Store in refrigerator.
5. Cook before serving - fry on a frying pan until golden brown.

Notes:

* oil emulsion: soy protein isolate/oil/water at 1:4:5.

Loukanika

132 calories per
100 g serving

Loukanika Sausage is a Greek fresh sausage made with lamb and pork and seasoned with orange rind. The Greek mountainous terrain is ill suited for raising cattle but perfect for animals such as goats and sheep. The best example is the famous Greek "Feta" cheese which is made from goat and sheep milk. Most recipes include spices like garlic, oregano, thyme, marjoram, and allspice. Dry red or white wine is often used.

Meat	Metric	US
lean pork	650 g	1.43 lb.
lamb	250 g	0.55 lb.
red wine	100 ml	⅜ cup

Ingredients per 1000 g (1 kg) of materials:

salt	15 g	2 ½ tsp.
pepper	2.0 g	1 tsp.
garlic	3.5 g	1 clove
allspice, ground	1.0 g	½ tsp.
thyme, dry leaf	2.0 g	1½ tsp.
oregano, dried	2.0 g	2 tsp.
orange peel, grated		2 tsp.
Sausage Maker fat replacer	4.0 g	1 tsp.

Instructions:

1. Grind meats through ⅜" plate.
2. Mix ground meat with wine and all ingredients.
3. Stuff into 32-36 mm casings, make 6" links.
4. Store in refrigerator or freeze for later use.
5. Cook before serving. The sausage can be fried, baked or boiled. You may place it in a skillet with water to cover, bring it to a boil and then simmer on lower heat for about 20 minutes. Keep the cover on.

Polish White Sausage

127 calories per
100 g serving

White Sausage (*Kiełbasa Biała Surowa*) is a popular Polish fresh sausage, always to be found on Easter tables and very often added into soups (*"żurek"*) with hard boiled eggs. Adding sausages into soups has been a long tradition in many countries, for example in Louisiana, sausages are added into everything. The recipe consists of the same ingredients and spices as in Polish Smoked Sausage, the only difference is that the White Sausage is not smoked. German equivalent - Weisswurst (white sausage) is made from veal and fresh pork bacon. It is flavored with parsley, onions, mace, ginger, cardamom, lemon zest and stuffed into 22 mm sheep casings.

Meat	Metric	US
lean pork	700 g	1.54 lbs.
lean beef	200 g	0.44 lbs.
cold water	100 g	3/8 cup

Ingredients per 1000 g (1 kg) of materials:

salt	15 g	2 ½ tsp.
pepper	2.0 g	1 tsp.
garlic	2.0 g	½ clove
marjoram	2.0 g	2 tsp.
Sausage Maker fat replacer	8.0 g	2 tsp.

Instructions:
1. Grind pork with 3/8"(10 mm) plate. Grind beef with the smaller plate - 3/16" or 1/8" (5-3 mm).
2. Mix beef and pork meat with water adding all ingredients.
3. Stuff the mixture hard into 32-36 mm hog casings making one long rope sausage.
4. Cook in water (176° F, 80° C) for 35 minutes before serving.

Potato Sausage

152 calories per
100 g serving

Potato Sausage with non fat dry milk is very similar to Swedish Potato Sausage. It is much easier to make as instead of boiling potatoes it calls for the addition of potato flour. Non fat dry milk effectively binds water and greatly improves the taste of low fat sausages. Adding potato flour, non fat dry milk, onions and water increases the yield by 40% making it not only great tasting but also a great value added product.

Meat	Metric	US
lean pork	600 g	1.43 lb.
lean beef	200 g	0.55 lb.
potato flour	80 g	½ cup
non fat dry milk	20 g	½ cup
water	100 g	3/4 cup

Ingredients per 1000 g (1 kg) of materials:

salt	15 g	2 ½ tsp.
carrageenan	5.0 g	1 tsp.
white pepper	6.0 g	3 tsp.
marjoram, ground	1.5 g	1 tsp.
ginger, ground	1.8 g	1 tsp.
nutmeg, ground	1.0 g	½ tsp.
cardamom, ground	1.0 g	½ tsp.
cloves, ground	1.0 g	½ tsp.
allspice, ground	1.0 g	½ tsp.
small onion, chopped	30 g	½ onion

Instructions:
1. Grind pork and onions through 3/8" (10 mm) plate.
2. Grind beef through 3/16" (5 mm) plate.
3. Add salt, spices, 1/2 of the water and start mixing with meat sprinkling potato flour and non fat dry milk powder. You could mix all ingredients with half of the water in a blender and then pour over the meat.
4. Add remaining water and keep on mixing until absorbed.
5. Stuff into large hog casings 36-40 mm or beef rounds.
6. Keep under refrigeration.
7. Cook before serving.

Notes:
Instead of potato flour, boiled or dry flaked potatoes can be added.

Tomato Sausage   172 calories per
100 g serving

Tomato sausage is made from pork and veal and it derives its flavor from tomatoes. Cracker meal or bread crumbs are used as fillers and a lot of sausage can be made from a few pounds of meat.

Materials	Metric	US
lean pork	600 g	1.32 lb.
veal	150 g	0.33 lb.
oil emulsion*	100 g	3.5 oz.
cracker meal	50 g	2 oz.
canned tomatoes	100 g	3.5 oz.

Ingredients per 1000 g (1 kg) of materials:

salt	12 g	2 tsp.
white pepper	3.0 g	1½ tsp.
carrageenan	5.0 g	1 tsp.
sugar	5.0 g	1 tsp.
nutmeg	2.0 g	1 tsp.
ginger	1.0 g	½ tsp.

Instructions:
1. Grind all meat through 3/16" plate (5 mm).
2. Mix meat with all ingredients together.
3. Stuff into 26-28 mm collagen, hog or sheep casings.
4. Store in a refrigerator or freeze for later use.
5. Cook before serving.

Notes:
*oil emulsion: soy protein isolate/oil/water at 1:4:5.
The flavor comes from tomatoes so don't overpower with spices.
Cracker meal: crumbled or smashed crackers that are either used as topping or as breading. May be substituted with bread crumbs.

Chapter 10

Cooked Sausages

Types of Cooked Sausages

This huge group of ready to eat sausages can be further subdivided by the degree of meat comminution:
- Regular, coarsely ground sausages.
- Finely comminuted sausages also known as emulsified sausages, eg. hot dog, frankfurter, bologna.
- Special sausages cooked in water such as head cheeses, liver and blood sausages where meats are cooked before stuffing and then the stuffed sausage is cooked again. Meats are simmered below the boiling point and the sausages are poached in hot water.

There are very few sausages that are not cooked:
- Fresh sausages.
- Traditionally fermented sausages like salami.
- Cold smoked sausages. They are either kept in a cooler or may be air dried.

They are well suited for making reduced or non-fat sausages but their manufacturing process requires more attention to detail.

Emulsified Sausages

Emulsified sausages are cooked sausages that have been finely comminuted to the consistency of a fine paste. In most cases they are smoked and cooked with moist heat (steamed or in hot water). The first emulsified sausage was probably the German frankfurter, followed by the Austrian wiener. In the 1800's German immigrants brought these recipes to America and originally these sausages were served like any other. The story goes that in 1904, a street vendor in St.Louis was selling his wieners on small buns. They were nicknamed the "red hots" as they were too hot to handle by his customers. Suddenly he got this great idea of making a bun that will fit the shape of the sausage and an all American favorite "hot dog" was born.

Emulsified sausages can be divided in two groups:

1. High quality products made at home such as Austrian wiener or Polish Serdelki, which are made from high quality meats and without chemicals. Beef, veal and pork are the meats commonly used. Beef frankfurter contains beef only. High quality products contain enough lean meat to absorb the necessary water without help from water retention agents.

2. Commercial products made from all types of meat trimmings (pork, beef, chicken, turkey), including machine separated meat. Chicken hot dogs, turkey hot dogs and all possible combinations can be found in a supermarket. A large number of chemicals, water binding agents, fats and water are added during manufacturing to compensate for lower meat grades.

The public prefers moist emulsified sausages and it is hard to imagine a hot dog or frankfurter that will feel dry. In commercial production meat is chopped in bowl cutters by rapidly moving blades which creates lots of friction. This action develops a significant amount of heat which will encourage the growth of bacteria. To prevent that, the manufacturer adds crushed ice to the meat in the chopper.

Emulsification will be successful if the following criteria are met:

• Enough lean meat has been selected. The lean meat is the main source of *myosin*. The more myosin extracted, the thicker and stronger protein coat develops around particles of fat.

• Enough *myosin* has been extracted. This depends on how vigorous the cutting process was and how much salt (and phosphates, if any) were added.

Too much fat, especially when finely comminuted, will create such a large surface area that *there will not be enough protein solution to coat all fat particles*. As a result pockets of fat will form inside of the sausage. Some moisture is lost during smoking, cooking, and storing, and this factor must be allowed for in the manufacturing process. To make up for those losses more water is added during chopping/emulsifying. Experienced sausage makers know that the meats used in the manufacturing of sausages exhibit different abilities at holding water. Lean meat can hold more water than fatty tissue. Organ meats such as heart, glands, pork and beef tripe, pork skin, or snout all have poor water holding capabilities. Red meat found in pork head exhibits good water holding capability. Generally speaking any lean red meat holds water well although beef is on top of the list.

- Beef - high
- Veal - medium
- Pork - medium

Beef meat can absorb significant amounts of water:

- Bull meat – up to 100%
- Shank meat – up to 70%
- Cow meat - up to 60%
- Cheek meat – up to 40%

In simple terms 100 lbs. of cow meat can absorb 60 lbs. of water and 100 lbs. of bull meat can absorb 100 lbs. of water. An average beef piece bought in a local supermarket should hold about 30-40% of added water. To make top quality emulsified sausages at home a combination of lean red muscle meats should be used. This does not mean that only best lean cuts of meat must be employed. Using meat trimmings is in fact encouraged. A typical frankfurter recipe consists of about 60% beef and 40% pork trimmings. Those trimmings may consist of cheaper grades of meat such as heart, cheek meat, pork or beef tripe, and fats. As long as lean beef is used to bind water, other "filler" meats may be added.

A commercial manufacturer can not afford the luxury of using only top quality meats and to keep costs down he has to use second grade meat trimmings. Keep in mind that there is nothing wrong with such meats from a nutritional point of view, but in order to successfully incorporate them in a sausage we have to resort to water binding agents which will help to absorb and hold water within the meat structure. If you study some original instructions for making emulsified sausages from earlier times when chemicals were not yet widely used, you will see that beef was always ground with a smaller plate than pork. This was done in order to fully extract meat proteins which allowed meat to absorb more water.

As finer meat particles are obtained, more protein is extracted and more water can be absorbed by the meat. The fats are not going to hold water and it makes little sense to emulsify them as fine as lean meat. That is why fat is added to the bowl cutter at the end. If show meats (larger pieces) or chunks of fat (Mortadella) are required, they will be mixed with an emulsified sausage mass in a mixer.

Manufacturing Process

Water plays an important part:

- It helps to extract water soluble proteins (*actin* and myosin) which contribute to better meat binding and strong emulsion.
- It helps to keep temperature down by adding ice to the bowl cutter.

Meat selection. Lean beef, veal, lean pork. Keep in mind that the color of the sausage will depend on the type of meat used (*myoglobin* content) and to a smaller degree on spices.

Fat

About 20% of fat is needed for good texture, taste and flavor. Hard and soft fats can be used. Pork fat, beef fat, mutton fat, chicken fat or even vegetable oils can be utilized. Beef and lamb fat have a very strong flavor which can be masked by a careful choice of spices.

Examples of typical low cost meat formulas:

Formula A. Beef trimmings 60% (80% lean, 20% fat),
Pork trimmings 40% (80% lean, 20% fat).

Formula B. Beef trimmings - 50% (80% lean, 20% fat),
Pork trimmings - 50% (80% lean, 20% fat).

Traditional curing. Meats should be properly cured with salt and sodium nitrite (Cure #1) using the dry curing method. This will produce a pink color so typical to frankfurters or bologna. The smaller meat particle size results in a shorter curing time and emulsified meats are often cured using the faster "emulsion curing" method.

Emulsion curing. Salt, spices, binders and sodium nitrite are added directly into a bowl cutter where they are mixed with minced meat. Crushed ice or ice cold water is slowly added and as a result an emulsified paste is obtained. This emulsified mix is then stuffed into casings but can not be submitted to smoking as the curing color has not developed yet. In this particular case meats have not been cured and more time is needed in order for the sodium nitrite to react with the meat. As the meat has been very finely comminuted, it is sufficient to hang stuffed sausages overnight in a refrigerator (38° F, 3-4° C). When taken out of refrigeration, they are kept for 1-2 hours at room temperature or in a warm smokehouse at around 50° C (122° F) without smoke. The reason is to dry out the sausage casings which may be moist (condensation) when removed from a cold refrigerator into a warmer room. It also provides an extra time for curing as sodium nitrite cures even faster at such high temperatures. The normal 2-3 days curing period has been eliminated. The curing method, "emulsion curing" may not be the best choice at home conditions, unless an extra refrigerator is available.

To lower costs, a commercial manufacturer tries to accomplish the entire curing process during meat cutting and emulsifying. This is possible due to the addition of sodium erythorbate or ascorbic acid, which accelerates the production of nitric oxide from sodium nitrite (Cure #1). Nitric oxide reacts with meat myoglobin rapidly producing nitrosomyoglobin. As a result the cured red color is obtained much faster and is more stable.

Grinding/Emulsifying. Commercial producers will perform the first stages of production entirely in a bowl cutter. This saves time and space, simplifies equipment and allows the introduction of huge amounts of water.

A typical emulsifying process:

1. Add beef to a bowl cutter rotating on low speed.
2. Add salt, sodium nitrite (Cure#1), phosphates (if used) and ingredients and 1/3 of finely crushed ice (less wear on knives). Cut on high speed.
3. Add lean pork trimmings and another 1/3 of ice.
4. Add last part of ice, all spices, color enhancers (ascorbic acid, sodium erythorbate etc), fat and fat pork trimmings. Cut and mix together.

Notes:

- Fat is added last as it does not absorb water and when finely chopped may smear.
- Ascorbic acid reacts sporadically when in direct contact with sodium nitrite. This is why sodium nitrite is added at the beginning and ascorbic acid last.
- About 2 - 3% salt and 0.3 - 0.5% phosphates should be added for maximum protein extraction.
- Salt soluble proteins are most effectively extracted from lean meat at 36 - 38° F (2 - 4° C).

Home Production

Grinding. Grind all meats with a coarse plate 3/8" (10 mm), refreeze and grind again through 3/16" (5 mm) or 1/8" (3 mm). Refreeze the mixture briefly and grind the third time through 1/8" (3 mm) plate.

Using Food Processor

A kitchen type food processor is the smaller brother of a commercial bowl cutter. It allows to effectively chop meat trimmings that contain a lot of connective tissue, the task which will be hard to perform with a manual grinder. The meat should be first ground in a grinder through 1/8" (3 mm) plate and then emulsified in a food processor. The grinding process can be performed a day earlier. Most processors come with a single cutting blade, some are equipped with two knives. In both cases a lot of heat is generated and crushed ice should be added.

Different meats can absorb different amounts of water but adding 25% of crushed ice may be a good estimate. Chop meat and fat gradually adding crushed ice until it is completely absorbed by the meat. If this process were performed at high temperatures the emulsion would be lost and the fat will separate from water.

A good comparison is the process of making mayonnaise or some butter sauces. If oil is added too fast to egg emulsion while whisking, the emulsion will break apart and oil will come out of the solution. If butter is added to emulsion too fast or at too high temperatures, the emulsion will be lost. The remedy is to add ice and vigorously whisk again. Adding some non-fat dry milk (3%), although not necessary, will strengthen the emulsion and will help the finished sausage retain moisture.

Mixing. Mix all ingredients with a cup of cold water and pour over minced meat. Start mixing, gradually adding flaked ice or cold water until a well mixed mass is obtained. We have been making wieners and frankfurters long before food processors came to be and there is no reason why we can't process them in the same way again.

Stuffing. Stuff hot dogs or frankfurters into sheep casings making 4-5" (10-12 cm) links. Hang them for 1 hour at room temperature to dry out the casings and then place the sausages in a smokehouse. The smoking step is very important during commercial manufacturing as sausages such as hot dogs or frankfurters are skinless (no casings). They are stuffed into cellulose casings and then smoked. This creates a hardened surface which becomes a sort of artificial casing. After smoking and cooking, sausages go through the machine that cuts cellulose casings lengthwise and then the casing is peeled off. The hardened surface of the sausage is strong enough to hold a sausage mass in one piece. At home the sausages are stuffed into sheepskin casings which are edible and it is entirely up to you whether to remove the casings or not. If it comes off clean (no meat attached) and easy you may remove it. A skinless fresh sausage can be produced by stuffing meat into cellulose casings. The sausage is then frozen and the casing stripped off.

Smoking. Freshly stuffed sausages are left for 1-2 hrs at room temperature or in a warm smokehouse at around 50° C (122° F) without smoke. The purpose of this step is to dry out the casings which should feel dry or tacky to the touch. We all know very well that we should not smoke wet meats or sausages. Sausages are smoked at 60-70° C (140-158° F) until a reddish-brown color is obtained. Smoking and cooking should be considered as one continuous operation.

Cooking. Cooking time depends directly on the temperature when the smoking has ended. For small diameter sausages such as hotdogs or frankfurters it should not be longer than 15 minutes. Emulsified sausages are heat treated with steam or hot water. At home conditions they will be submerged in hot water at 75° C (167° F). Frankfurters are thin sausages and 15 minutes cooking time is plenty. Keep in mind that they have been smoked at 60-70° C (140-158° F) for about 45 minutes and are already warm and partly pre-cooked. If a sausage diameter is larger, let's say Mortadella, 60 mm, you may cook it at 75 – 78° C (167 – 172° F) for 60 minutes. A very large bologna sausage may be smoked for 3-5 hours and cooked for 5 hours more. A rule of thumb dictates 10 min for each 1 cm of diameter of the sausage. There is no need for estimating time when a thermometer is used and cooking stops when the internal temperature of the sausage reaches 68-70° C (154-158° F).

Cooling. Dip sausages in cold water to cool them down. You may have to change the water once or twice depending on the size of the container and amount of production. If possible shower them or dip them very briefly with hot water to remove any grease on the surface. Hang them and wipe off any fat with a wet cloth. The reason for cooling is to bring the temperature down outside the Danger Zone (50-30° C, 122-86° F) when most bacteria find favorable conditions to grow. Although the cooking process kills 99% of bacteria, nevertheless new bacteria which are present all around will start multiplying again on the surface of the sausage. It is in our interest to bring the temperature below 30° C (86° F) as soon as possible. The sausages can be hung between 25-30° C (77-86° F) as at those temperatures moisture and heat evaporate from the surface rapidly. Then the sausages may be placed in a refrigerator.

Storing. In refrigerator.

Spices and additives. Aromatic seeds such as cloves, ginger, allspice, cinnamon, and nutmeg are commonly added to emulsified sausages. Other popular spices are white pepper, coriander and celery seed. The following additives can be used in emulsified products: non fat dry milk, starch, soy protein isolate or concentrate, egg whites, phosphates and ascorbates.

Making Different Sausages

1. Often more than one sausage type is produced at the same time. In such a case the emulsified mixture becomes a sausage mass that *becomes a base for different sausages*. Of course besides salt, nitrite and phosphate, no other ingredients are added when making the base.

2. Lean meat is manually cut into larger pieces or ground through a coarse grinder plate. The fat can be diced into 1/8" cubes. Those bigger parts will become *the show meat* in a finished sausage.

3. Emulsified sausage base is mixed with other ingredients and stuffed into casings. Ingredients such as olives, pistachio nuts, and whole peppercorns may be added as well.

4. The sausage mass is stuffed into casings and cooked in water.

Bologna
(reduced-fat)

184 calories per
100 g serving

Bologna and frankfurter are smoked and cooked emulsified sausages which are similar. Many producers use the same formula and processing steps for both sausages. The main difference is the size of the casings as bologna is a much bigger sausage. It is an American equivalent of Italian Mortadella with no visible pieces of fat.

Meat	Metric	US
lean beef	700 g	1.54 lb.
oil emulsion*	200 g	0.44 lb.
potato starch	20 g	3 Tbsp.
water	80 g	1/3 cup

Ingredients per 1000 g (1 kg) of materials:

salt	18 g	3 tsp.
Cure #1	2.5 g	½ tsp.
carrageenan	5.0 g	1 tsp.
phosphate**	3.0 g	½ tsp
sodium erythorbate**	0.3 g	use scale
paprika	2.0 g	1 tsp.
allspice	2.0 g	1 tsp.
white pepper	2.0 g	1 tsp.
coriander	2.0 g	1 tsp.

Instructions:
1. Grind meat through 3/16" plate (5 mm).
2. In food processor chop ground meat, water, salt, phosphate, cure #1 and sodium erythorbate.
3. Add starch and spices and remix. Add oil emulsion and remix.
4. Stuff firmly into 40-60 mm beef middles, fibrous or cellulose casings.
5. Hang at room temperature for one hour.
6. When sausages feel dry to touch, apply hot smoke 50-60° C (120-140° F) for 2-3 hours.
7. Cook in smokehouse or in water to 160° F (72° C) internal meat temperature.
8. Shower with or immerse in cold water for 10 minutes.
9. Store in refrigerator.

Notes:
* oil emulsion: soy protein isolate/oil/water at 1:4:5.
** Sodium erythorbate and phosphate are not absolutely necessary, although highly recommended.

Chinese Sausage

187 calories per
100 g serving

Chinese sausage is a dried, hard sausage usually made from fatty pork. Ingredients like monosodium glutamate, soy sauce and sugar are added to the sausages in very high levels. The addition of selected Chinese rice wines or even scotch or sherry are common for certain quality products. The most popular spice is cinnamon since Chinese manufacturers believe that it acts as a preservative.

Meat	Metric	US
lean pork	700 g	1.54 lb.
oil emulsion*	150 g	0.33 lb.
potato starch	20 g	3 Tbsp.
sugar	50 g	4 Tbs.
rice wine	30 ml	2 Tbsp.
cold water	50 ml	3 Tbsp.

Ingredients per 1000 g (1 kg) of materials:

soy sauce	30 g	⅛ cup
Cure #1	2.0 g	1/3 tsp.
monosodium glutamate	3 g	½ tsp.
cinnamon	1 g	½ tsp.
pepper	2.0 g	1 tsp.
garlic	3.5 g	1 clove

Instructions:
1. Grind pork through the 3/8" (10 mm) plate.
2. Mix ground meat with all ingredients.
3. Stuff into 22-26 mm sheep casings and make 5" - 6" long links.
4. When sausages feel dry to touch, apply hot smoke 50-60° C (120-140° F) for 30 minutes.
5. Cook in smokehouse or in water to 160° F (72° C) internal meat temperature.
6. Shower with or immerse in cold water for 5 minutes.
7. Store in refrigerator.

Notes:
* oil emulsion: soy protein isolate/oil/water at 1:4:5.

Coney Island Frank

(reduced-fat)

164 calories per
100 g serving

This sausage was very popular in the Coney Island amusement park and other parks in New York City where it was roasted over charcoal fires.

Meat	Metric	US
lean beef	600 g	1.32 lb.
lean pork	200 g	0.44 lb.
oil emulsion*	100 g	0.22 lb.
potato flour	30 g	1 oz.
water	70 g	1/3 cup

Ingredients per 1000 g (1 kg) of materials:

salt	18 g	3 tsp.
Cure #1	2.5 g	½ tsp.
pepper	2.0 g	1 tsp.
gelatin	10.0 g	2 tsp.
red pepper	1.0 g	½ tsp.
nutmeg	1.0 g	½ tsp.

Instructions:

1. Grind meats with 3/16" plate (5 mm). Refreeze and grind again preferably through 1/8" (3 mm) plate.
2. Mix lean beef with all ingredients adding cold water. Add lean pork and remaining cold water and mix well. Add oil emulsion and mix everything together.
3. Stuff into 24-26 mm sheep casings.
4. Hang for one hour at room temperature.
5. When sausages feel dry apply hot smoke 60-70° C (140-158° F) for about 60 minutes until brown color develops.
6. Cook in hot water, at 80° C (176° F) for about 20 minutes.
7. Immerse sausages in cold water for 5 minutes.
8. Keep in a refrigerator.

Notes:
* oil emulsion: soy protein isolate/oil/water at 1:4:5.

Frankfurter
(reduced-fat)

175 calories per
100 g serving

Materials	Metric	US
lean beef	650 g	1.43 lb.
soy protein isolate	20 g	3 Tbsp.
vegetable oil	80 g	1/2 cup
potato flour	20 g	4 tsp.
cold water	230 g	1 cup.

Ingredients per 1000 g (1 kg) of materials:

salt	15 g	2½ tsp
cure #1	2 g	1/3 tsp.
carrageenan	5.0 g	1 tsp.
white pepper	3 g	1½ tsp.
nutmeg, ground	1.0 g	½ tsp.
coriander, ground	2.0 g	1 tsp.
garlic, smashed	7.0 g	2 cloves
sodium erythorbate*	0.3 g	use scale
phosphate*	3.0 g	½ tsp

Instructions:
1. Grind beef through a small plate (1/8", 3 mm).
2. In a food processor, start chopping ground meat, cure #1, phosphate, erythorbate and cold water. Add gradually oil, spices, flour and emulsify.
3. Stuff into 22-26 mm sheep casings.
4. Hold at room temperature for 30 minutes.
5. Smoke at 65° C (150° F) for 30-40 minutes.
6. Cook sausage in water at 176 F (80 C), about 15-20 minutes.
7. Cold shower or cool in cold water. Store in refrigerator.

Notes:
* Sodium erythorbate and phosphate are not absolutely necessary, although highly recommended.

Hot Dog

(non-fat, extended sausage)

121 calories per
100 g serving

Materials	Metric	US
lean pork	500 g	1.1 lb.
potato starch	20 g	3 Tbsp.
soy protein isolate (SPI)	20 g	3 Tbsp.
water	100 g	0.22 lb.
vegetable protein (TVP)	90 g	3 oz.
water (for TVP)	270 g	1-1/8 cup

Ingredients per 1000 g (1 kg) of materials:

salt	18.0 g	2 tsp.
cure #1	2 g	1/3 tsp.
carrageenan	5.0 g	1 tsp.
phosphate*	3.0 g	½ tsp
sodium erythorbate*	0.3 g	use scale
pepper	2.0 g	1 tsp.
nutmeg, ground	1.0 g	½ tsp.
paprika	1.0 g	½ tsp.
coriander, ground	2.0 g	1 tsp.
dextrose	10.0 g	2 tsp.
garlic	3.5 g	1 clove

Instructions:

1. Soak TVP in cold water for 30 minutes.
2. Grind pork through a small plate (1/8", 3 mm).
3. In a food processor chop 100 g of cold water, ground meat, salt, phosphate, cure #1, and sodium erythorbate. Add SPI and remix . Add rehydrated TVP and all other ingredients and emulsify all together.
4. Stuff into 22-26 mm sheep or cellulose casings.
5. Hold at room temperature for 30 minutes.
6. Smoke at 65° C (150° F) for 30-40 minutes.
7. Cook sausage in water at 176° F (80° C), about 15-20 minutes.
8. Cold shower or cool in cold water. Store in refrigerator.

Notes:

* Sodium erythorbate and phosphate are not absolutely necessary, although highly recommended.

Kabanosy   154 calories per
                               100 g serving

Kabanosy is a famous Polish sausage and probably the finest meat stick in the world. The name Kabanosy comes from the nickname "kabanek" given to a young fat pig no more than 120 kg (264 lbs.) that was fed mainly potatoes in the Eastern parts of XIX Poland.

Meat	Metric	US
lean pork	800 g	1.76 lb.
oil emulsion*	100 g	0.22 lb.
water	100 g	0.22 lb.

Ingredients per 1000 g (1 kg) of materials:

salt	15 g	2 ½ tsp.
Cure #1	2.5 g	½ tsp.
Sausage Maker Fat Replacer	8.0 g	2 tsp.
sodium erythorbate**	0.3 g	use scale
pepper	2.0 g	1 tsp.
sugar	1.0 g	1/5 tsp.
nutmeg	1.0 g	½ tsp.
caraway	1.0 g	½ tsp.

Instructions:
1. Grind lean pork with 3/8" (10 mm) plate.
2. Mix ground meat with water, cure #1 and spices until the mass feels sticky. Add oil emulsion and remix all together.
3. Stuff mixture into 22-26 mm sheep casings. Link sausage into 60-70 cm (24-27") links so when hung on a smoking stick the individual links (half of the meat stick) will be about one foot long.
4. Leave sausages at room temperature for 30-60 min.
5. When sausages feel dry to touch, apply hot smoke 50-60° C (120-140° F) for 45 minutes.
6. Cook in smokehouse or in water to 160° F (72° C) internal meat temperature.
7. Shower with or immerse in cold water for 10 minutes.
8. Store in refrigerator.

Notes:
* oil emulsion: soy protein isolate/oil/water at 1:4:5.
** Sodium erythorbate is not absolutely necessary, although it will promote development of a strong color.

Krakowska Sausage
(Kielbasa krakowska krajana)

160 calories per
100 g serving

This sausage has always been one of the top sellers in Poland. The name relates to the city of Krakow, one of the oldest cities in Europe. The middle part of the name "krajana" implies that the meat was manually cut into pieces. It goes by many similar names for example Krakauer Sausage.

Meat	Metric	US
lean pork (show meat)	800 g	1.76 lb.
oil emulsion*	100 g	0.22 lb.
potato starch	10 g	4 tsp.
non-fat dry milk	10 g	3 tsp.
cold water	80 g	1/3 cup

Ingredients per 1000 g (1 kg) of materials:

salt	18 g	3 tsp.
Cure #1	2.5 g	½ tsp.
carrageenan	5.0 g	1 tsp.
Sausage Maker Fat Replacer	8.0 g	2 tsp.
pepper	2.0 g	1 tsp.
sugar	2.5 g	½ tsp.
nutmeg	1.0 g	½ tsp.

Instructions:

1. Manually cut lean pork show meat into 2" (5 cm) cubes. Mix with salt and Cure #1, place in container and refrigerate for 24 hours. This curing process will develop strong pink color of the show meat.
2. Mix all ingredients with cold water. Pour over show meat pieces and mix together.
3. Add oil emulsion and mix everything well together.
4. Stuff firmly into 100-120 mm (4-5") beef bungs or synthetic fibrous casings and tie the ends with twine forming a hanging loop on one end. Make 14-16" long sections. Lace up sausages with two lengthwise loops and loops across the casing every 2 inches. Prick any visible air pockets with a needle.
5. Hang at room temperature for 2 hours.
6. Smoke with hot smoke for 120-150 min until casings develop a light brown color with a pink tint.
7. Cook in water at 167°F, 75° C, until internal temperature of the meat becomes 68-70°C (154-158°F). This will take about 2 hours.
8. Shower with cold water for about 10 min, air dry and place in refrigerator.

Notes:

* oil emulsion: soy protein isolate/oil/water at 1:4:5.

Mortadella Lyoner
(reduced-fat)

146 calories per
100 g serving

Meat	Metric	US
lean pork	350 g	0.77 lb.
lean beef	350 g	0.77 lb.
oil emulsion*	100 g	0.22 lb.
non fat dry milk	20 g	2 Tbsp.
cold water	180 g	3/4 cup

Ingredients per 1000 g (1 kg) of materials:

salt	18 g	3 tsp.
Cure #1	2.0 g	1/3 tsp.
carrageenan	5.0 g	1 tsp.
phosphate**	3.0 g	½ tsp.
sodium erythorbate**	0.3 g	use scale
white pepper	2.0 g	1 tsp.
mace	0.5 g	¼ tsp.
coriander	0.5 g	¼ tsp.
ginger	0.5 g	¼ tsp.
cardamom	0.5 g	¼ tsp.
sweet paprika	1.0 g	½ tsp.
onion powder	2.0 g	1 tsp.

Instructions:
1. Grind all meats with ⅛" (3 mm) grinder plate.
2. In a food processor chop ground meat, water, salt, phosphate, cure #1 and sodium erythorbate.
3. Add spices, flour and oil emulsion and remix.
4. Stuff into 60 mm plastic waterproof casings.
5. Cook in water at 167-176 °F, 75-80° C for 60 minutes.
6. Cool in cold water and refrigerate.

Notes:
* oil emulsion: soy protein isolate/oil/water at 1:4:5.
** Sodium erythorbate and phosphate are not absolutely necessary, although highly recommended.

Moscow Sausage

153 calories per
100 g serving

This is a hot smoked version of the Moscow sausage which was originally cold smoked and not cooked.

Meat	Metric	US
lean beef	750 g	1.65 lb.
oil emulsion*	100 g	0.22 lb.
potato flour	20 g	4 tsp.
potato starch	10 g	4 tsp.
water	120 g	½ cup

Ingredients per 1000 g (1 kg) of materials:

salt	18 g	3 tsp.
Cure #1	2.0 g	1/3 tsp.
carrageenan	5.0 g	2 tsp.
pepper	2.0 g	1 tsp.
sugar	2.0 g	½ tsp.
nutmeg	1.0 g	½ tsp.

Instructions:

1. Grind beef with 3/16" (5 mm) plate.
2. Mix ground beef, salt, cure #1, and all spices with water. Mix until all water is absorbed by the mixture. Then add flour, starch, oil emulsion and mix everything together.
3. Stuff into beef middles or fibrous synthetic casings 40-60 mm and form 12" (30 cm) long links.
4. Hang at room temperature for 60 min.
5. Apply hot smoke for 120 minutes.
6. In the last stage of smoking the sausage is baked at 75-90° C (167-194° F) until internal meat temperature is 68-70° C (154-158° F).
7. Shower with cold water for about 5 min.
8. Store in refrigerator.

Notes:
* oil emulsion: soy protein isolate/oil/water at 1:4:5.

Mysliwska - Hunter's Sausage

144 calories per 100 g serving

Mysliwska Sausage - Hunter's Sausage is made of pork and beef. A hunter carried a big hunting bag where he kept the necessary tools and food that had to last for a number of days. Mysliwska Sausage was a relatively short, well smoked sausage that would make an ideal food or snack in those circumstances. Hunter's Sausage is popular in many countries, for example in Germany it is called Jadgwurst and in Italy Cotechino. Prolonged smoking and juniper berries give the sausage its unique character.

Meat	Metric	US
lean pork,	650 g	1.43 lb.
lean beef	100 g	0.22 lb.
vegetable oil	30 g	2 Tbsp.
potato flour	20 g	4 tsp.
cold water	100 g	½ tablespoon

Ingredients per 1000 g (1 kg) of materials:

salt	18 g	3 tsp.
Cure #1	2.5 g	½ tsp.
gelatin	10.0 g	2 tsp.
Sausage Maker fat replacer	4.0 g	1 tsp.
pepper	2.0 g	1 tsp.
sugar	1.0 g	1/5 tsp.
garlic	3.5 g	1 clove
juniper	1.0 g	½ tsp.

Instructions:

1. Grind lean pork with ½" (13 mm) plate. Grind beef twice through ⅛" (2 - 3 mm) plate.
2. Add cold water into the ground beef and mix well with all ingredients except oil. Add pork and mix all together. Add oil and mix all together.
3. Stuff mixture into 32 mm hog casings and form 7 - 8" (18-20 cm) links.
4. Hang sausages at room temperature for 2 hours.
5. Sausage is hot smoked in a few distinct stages:
   - At about 122° F (50° C) for 80-90 min. You can keep on increasing the smoking temperature gradually up to 176° F (80° C).
   - At 176 - 194° F (80 - 90° C) for 25 min until the internal temperature of 154 - 158° F (68 - 70° C) is reached. The color of the sausage should be brown.
6. Shower with cold water for about 5 min and place in refrigerator.

Polish Smoked Sausage
(reduced-fat)

158 calories per
100 g serving

Materials	Metric	US
lean pork	800 g	1.76 lb.
oil emulsion*	100 g	0.22 lb.
water	100 g	2 Tbsp.

Ingredients per 1000 g (1 kg) of materials:

salt	18.0 g	3 tsp.
cure #1	2.5 g	½ tsp.
carrageenan	5.0 g	1 tsp.
dextrose	10.0 g	2 tsp.
pepper	3.0 g	1 tsp.
garlic	3.5 g	1 clove
marjoram	1.0 g	⅔ tsp.

Instructions:

1. Grind meat through 3/8" (10 mm) plate. Add salt and Cure 1 and mix well with meat.
2. Mix dextrose, spices and fat replacer with ground meat.
3. Add oil emulsion and mix all together.
4. Stuff mixture into 32 - 36 mm hog casings and form 12" links.
5. Hang on smoke sticks for 1-2 hours at room temperature OR
6. Place sausages in a preheated smoker at 120° F (49° C) with draft dampers fully open.
7. When casings feel dry partially close the exit smoke damper and apply smoke for 60 minutes. Keep on increasing the smoking temperature until you reach 170° F (76° C). Sausage is done when the internal temperature reaches 154° F (68° C).
8. Remove from smoker and shower with water or immerse sausages in cold water.
9. Store in refrigerator.

Notes:
* oil emulsion: soy protein isolate/oil/water at 1:4:5.

Polish Smoked Sausage
(non-fat)

124 calories per
100 g serving

Materials	Metric	US
lean pork	850 g	1.87 lb.
water	150 g	2 Tbsp.

Ingredients per 1000 g (1 kg) of materials:

salt	18.0 g	3 tsp.
cure #1	2.5 g	½ tsp.
Sausage Maker fat replacer	8.0 g	2 tsp.
carrageenan	5.0 g	1 tsp.
dextrose	10.0 g	2 tsp.
pepper	3.0 g	1 tsp.
garlic	3.5 g	1 clove
marjoram	1.0 g	⅔ tsp.

Instructions:
1. Grind meat through 3/8" (10 mm) plate.
2. Add salt and Cure 1 and mix well with meat.
3. Mix dextrose, spices, fat replacer with ground meat and water.
4. Stuff mixture into 32 - 36 mm hog casings and form 12" links.
5. Hang on smoke sticks for 1-2 hours at room temperature OR
6. Place sausages in a preheated smoker at 120° F (49° C) with draft dampers fully open.
7. When casings feel dry partially close the exit smoke damper and apply smoke for 60 minutes. Keep on increasing the smoking temperature until you reach 170° F (76° C). Sausage is done when the internal temperature reaches 154° F (68° C).
8. Remove from smoker and shower with water or immerse sausages in cold water.
9. Store in refrigerator.

Pork Curry Sausage
(reduced-fat)

166 calories per
100 g serving

Pork curry sausage is an emulsified and cooked sausage which is basically frankfurter flavored with curry.

Meat	Metric	US
lean pork	800 g	1.76 lb.
oil emulsion*	100 g	0.22 lb.
non-fat dry milk	20 g	2 Tbsp.
potato starch	10 g	4 tsp.
water	70 g	1/3 cup

Ingredients per 1000 g (1 kg) of materials:

salt	15 g	2 ½ tsp.
carrageenan	5.0 g	1 tsp.
white pepper	2.0 g	1 tsp.
curry powder	2.0 g	1 tsp.
ginger	0.5 g	⅓ tsp.
cardamom	2.0 g	1 tsp.
coriander	2.0 g	1 tsp.
nutmeg	2.0 g	1 tsp.
grated lemon peel	1.0 g	½ tsp.

Instructions:

1. Grind meat through 3/16" plate (5 mm). Refreeze and grind again.
2. Mix salt, spices, non-fat dry milk, potato starch and cold water. Add ground pork and mix all together. Add oil emulsion and mix all together.
3. Stuff firmly into 28-32 mm hog casings.
4. Cook in water, at 176° F, 80° C for 30 minutes.
5. Cool in cold water for 5 minutes.
6. Keep in a refrigerator.

Notes:
* oil emulsion: soy protein isolate/oil/water at 1:4:5.

Serdelki
(reduced-fat)

156 calories per
100 g serving

Serdelki is the Polish equivalent of a wiener. This is a fine textured emulsified sausage like a hot dog or frankfurter.

Meat	Metric	US
pork	500 g	1.10 lb.
beef	250 g	0.55 lb.
oil emulsion*	100 g	0.22 lb.
potato starch	20 g	3 Tbsp.
non-fat dry milk	10 g	3 tsp.
cold water	120 g	½ cup

Ingredients per 1000 g (1 kg) of materials:

salt	18 g	3 tsp.
Cure #1	2.0 g	1/3 tsp.
carrageenan	5.0 g	1 tsp.
white pepper	2.0 g	1 tsp.
nutmeg	1.5 g	1 tsp.
garlic	3.5 g	1 clove

Instructions:
1. Grind meats through 3/16" (5 mm) plate.
2. Mix everything together adding water and all ingredients. You can use a food processor.
3. Stuff firmly into 32-34 mm hog casings, or 28-30 mm sheep casings.
4. Hang at room temperature for one hour.
5. When sausages feel dry to touch, apply hot smoke 50-60° C (120-140° F) for 1 hour.
6. Cook in water, at 176° F, 80° C for 30 minutes.
7. Shower with or immerse in cold water for 5 minutes.
8. Store in refrigerator.

Notes:
* oil emulsion: soy protein isolate/oil/water at 1:4:5.

Ukrainian Sausage

166 calories per
100 g serving

A traditional heavily smoked sausage that is cooked in water from the Poland's neighbor in the East.

Meat	Metric	US
lean beef	700 g	1.54 lb.
oil emulsion*	150 g	0.33 lb.
non-fat dry milk**	20 g	2 Tbsp.
carrageenan**	10 g	2 tsp.
water	120 g	½ cup

Ingredients per 1000 g (1 kg) of materials:

salt	18 g	3 tsp.
Cure #1	2.5 g	½ tsp.
pepper	2.0 g	1 tsp.
paprika	2.0 g	1 tsp.
allspice	2.0 g	1 tsp.
garlic	3.5 g	1 clove
marjoram	2.0 g	1½ tsp.

Instructions:

1. Grind beef with 3/16" (5 mm) plate.
2. Mixed ground beef with water, add all other ingredients, except oil emulsion. Add oil emulsion and mix everything together.
3. Stuff mixture into 36 mm hog casings or beef rounds.
4. Hang at room temperature for two hours to dry.
5. Smoke with hot smoke 90-120 minutes.
6. Cook for 40 minutes in water at 167°-176° F (75°-80° C).
7. Immerse in cold water for 5 minutes.
8. Store in refrigerator.

Notes:

* oil emulsion: soy protein isolate/oil/water at 1:4:5.
** carrageenan and non-fat dry milk may be replaced with 20 g potato starch and 10 g powdered gelatin.

Wiener
(reduced-fat)

171 calories per
100 g serving

The wiener is a cured, smoked and cooked sausage. It is a ready to eat sausage or it may be boiled, fried or grilled for serving. The wiener originated about 300 years ago in Vienna, Austria and German immigrants brought this technology to the USA. The terms frankfurter, wiener or hot dog are practically interchangeable today.

Meat	Metric	US
lean pork	400 g	0.88 lb.
veal	300 g	0.66 lb.
oil emulsion*	150 g	0.33 lb.
potato flour	30 g	2 Tbsp.
water	120 g	½ cup

Ingredients per 1000 g (1 kg) of materials:

salt	18 g	3 tsp.
Cure #1	2.0 g	⅓ tsp.
carrageenan	5.0 g	1 tsp.
phosphate*	3.0 g	½ tsp.
sodium erythorbate**	0.3 g	use scale
paprika	2.0 g	1 tsp.
white pepper	2.0 g	1 tsp.
coriander	2.0 g	1 tsp.
mace	0.5 g	⅓ tsp.
onion powder	1.0 g	½ tsp.

Instructions:
1. Grind meats through 3/16" plate (5 mm).
2. In a food processor chop ground meat, water, salt, phosphate, cure #1 and sodium erythorbate.
3. Add spices and oil emulsion and remix.
4. Stuff firmly into 24-26 mm sheep casings.
5. Hang at room temperature for 30 minutes.
6. When sausages feel dry to touch, apply hot smoke 50-60° C (120-140° F) for 45 minutes.
7. Cook in smokehouse or in water to 160° F (72° C) internal meat temperature.
8. Shower with or immerse in cold water for 10 minutes.
9. Store in refrigerator.

Notes:
* oil emulsion: soy protein isolate/oil/water at 1:4:5.
** Sodium erythorbate and phosphate are not absolutely necessary, although highly recommended.

Chapter 11

Liver Sausages

Liver sausages can be classified as:

- Regular liver sausages - coarsely comminuted through 5 mm grinder plate and cooked in water.
- Delicatessen type liver sausages - finely comminuted through 2 mm grinder plate and emulsified.
- Pâtés - liver sausages which are not stuffed, but placed in molds and baked or cooked in water. Molds are often lined with pastry and pâtés are covered with decorations and gelatin.

Composition of a Liver Sausage

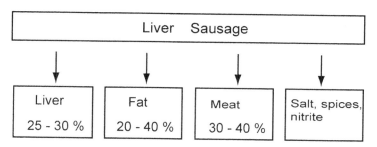

Fig. 11.1 Composition of a liver sausage. Raw liver is a natural emulsifier which helps to combine fat with water.

Liver is an organ that works hard by filtering blood and as an animal grows older, the liver becomes darker and might develop a slightly bitter taste. Think of it as it were a filter that would become dirtier in time, the difference is that not the dust, but atoms of heavier materials like iron or copper will accumulate in time within its structure. Calf are slaughtered at the age of 4 months, a pig at 6 months, but a cow may live a few years. Because it is older the cow's liver or blood are of much deeper color and will induce a darker color to a finished sausage.

On the other hand veal, pork or poultry liver will make a sausage lighter and will make it taste better. This does not mean that you can not use beef liver at all and up to 25% of beef liver may be mixed with other livers without compromising the final taste. As the name implies a liver is an essential ingredient in the recipe but which one is the best?

Liver source	Description
Veal	Excellent. Light color, great taste, more expensive.
Pork	Very good.
Lamb and goat	Good. Up to 50% can be mixed with pork liver.
Beef	Poor. Can be mixed with other livers but should not account for more than 25% of the total liver mass. Dark color.
Goose	Very good.
Chicken, turkey, duck	Good. Can be mixed with pork liver in any proportions.
Rabbit	Very good. Can be mixed with pork liver in any proportions.
Venison and wild game	Not suitable.

As you can see you can control the quality and color of your sausage by choosing the type of liver used. The way you will process liver, fat and meats will have the biggest impact on the quality of your sausage and the selected spices will add the final touch.

Best liver sausages are made from livers of young animals. Up to 25% of beef can be added as it is tougher and will darken liver sausage. Poultry such as goose, duck or turkey will make a fine liver sausage, but chicken liver is not the best choice.

Liver must NOT be cooked. In many recipes liver is cooked briefly (blanched) in hot water for up to 5 min to remove any leftover blood but there is no real need for that. Blanching will cook some of the liver proteins and less of them would be available for emulsifying fat and water. Instead, liver can be rinsed and soaked in cold water for one hour to get rid of any traces of blood and remaining gall liquid. Soaking liver in milk is an old remedy for the removal of some of the liver's bitterness which can be noticeable in beef liver.

Materials, 100 g portion				
Name	Protein (g)	Fat (g)	Energy (cal)	Cholesterol (mg)
Pork liver	21.39	3.65	134	301
Beef Liver	20.36	3.63	135	275
Veal Liver	19.93	4.85	140	334
Chicken Liver	16.92	4.83	119	345
Turkey Liver	17.84	16.36	228	331
Duck Liver	18.74	4.64	136	515
Goose Liver	16.37	4.28	133	515
Source: USDA Nutrient database				

Meat Selection

Meats used for commercially made liver sausages are first cured with sodium nitrite to obtain a pinkish color and the characteristic cured meat flavor. Liver sausages made at home in most cases employ meats that are not cured with sodium nitrite and the color of the sausage will be light yellow. That will largely depend on the type of liver and spices used. It is advantageous, especially when making coarse type liver sausage, to use meats with a lot of connective tissues such as pork head meat, jowls (cheeks) or skin. Those parts contain a lot of collagen which will turn into gelatin during heat treatment. During subsequent cooling this gelatin will become a gel and that will make the sausage more spreadable with a richer mouthful texture. Meats commonly used in commercial production are pork head meat, jowls, meat trimmings and skin. Although pork head meat may not appeal to most people as a valuable meat, it is high in fat and connective tissues and contains more meat flavor than other cuts. For those reasons it is a perfect meat in liver or head cheese production.

If skinless pork jowls or skinless head meat is used about 5-10% of skins are added to the meat mass. Keep in mind that too many skins may make the texture of your sausage feel rubbery. As long as the proper proportion of liver and fat are observed the remaining meats can be of any kind: pork, beef or veal.

Fat

Liver sausages contain a large percentage of fat (20-40%) which largely determines their texture and spreadability. Any pork fat such as a hard fat (back fat, jowls), soft fat (belly), or other fat trimmings is fine. Beef fat or pork flare fat (kidney) are not commonly used as they are hard and not easy to emulsify. To make fine spreadable liver sausage, fat should be dispersed in the liquid state at warm temperatures. To achieve a final chopping temperature of around 95° F, (35° C), fat or fat trimmings are usually poached at 176° F (80° C). Then when still warm they are ground. Liver and lean meat are emulsified at cool (or room) temperature. Then warm ground fats are mixed with liver, lean meat and spices together.

Salt, Spices and Other Ingredients

Liver sausages contain less salt than other sausages, the average being 12-18 g (1.2-1.8%) of salt per 1 kg of meat. Those sausages are of a much lighter color and for that reason white pepper is predominantly used as it can not be seen. Home made style liver sausages and pâtés are usually made without sodium nitrite and the final color remains greyish in sharp contrast to pinkish commercial products. Sodium nitrite has some effect on extending the shelf life of the product and for that reason alone it is used by commercial processors.

Most liver sausages are not smoked and for a home sausage maker there is no need to use nitrite. If a smoked flavor is desired, sodium nitrite will have to be added as the sausage will be lightly smoked with cold smoke. Liver sausages are cold smoked (< 68° F, 20° C) after being cooked in water. The main purpose of smoke is to impart a smoky flavor to a product. Hot smoking has little effect on the preservation of a product and must still be considered perishable.

Fresh onions are frequently used in home made liver sausages but are a poor choice in canned products and can create a sour taste. Milk or sweet cream is often added for a milder taste. Like in other sausages, sugar may be added to offset the salty taste. Vanilla is often added to create an aromatic sweet taste. Commonly used spices are: nutmeg, mace, allspice, marjoram, white pepper, sweet paprika and ginger. Port or brandy are often added.

Home Production

Precooking meat. Commercial plants cure meats with sodium nitrite regardless whether they will be smoked or not. Liver sausages made at home contain meats that are traditionally not cured although if a smoked product is desired, sodium nitrite should be added. Pork skin should be clean without any remaining hair or excess fat. They are cooked at 85°-90° C (185-194° F) in a separate vessel as a much longer cooking time is needed. If the skins are under cooked, they will be hard to emulsify and hard pieces will be visible in a finished sausage. If overcooked, they will break into pieces. When the skins are properly cooked they should hold their shape but you should be able to put your finger through them.

Pork heads are normally cut in halves and are cooked at 85-90° C (185-194° F) until all meat and fat can be removed by hand. If they fall off the bones by themselves that means that the pork head was overcooked. All cartilage and gristle must also be removed. If pork head meat will not be used the same day it should be frozen. If jowls came attached to the head, they must be removed and cooked separately as different times are involved. Fats and other meats are cooked at 85-90° C (185-194° F) until internal meat temperature reaches 70° C (158° F). *Don't discard leftover meat stock* (from cooking meats), it can be added to meat mass during emulsifying or grinding (about 0.1 liter - 0.2 liter, or 1/2 cup) per 1 kg of meat.

Grinding. Warm pre-cooked meat should be minced with a small grinder plate 3-5 mm (1/8-3/16"). Liver is ground cold. As it contains a lot of water and blood, the ground liver is easily emulsified. Grinding of meats, especially liver with a small plate increases the surface area and improves spreadability.

Emulsifying. To achieve a fine texture, ingredients that compose a liver sausage are cut in a bowl cutter which requires crushed ice or cold water. During the comminution process the fat cells become ruptured and the free fat is released. Fat does not dissolve in water or mix with it well. The purpose of emulsion is to bond free fat, meat and water together so they will not become separated.

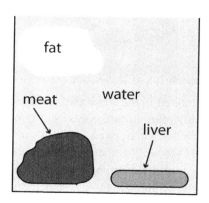

Natural emulsifiers that help to emulsify sausages are: egg protein, blood plasma, soy protein and sodium caseinate (milk protein). Commercial plants use chemical emulsifiers such as monoglycerides and diglycerides.

Fig. 11.2 Components of liver sausage which must be mixed together.

If emulsification is not done right, the finished product might display pockets of fat. To prevent that experienced sausage makers massage cooked and still warm sausages between their thumb and index fingers. The sausage will have a more delicate texture and will be more spreadable if grinding is followed by emulsifying. Meats that were previously ground are emulsified in a kitchen food processor until a smooth paste is obtained. Liver is emulsified separately until air bubbles appear on the surface. Even if meat and fat are ground only, it is a good idea to at least emulsify the liver. If no food processor is available, grind meats and liver twice through the fine grinder plate.

Mixing. Meat, fat and liver are mixed together with salt and spices. Between 10-20% meat stock may be added now. This can be performed in a food processor.

Stuffing. Meat mass should be warm (35-40° C, 95-104° F) and not too dense. The casings are filled rather loose. Beef middles or natural hog casings are often used, synthetic waterproof casings can be used as well but will not allow smoke to go through. It is impractical to use a grinder with a stuffing tube to stuff casings as the sausage mass is very thin. A common approach is to attach a casing to a funnel and to pour the sausage mass from a large cup or fill the funnel with a ladle. Due to its weight the sausage mass will fall down by itself into the casing and no pushing is required. This way one continuous coil of loosely filled sausage can be made in a short time and it can be easily subdivided into individual links or rings.

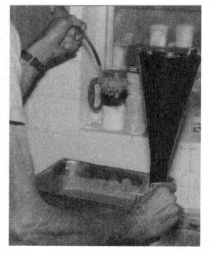

Photo 11.1 Filling casings.

Cooking. Better quality sausages are cooked in the stock that has been obtained during cooking meats. Cooking temperature stays below the boiling point, usually about 176° F (80° C) otherwise casings may burst open. After a while the layer of fat would accumulate on the surface of the stock. It is a good idea to remove this fat when using stock for poaching sausages. The reason is that the top sausages may

burst open due to the fat's higher temperature than that of water. Cooking water absorbs meat
flavor and is usually saved for
making soup.

Photo 11.2 Cooking sausages.

Cooling. Sausages are usually rinsed with tap water and then placed
in cold water. Then they are spread on the table to cool. Finely comminuted liver sausage may be gently massaged at this stage between
the thumb and index finger. This will prevent the possibility of accumulating pockets of fat inside of the sausage. When the sausages are
cool, they are placed in a refrigerator.

Smoking. Once the sausages have cooled down to 30° C (86° F) they
are sometimes submitted to a short (30 min) cold smoking process
(20 - 30° C, 68 - 86° F) to impart the generally liked smoky flavor to a
product. This will also provide an additional degree of preservation on
the surface of the sausage against bacteria. After smoking, sausages
must be placed in a refrigerator.

Storing. Liver sausages should be kept at the lowest temperatures
above the freezing point possible: 0 - 2° C (32 - 34° F) although in a
home refrigerator the temperatures of about 3 - 4° C (38 - 40° F) can
be expected.

Times between grinding/emulsifying, mixing and stuffing should be
kept to the minimum. Longer delays will lower the temperature of
the sausage mass considerably, which should stay at least at 35° C
(95° F) as at below this temperature fat particles will clump together.
That prevents them from being properly coated by emulsified liver
protein and increases the risk of fat separation during the cooking process. Another reason for keeping short processing times is that a warm
sausage mass surface area is high in moisture and sugar (liver may
contain up to 8% of glycogen which is a kind of glucose sugar) that
makes a perfect breeding ground for bacteria. If pre-cooked meats are
to be processed at a later date they should be frozen. Then they should

be thawed and re-heated in hot water before going into the grinder. Fresh or chilled liver tastes better than a previously frozen one. Liver sausages are quite easy to make and they taste delicious. Although they require an additional processing step (meat pre-cooking), all labor is done within boundaries of the kitchen and that makes it easy and enjoyable. In most cases the smoking process is eliminated altogether and there is no need to go outside to check on smoke.

Beef tripe is white in color and tripe stews are popular in many countries: "flaczki" in Poland or "Sopa de Mondongo" in any Spanish speaking country. Although tripe has practically no meat binding nor water holding properties, it is a nutritious material. About 10% cooked and finely ground beef tripe can be added to liver sausage. As the tripe is white, the sausage will develop a lighter color too.

Materials, 100 g portion				
Name	Protein (g)	Fat (g)	Energy (cal)	Cholesterol (mg)
Beef, tripe, raw	12.07	3.69	85	122
				Source: USDA Nutrient database

Pâtés (French for "pie") may be considered a type of liver product whose composition resembles a liver sausage but the product is baked in the oven ("pâtè") or placed in molds which becomes a "terrine." Frequently duck and venison meats are used. Very often those molds are inserted in a bigger dish filled with water and then baked. Some are placed in molds lined up with pastry and the pastry lid is placed on top. Often gelatin and decorative fruits are added and brandy or port wine are incorporated. As they are not stuffed in casings, we don't consider them to be sausages. For those interested in learning more, the best advice is to get a good cook book that will cover the subject of "charcuterie".

Foie Gras (in French "fat liver") is made only with 80% of goose or duck liver with no other meats added.

People who object to eating pork on religious reasons can still make liver sausages utilizing poultry and beef livers and replacing pork fat with oil. The rules of the game remain the same: to make a quality sausage you need liver, fat (oil), meat and spices. There is no need to worry about fat particles clumping together at below 35° C (95° F) as oil will remain in its liquid state.

Surprisingly good liver sausages can be made without adding animal fat. Soy protein isolate, vegetable oil, gelatin, starch, carrageenan, or konjac flour will help glue all the components together. As very little fat (oil) is added, there is an abundance of protein to coat oil particles and bind them with water, creating an emulsion. Gelatin works very well, but is an animal product and its use may be questionable in kosher and vegetarian sausages. All other additives are of plant origin.

Adding carrageenan results in a firm texture and good sliceability. It must be noted that adding more than 1% will make a sausage hard and kind of rubbery. That is adding carrageenan at 0.5% (5 g per 1 kg of material) is a very good starting point. Konjac flour mixes with cold water extremely well and gelatinizes easily. It provides a slippery, fatty sensation, but it does not create as firm of a texture as carrageenan does. Konjac flour should be supplemented with potato starch, gelatin or carrageenan.

Adding Sausage Maker's fat replacer which consists of konjac, xanthan and microcrystalline cellulose will help mimic the feeling of fat. Carrageenan works well with non fat dry milk, but adding dry milk will create a much lighter color. Bread crumbs and flour are good filler material.

Braunschweiger Liver Sausage
(extended)

183 calories per
100 g serving

Meat	Metric	US
pork or veal liver	450 g	0.99 lb.
oil emulsion*	200 g	0.44 lb.
potato flour	20 g	4 tsp.
potato starch	20 g	8 tsp.
non-fat dry milk	10 g	3 tsp.
textured vegetable protein	60 g	2 oz.
(water for TVP)	180 g	3/4 cup
cold water	60 g	1/4 cup

Ingredients per 1000 g (1 kg) of materials:

salt	15 g	2 ½ tsp.
carrageenan	5 g	1 tsp.
Sausage Maker fat replacer	4 g	1 tsp.
pepper	4.0 g	2 tsp.
marjoram	2.0 g	1 tsp.
nutmeg	1.0 g	½ tsp.
onion powder	1.0 g	½ tsp.

Instructions:
1. In food processor, chop sliced raw liver with salt until bubbles appear.
2. Add cold water, rehydrated TVP, flour, starch, all ingredients and mix.
3. Add oil emulsion and blend all together.
4. Stuff in 36 mm casings.
5. Cook sausages in preheated water at 176 - 185° F (80 - 85° C) until an internal temperature of 160° F (72° C) is reached. The required time is about 35 minutes.
6. Cool in cold water for 10 min, drain and air dry.
7. Store in refrigerator.

Notes:
* oil emulsion: soy protein isolate/oil/water at 1:4:5.

Liver Sausage

185 calories per
100 g serving

Materials	Metric	US
lean pork	350 g	0.77 lb.
pork liver	350 g	0.77 lb.
oil emulsion*	200 g	0.44 lb.
non-fat dry milk	20 g	2 Tbsp.
broth	80 g	1/3 cup

Ingredients per 1000 g (1 kg) of meat:

	Metric	US
salt	15 g	2 ½ tsp.
cure #1**	2.0 g	1/3 tsp.
sodium erythorbate***	0.5 g	use scale
carrageenan****	5 g	1 tsp.
Sausage Maker fat replacer	8 g	2 tsp.
pepper	4.0 g	2 tsp.
marjoram	2.0 g	1 tsp.
nutmeg	1.0 g	½ tsp.
ginger	0.5 g	1/3 tsp.
onion powder	1.0 g	½ t s p .

Instructions:

1. Pre-cook pork meat (not livers) in simmering water until soft, save broth.
2. Grind pork meat through 3/16" (5 mm) plate.
3. In food processor, chop raw liver with salt.
4. Add broth, ground pork, dry milk, all ingredients and chop.
5. Add oil emulsion and mix until emulsified.
6. Stuff loosely into 36 mm diameter hog or cellulose casings.
7. Cook sausages in preheated water at 176 - 185° F (80 - 85° C) until an internal temperature of 160° F (72° C) is reached. The required time is about 35 minutes.
8. Cool in cold water for 10 min, drain and air dry. If smoky flavor is desired, the sausages may be *cold smoked* (<68° F, 20° C).
9. Store in refrigerator.

Notes:

* oil emulsion: soy protein isolate/oil/water at 1:4:5.
** cure #1 develops pink color.
*** sodium erythorbate accelerates development of pink color.
**** carrageenan improves texture and sliceability.

Liver Sausage - White   188 calories per 100 g serving

White liver sausage exhibits a much lighter color than other sausages due to the careful selection of meats.

Meat	Metric	US
veal or pork livers	300 g	0.66 lb.
lean pork	300 g	0.66 lb.
oil emulsion*	200 g	0.44 lb.
beef tripe, cooked	100 g	0.22 lb.
non-fat dry milk	20 g	2 Tbsp.
potato starch	20 g	8 tsp.
broth	60 g	1/4 cup

Ingredients per 1000 g (1 kg) of materials:

salt	18 g	3 tsp.
carrageenan	5 g	1 tsp.
Sausage Maker fat replacer	4 g	1 tsp.
white pepper	4.0 g	2 tsp.
sugar	2.0 g	½ tsp.
coriander	2.0 g	1 tsp.
cardamom	2.0 g	1 tsp.
nutmeg	1.0 g	½ tsp.
cinnamon, ground	1.0 g	½ tsp.
onion powder	1.0 g	½ tsp.
carrageenan	5 g	1 tsp.

Instructions:

1. Pre-cook pork meat (not livers) in simmering water until soft, save broth.
2. Grind pork meat and cooked tripe through 3/16" (5 mm) plate.
3. In food processor, chop raw liver with salt.
4. Add broth, ground pork, tripe, dry milk, starch, all ingredients and chop.
5. Add oil emulsion and mix until emulsified.
6. Stuff loosely into 36 mm diameter hog or cellulose casings.
7. Cook sausages in preheated water at 176 - 185° F (80 - 85° C) until an internal temperature of 160° F (72° C) is reached. The required time is about 35 minutes.
8. Cool in cold water for 10 min, drain and air dry.
9. Store in refrigerator.

Notes:
* oil emulsion: soy protein isolate/oil/water at 1:4:5.

Liver Sausage with Flour

198 calories per
100 g serving

Materials	Metric	US
lean pork	350 g	0.77 lb.
pork liver	250 g	0.55 lb.
oil emulsion*	200 g	0.44 lb.
broth	80 g	80 ml
wheat flour	50 g	3 Tbsp.
bread crumbs	40 g	5 Tbsp.
onion, chopped	30 g	½ small onion

Ingredients per 1000 g (1 kg) of meat:

salt	15 g	2 ½ tsp.
carrageenan	5 g	1 tsp.
Sausage Maker fat replacer	4 g	1 tsp.
pepper	2.0 g	1 tsp.
marjoram	2.0 g	1 tsp.
ginger	0.5 g	⅓ tsp.
nutmeg	1.0 g	½ tsp.
allspice	2.0 g	1 tsp.

Instructions:

1. Pre-cook pork meat (not livers) in simmering water until soft, save broth.
2. Fry onions in oil until golden. Do not make them brown.
3. Grind pork meats and fried onions through 2 mm plate (1/8"). Slice liver in smaller pieces and grind through 2 mm (1/8") plate.
4. Mix ground meat with liver, spices, flour, bread crumbs and broth. Add emulsion and remix.
5. Stuff loosely into 36 mm diameter hog or cellulose casings.
6. Cook sausages in preheated water at 176 - 185° F (80 - 85° C) until an internal temperature of 160° F (72° C) is reached. The required time is about 35 minutes.
7. Cool in cold water for 10 min, drain and air dry.
8. Store in refrigerator.

Notes:
* oil emulsion: soy protein isolate/oil/water at 1:4:5.

Liver Sausage with Rice

154 calories per
100 g serving

Liver sausage with rice is a popular sausage in many East-European countries.
Rice is a common filler in many Asian sausages.

Materials	Metric	US
lean pork	450 g	0.99 lb.
pork liver	250 g	0.55 lb.
rice	100 g	3.5 oz.
oil emulsion*	100 g	0.22 lb.
broth	70 g	80 ml
onion, chopped	30 g	½ small onion

Ingredients per 1000 g (1 kg) of meat:

salt	15 g	2 ½ tsp.
carrageenan	5 g	1 tsp.
Sausage Maker fat replacer	8 g	2 tsp.
pepper	2.0 g	1 tsp.
marjoram	2.0 g	1 tsp.
ginger	0.5 g	⅓ tsp.
nutmeg	1.0 g	½ tsp.
allspice	2.0 g	1 tsp.
powdered gelatin	10 g	2 ½ tsp.

Instructions:

1. Cover meats (not livers) with water and simmer in water until soft, save broth.
2. Cut blood veins out of livers and place them in cold water until all traces of blood are removed. Blanch livers in water at around 158° F (70° C) for 5 min.
3. Cook rice (don't overcook), then rinse in cold water and drain.
4. Fry onions in oil until golden. Do not make them brown.
5. Grind pork meats and fried onions through 2 mm plate (1/8"). Slice liver in smaller pieces and grind through 2 mm (1/8") plate.
6. Mix ground meat with liver, spices, rice and broth. Add emulsion and remix.
7. Stuff loosely into 36 mm diameter hog or cellulose casings.
8. Cook in preheated water at 176 - 185° F (80 - 85° C). until an internal temperature of 160° F (72° C) is reached. The required time is about 35 minutes.
9. Cool in cold water for 10 min, drain and air dry.
10. Store in refrigerator.

Notes:
* oil emulsion: soy protein isolate/oil/water at 1:4:5.

Chapter 12

Head Cheeses and Meat Jellies

In English, the name *head cheese* doesn't sound appealing and it prevents many people from trying the product. In other languages it sounds more pleasant, without the word *"head"* being part of the name. When vinegar is added, it is called "souse" and this already sounds much better. Head cheese, brawn, or souse are not cheeses, but rather jellied loaves or sausages that may or may not be stuffed into large diameter casings. They can be easily found in places that cater to Central Europeans, Eastern Europeans and Italians.

Traditionally head cheese was made entirely from the meat of the head of a hog, cured and stuffed in large beef bungs or in pork stomachs. We may find this choice of meat today less appealing, forgetting at the same time the fact that pork head meat is highly nutritional and flavorsome. Bear in mind that the head is boiled first until the meat easily separates from the bones and then it looks like any other meat. Let's look back into the history of making head cheese. The following comes from an old booklet "Meat Production on the Farm" by the E.H.Wright Company, Lt., Kansas City, Missouri.

"Head cheese is supposed to be better when made from the head of the hog alone; but the odds and ends can be included without harming the product. The head must be shaven clean, the snout skinned and the nostrils cut off just in front of the eyes. The eyes and ear drums should be removed and the fattest part of the head cut away for lard. Great care must be taken in soaking and rinsing the head to free it from all dirt. Boil the head until the meat comes off the bones. The heart and tongue may also be included, if desired. Take out the meat and chop it fine, saving the liquor which will be needed again.

For every twenty-five pounds of meat, use three-fourths pound of salt, one and one-half ounces of black pepper, one half ounce of red pepper, two ounces of ground cloves and one gallon of the liquor in

*which the head was cooked. Mix these thoroughly with the finely
ground meat and stuff into large casings, boil them again in the liquor
in which the head was cooked, until they float. Place them in cold
water about fifteen minutes, drain and lay away in a cool place. If the
meat is not stuffed it should be packed in shallow vessels and kept cool
until used."*

Persons living in metropolitan areas can not buy pork head anyhow but still can make a great tasting product by using pork picnic
and pigs feet. Nowadays head cheese can include edible parts of the
feet, tongue, and heart. Many of us have made a head cheese before
without even realizing it, although pork head meat was not a part of
the recipe.

*Every time we cook meat stock or chicken soup based on bones
we are making a weak version of a head cheese. The reason the soup
does not become a meat jelly is because there is too much water in it.*

If this stock would simmer for a long time, enough water will be
lost, and the resulting liquid, when cooled will solidify and become
a jelly. In the past, after the first and second World War, or even in
most countries today, people had no opportunity to buy a commercially made gelatin. And this is why those unappealing cuts of meat
like pork head, jowls, skins, hocks, legs and fatty picnic legs started
to shine. You can not make the real head cheese by using noble cuts
like hams, tender loins or other tender lean meats. Those cuts don't
contain enough connective tissues (collagen) in order to make natural
gelatin. *You can use them, but a commercial grade gelatin must be
added* and of course the taste and flavor of the finished product will be
less satisfactory although the resulting jelly will be very clear. Making
head cheese is quite easy as the procedure does not involve the use of
special equipment like a grinder or stuffer. Every kitchen contains all
utensils that will be needed.

Any professional cookbook lists wonderful meat jellies that incorporate different cuts of meats. They are often garnished with fruits and
vegetables. Don't your kids eat fruit jello? You can make your own by
mixing commercial gelatin with water and adding fruit to it. Gelatin
and glue are derived from a protein called collagen. You may not realize
it, but every time you lick quality ice cream, you eat gelatin that came
from hides, bone, tendon, skin and connective tissues rich in collagen.

Types of Head Cheeses

- Regular head cheese - pork head meat, jowls, skins, snouts, pigs feet, gelatin.

- Tongue head cheese - in addition to the above mentioned meats the tongue added. It should be cured with salt and nitrite in order to develop a pink color.

- Blood head cheese - head cheese made with blood. Such a head cheese is much darker in color.

- Souse - a typical head cheese to which vinegar has been added. Similar to sulz but not limited to pig's feet only. Most people eat head cheese with vinegar or lemon juice anyway so it comes as no surprise that vinegar would be added to head cheese during manufacture. It also increases the keeping qualities of the sausage as all foods containing vinegar last longer. Souse contains more jelly than a regular head cheese. In addition pimentos, green peppers or pickles are often added for decoration. Both sulz and souse contain about 75% of meat, 25% of jelly and around 3% of vinegar.

- Sulz - original head cheese made of pigs feet with the bone in. Later bones were removed to facilitate slicing. This name can be found in some older books. It was made with pig's feet only but often snouts and pig skins were added as well. Meat jellies made from pig's feet are still popular in many European countries, for example in Poland where they are known as pig's feet in aspic (*Nóżki w Galarecie*). Pickled pigs feet which are sold today are basically sulz in vinegar.

Head cheese, souse and sulz are all very similar, the main difference is that souse and sulz contain vinegar and more gelatin.

Manufacturing Process

Meat selection. Traditionally made head cheese requires meats with a high collagen content to produce a natural gelatin. Meat cuts such as pork head, hocks and skins are capable of producing a lot of natural gelatin. In addition tongues, hearts, snouts and skins are also used as filler meats. Commercially made products don't depend on natural gelatin and use commercially produced gelatin powder instead. It is a natural product which is made from bones (pork and beef) and skins. Before meats will be submitted to cooking in hot water a decision has to be made whether the meats will be cured or not. Commercial producers will invariably choose to cure meats with nitrite in order to obtain a typical pink color.

Meats that were traditionally used for head cheeses were:

- Pork heads (cured or not), often split in half - boiled in hot water at about 194° F (90° C) until meat was easily removed from bones by hand. They should be first soaked for 1-2 hours in cold water to remove any traces of coagulated blood.

- Pork hocks (cured or not) - boiled at about 194° F (90° C) until meat was easily removed from bones by hand.

- Skins. Pork skin should be clean without any remaining hair or excess fat. They are cooked at 185-194° F (85-90° C) until soft and require a longer cooking time. Pork shanks with meat (picnic), cured or not - boiled in hot water at about 194° F (90° C) until soft.

- Lean pork trimmings (cured or not) - boiled in hot water at about 194° F (90° C) until soft.

- Hearts (cured or not) - boiled in hot water at about 194° F (90° C) until soft. Hearts are first cut open and any remaining blood is rinsed away in cold water. The heart is a very hard working muscle and will be of a dark red color due to its high content of *myoglobin*. It should be diced into small diameter pieces (1/4", 5-6 mm) otherwise it will stand out.

- Tongues (cured or not) - boiled in hot water at about 194° F (90° C) until soft. Pork or beef tongues are very often used but the outer skin on the tongues must be removed due to its bitter taste. It is easily accomplished once the tongues are submerged for a few minutes in hot water.

Curing meats. Traditionally made products may employ meat curing with nitrite or not. If meats are not cured with sodium nitrite the product will be of grey color but a hobbyist does not care much about the fact. Curing pork head or legs is a hassle that requires extra space in a cooler, needs dedicated containers and will take some time.

Head cheeses are not smoked so there is very little need for sodium nitrite at least for safety reasons. A commercial producer will cure meats as he is mainly concerned with the profit. The product must look pretty and must have a long shelf life otherwise supermarkets will not carry it. As a customer judges a healthy looking meat product by its red or pink color (poultry meat is an exception) the commercial producer must cure meats and add nitrite to achieve this desired color. Another incentive for a commercial plant to cure meats is that they gain weight and that leads to increased profits.

Cooking meats and making broth. This is basically one easy process but certain rules must be observed. Head cheese differs from other sausages in that meats are cooked before stuffing:

• All meats, skin included are cooked until soft.
• Meat is separated from bones.

Meats should be covered with 1-2 inches of water and simmered below the boiling point for 2-3 hours. The skins should be boiled separately until soft but still in one piece. When still warm, cooked meats should be removed from bones and cooled down. The skins are cut into strips. The resulting meat broth should be filtered though 2-3 layers of cheese cloth until clarified. The better clarity obtained, the better looking cheese head will be produced. Such a jelly is a fat free and rich in protein product.

When too much water was used it is possible to end up with a broth that will contain not enough gelatin and will not set. This may be corrected by additional boiling of the meat stock. As more water evaporates from the stock, the resulting meat broth gets concentrated and when cool it will become a jelly. If this does not work you will have to re-heat the jelly, strain the hot gelatin and add a packet of a commercial gelatin. Then re-arrange meats on a plate and pour the hot gelatin over them. This will become a serious issue if the meat was stuffed into the casing.

When in doubt it is safer to add powdered gelatin straight from the beginning than to create unnecessary extra work for yourself. As an extra precaution you may test your meat broth before it is added to the casing. Place some of it in a refrigerator and see whether it solidifies within one hour. If not enough collagen is present, for example mainly lean meats were used, little gelatin will be produced and the resulting meat stock will not solidify. This can be easily corrected by adding commercial gelatin.

For best results mix powdered gelatin with the existing meat broth and not with water. Water will dilute the flavor of the broth.

Cutting meats. The grinder is usually not employed as this will extract proteins and will break the fat's structure. *As a result a cloudy stock will be obtained.* Meats are much easier to cut into smaller pieces when chilled. After they are cut, it is a good idea to rinse them briefly in hot water as *this will eliminate unnecessary grease that would normally cloud the jelly.* Until now the process of making head cheese or meat jelly has been the same. What differentiates them is that head cheese being a sausage is stuffed into casings and meat jelly is not.

Mixing. Meats are mixed with all other ingredients. Although the recipe provides the amounts of all ingredients, nevertheless due to precooking meats in water, then washing them with hot water later on, it is recommended to taste the mixture and refine the recipe if needed. *Do not mix meat and jelly together before stuffing.* The hot jelly will draw some of the juices out of the meat and the jelly becomes cloudy. A good idea is to scald meat with hot water to remove any grease that might cloud the gelatin.

Stuffing. Head cheese was traditionally stuffed into pig stomach. Pig stomach is a one unit chamber of uniform oval shape with two easy to saw openings. Stomachs of a cow or a sheep are basically three stomachs in one unit. The shape of those stomachs is irregular and not easy to fill. After filling, the stomach's opening had to be sewn with butcher's twine. Today, head cheese is stuffed into a large diameter synthetic casing, preferably a plastic one that will prevent loss of aspic during cooking. The tied or clipped at the bottom casing is held vertically and meat pieces are placed first. Then a gelatin, from naturally produced meat broth or made from a commercial powder, is carefully poured down into the casing. This is normally done through a big funnel using a ladle. The casing is tied or clipped on the top and head cheese is ready for cooking.

Cooling. After cooking head cheese should be left at room temperature for a few hours. After that the head cheese was placed between two wooden boards. The top board was weighted and the sausage was stored overnight in a refrigerator. This permanently flattened the head cheese and gave it a rectangular shape with rounded corners.

Photo 12.1 Head cheese.

Photo 12.2 Head cheese.

 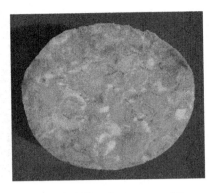

Photo 12.3 Head cheese with tongues.

Photo 12.4 Head cheese with smaller size filler meat.

Ingredients. Amount of salt varies between 1.5-2% which is the same as for a typical sausage. Commonly used spices: pepper, nutmeg, mace, allspice, cloves, marjoram, cardamom, onions, garlic, caraway, thyme, ginger.

Meat jellies

Meat jellies are much easier to make than head cheeses as they don't have to be stuffed which greatly simplifies the procedure. In addition no secondary cooking is needed. Cooked meats are arranged on the bottom of the container, meat broth is carefully poured over it and left for cooling. It basically becomes a meat jelly.

Meat jelly although technically not a sausage, follows the same rules of production as a head cheese. They fit more into general cuisine and many fancy products can be created based on one's ingenuity and imagination. They are basically more refined products where the looks of the products play an important role. Because of that they contain solid chunks of lean "show meat" and use commercial gelatin in order to obtain perfectly clear jelly. Different meats can be incorporated in meat jellies, for example fish fillets, skinless and boneless chicken breast, diced ham etc. As a rule meat jellies don't include low value meat products like skins, snouts, or hearts. Chicken breast or fish fillets will make a great show meat in any meat jelly.

Meat jellies can be easily decorated:

- A thin layer of hot gelatin is placed in a form or any dish or plate and allowed to set in a cooler.
- Decorative items are placed on top of the set gelatin.
- A new layer of gelatin is poured on top and allowed to set in a cooler.
- Meat and the remaining gelatin are placed on top and allowed to set in a cooler.
- When ready for consumption the form is briefly placed in hot water which melts a thin layer of gelatin and turning the form upside down will release the meat jelly with decorations being on top.

Decorative pieces such as slices of oranges, apples or hard boiled eggs are used. Herbs, cubed cheese, cracked pepper, slices of pickle, carrots, peas, corn, and green scallions are often used in meat jellies.

Photo 12.5 Diced ham jelly made with commercial gelatin. Sliced hard boiled eggs used for decoration.

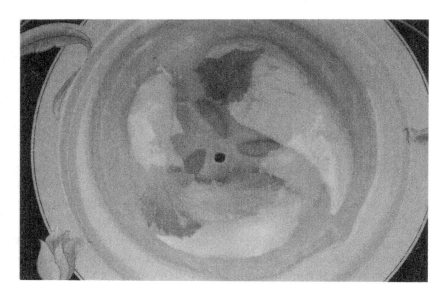

Photo 12.6 Chicken jelly made with commercial gelatin.

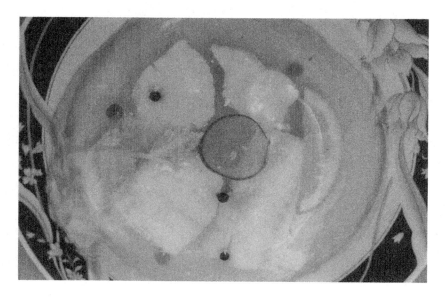

Photo 12.7 Fish jelly made with commercial gelatin.

Gelatin

Natural gelatin produced from meat stock such as the one used for head cheese manufacture. Natural stock will not be as clear as the one made by dissolving commercial gelatin powder with water. The main reason the natural stock is often cloudy is that it is boiled and not simmered. *Do not to boil the stock, always simmer.* If you cook your stock gently, below the boiling point, the fat will not emulsify in water and the stock will remain clear.

Natural gelatin that is obtained from the natural stock has a superior taste and flavor that comes from boiling its meats and ingredients. The ingredients such as peppercorns, bay leaf, pimentos, and soup greens are often added to create a better flavor.

Clarifying stock. The natural stock can be clarified to obtain a clearer version with almost no fat. This is a basic cooking technique that every cook is familiar with.

1. Once when the stock cools down a little, the fat will accumulate on the surface and can be easily scooped up and discarded.

2. Then the liquid can be strained through a cheese cloth.

3. For every quart of stock, lightly beat 3 egg whites with 2 Tbsp of water and 1 tsp of vinegar.

4. Add the egg white mix to the stock. Bring stock to boil, then reduce heat and simmer for 20 minutes. Stir constantly with the soup ladle. Do not boil. The egg white will attract fat and impurities and will coagulate. It may float on top of the stock, which should be much clearer now.

5. Let it cool for 15 minutes.

6. Put several layers of cheese cloth in colander and pour the stock carefully over it.

7. Refrigerate stock overnight. Skim any remaining fat off the top. Now you have crystal clear stock with plenty of protein, *little fat* and great flavor.

Photo 12.8 Home made meat jelly with natural gelatin. The fat layer on top is left on purpose as it will be spread on bread. This is very tasteful fat that has been obtained by boiling meats with vegetables and spices. Of course when you clarify the stock, there will be hardly any fat remaining.

Commercial gelatin is just a powder that was obtained from skins, hooves, and other meat cuts that contain a lot of connective tissue. It has no flavor, but is very clear and convenient to apply. A little salt and white vinegar should be added to give it some character. Packets of powdered gelatin are available in every supermarket and all that is required is to mix it with water. Gelatin use is not limited to meats, and you can use it with fruits and juices as well. The size of the packet will dictate how much water is needed. Usually, 1 part of gelatin to 6 parts water will produce a good jelly. If more powder is added the jelly will be much thicker.

To make a jelly:

1. Pour the gelatin into a container with cold water and let it stand until the gelatin absorbs the water. Do not stir.
2. Place this container inside another vessel filled with hot water.
3. Heat the water until the gelatin solution reaches 160° F (72° C).
Note: if gelatin solution is heated above 160° F, it will lose its binding power.

Useful Information

Head cheeses, liver sausages and blood sausages belong to a special group of products that incorporate less noble cuts of meat that will be much harder to sell to the public at least in their original form. What separates those products from other common sausages is the fact that meats are precooked before being stuffed into casings and then they are submitted to a hot water cooking process. Another peculiarity is that all those products are often made *without being stuffed into casings* and:

- Head cheeses are placed in forms, boiled in water and they become meat jellies.
- Head cheese is usually eaten cold or at room temperature as a luncheon meat.
- Head cheese freezes very well.
- Diced meats must be washed with hot water to remove any fat particles from the surface and then drained. This will make them look sharp in jelly.
- Gelatin should be soaked in cold (room temperature) water for about 15 min to swell and then mixed with hot water.
- Commercial gelatin should be used as it produces a very clean, transparent jelly. Traditionally made meat jelly of pork and beef meat may use natural gelatin (broth) as the looks of the product are less important. Lean cuts of meat such as hams, pork loins, chicken breast or fish fillets will look much better in a clean, commercially made gelatin. On the other hand the natural meat broth may be cloudy sometimes but it has a superior taste.
- Commercial gelatin packets come with instructions and are available in every supermarket, for example Knox® brand. If a jelly does not want to set in because gelatin was made too thin, reheat your weak jelly, strain it and reinforce it with an

extra packet of gelatin. Then pour your stronger and warmer gelatin over the meat.

- Meat jellies can be made of lean meats and will taste good even if little salt is added (1.0 %)
- The gelatin is often made with wine, brandy and other spirits to create a high quality product.
- Show meat, for example tongues, may be cured in order for meat to develop a pink color.

Traditionally made head cheese or meat jelly may look less pretty but will be a product of much higher quality due to the following reasons:

- No chemicals are added.
- No water is pumped into the product (stronger meatier flavor).
- It contains the natural broth. Commercially prepared gelatin is a combination of neutrally flavored powder (natural glue) and water and natural broth is a combination of natural glue plus highly flavored meat stock that remains after cooking bones. On cooling this gelatin will subsequently become a jelly and accounts for about 30% of the total weight of the product. What would you prefer to have in your head cheese or meat jelly: 30% of water or 30% of meat broth?

It is a good idea to add some vinegar to low fat and low salt head cheese as this slows down the growth of bacteria and will extend the shelf life of the product.

Photo 12.9 You will save yourself a lot of time and money by buying a pound of gelatin from places like The Sausage Maker, Buffalo, NY.

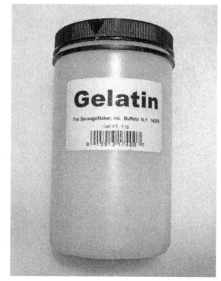

The following recipes were calculated using these figures:

cooked meat - 240 calories per 100 g serving.
meat stock - 10 calories per 100 g serving.

Chicken Meat Jelly

105 calories per
100 g serving

Materials:

chicken breasts,   1000 g   2.20 lb
fully cooked

Instructions:

1. Make 1 liter/quart gelatin. Add 1 Tbsp. white vinegar and 1 Tbsp. white wine.

2. Pour a small amount of hot gelatin on the bottom of the container, then place it in a refrigerator.

3. Once the solution hardens, place a slice of orange, hard boiled egg, carrot, apple or any decoration of your choice on top of the solid gelatin.

4. More hot gelatin is added again to set the slices of fruit in place and the container is placed in the refrigerator again.

5. Once the solution solidifies it is removed from the refrigerator and the whole pieces of cold chicken breast are placed into the container.

6. The container is filled with gelatin and placed in the refrigerator overnight for the jelly to solidify.

7. Before serving the container is flipped upside down so that the entire product drops out. It helps to dip the container first for a short while in hot water to melt a tiny amount of gelatin that is attached to the container inside.

Head Cheese - City   174 calories per
                                   100 g serving

Head cheese also known as brawn or souse is a jellied meat sausage that is stuffed in a large diameter casing or it may be placed in a form becoming a jellied meat loaf. Traditionally made head cheese employed meats that were rich in collagen, which was required to produce a natural gelatin (broth), that after cooling became a jelly. The best meat was highly flavored pork head meat and pork legs and feet (hocks). A person living in a large city may not be able to find these cuts anymore but intelligent substitutions can easily be made by buying commonly available supermarket carried meats and the final product will be of very high quality yet much easier to make. The easiest way to make a head cheese is to think in terms of cooking a heavy meat broth which may or may not be stuffed into casings.

Meat	Metric	US
cooked pork picnic, hocks,	700 g	1.54 lb.
meat stock	300 g	300 ml

Ingredients per 1000 g (1 kg) of meat:

salt	15 g	2½ tsp.
white pepper	2.0 g	1 tsp.
allspice, ground	2.0 g	1 tsp.
garlic	3.5 g	1 clove

Instructions:

Making Broth

1/2 pork picnic (front leg) or pork butt. The amount of boiled meat available for further processing will be about 2.2 lbs. (1 kg). Picnic meat is fattier with more connective tissues (collagen) and will produce more gelatin than a butt. The butt has only one little bone and its meat is leaner than a picnic and a commercial gelatin (natural product made from bones and skins) will have to be added.

Two pig feet (hocks). If you use hocks and picnic, enough natural gelatin (broth) should be produced to create jelly on cooling. If pork butt is the only meat used, you will have to use powdered gelatin.

3 bay leaves
1 stalk celery
1 carrot
Salt and pepper to taste
1 package of gelatin (if needed)

1. Place meats and other ingredients in a pot and cover with about two inches of water. Cook below boiling point for about 3 hours or until meat separates easily from bones. Strain liquid and save for later. Clarify the stock if making a reduced-fat product.

2. Separate meats from bones. It is easier to perform this task when meats are still warm. Cut meats into smaller pieces. It is easier to cut them when they are chilled. Normally the leaner the meat the larger diameter the cut. Fatter meats and fat will be chopped into smaller pieces. Don't use fat cuts when making the reduced-fat version.

3. Dissolve gelatin in 1/4 cup room temperature water and add to your hot meat broth.

4. Mix meats with meat broth/gelatin and add garlic and salt and pepper to taste. Head cheese does not require much salt and a low sodium product can be made.

5. Now you can go two different ways:

a. pour your head cheese into containers, let them sit for 2 hours at room temperature and then place in a refrigerator. Keep it there for 12 hours to give the head cheese time to set.

b. stuff with a ladle into large diameter waterproof casings, clip the ends and cook (simmer) in hot water at about, 185° F (85° C). A rough estimate will be about 20 min for each ½" (12 mm) of diameter of a casing. Or using a thermometer cook to 160° F (72° C) internal meat temperature. Then place at room temperature for about 2 hours for gelatin to set. Place for 12 hours in a refrigerator to complete setting.

Notes:

Don't add garlic when making broth as it loses its flavor very rapidly when being cooked. Add garlic when mixing meats with gelatin.

It is easy to add a degree of sophistication to your product by decorating your gelatin.

Head cheese is normally removed from containers and turned upside down. This way any decoration will rest on top of the product. It is eaten cold with bread and some vinegar or lemon juice is sprinkled on top of it.

Head cheese that was stuffed in casings is sliced and eaten like any other regular sausage.

Head Cheese - Italian

191 calories per
100 g serving

Although of Italian origin this head cheese has been always popular in Poland.

Meat	Metric	US
cooked pork cuts (with bones), hocks, picnic	600 g	1.32 lb.
cooked beef (boned)	150 g	0.33 lb.
pork skins	50 g	0.22 lb.
meat stock	200 g	200 ml

Ingredients per 1000 g (1 kg) of meat:

salt	15 g	2½ tsp.
pepper	4.0 g	2 tsp.
caraway seeds	4.0 g	2 tsp.

Instructions:
1. Slow cook meats in a small amount of water. After cooking remove meat from pork heads and spread all meats apart on a flat surface to cool. Save meat stock and clarify to remove fat.
2. Separate meat from bones when still warm.
3. Mix all meats with spices adding 100 g of meat stock.
4. Stuff mixture not too tight into beef bungs.
5. Cook at 176°F (80°C) for 90-150 min (depending on size) until the internal temperature of the meat reaches 154-158°F (68-70°C). Remove air with a needle from pieces that swim up to the surface.
6. Spread head cheeses on a flat surface and let the steam out.
7. After cooling clean head cheeses of any fat and aspic that accumulated on the surface, even them out and cut off excess twine. Store in refrigerator.

Note:
Commercial producers will cure heads with nitrite in order for meat to develop a pink color.

Meat Jelly

143 calories per
100 g serving

Meat	Metric	US
lean pork, ham or lean pork butt	1000 g	2.20 lb.

Ingredients:		
salt	15 g	2½ tsp.
Cure #1	2.5 g	½ tsp.
white vinegar	15 g	1 Tbsp.
gelatin	as needed	

Instructions:

1. Cut lean meat into 1" (5 cm) cubes. Mix with salt and Cure #1. Pack tightly in a container, cover with a cloth and place for 2-3 days in refrigerator.

2. Cook meat until 154-160° F (68-72° C) internal temperature is reached.

3. Make 1 liter/quart gelatin. Add 1 Tbsp. white vinegar and 1 Tbsp. white wine.

4. Pour a small amount of hot gelatin on the bottom of the container, then place it in a refrigerator.

5. Once the solution hardens, place a slice of orange, hard boiled egg, carrot, apple or any decoration of your choice on top of the solid gelatin.

6. More hot gelatin is added again to set the slices of fruit in place and the container is placed in the refrigerator again.

7. Once the solution solidifies it is removed from the refrigerator and the diced lean meat cubes are placed into the container.

8. The container is filled with gelatin and placed in the refrigerator overnight for the jelly to solidify.

9. Before serving the container is flipped upside down so that the entire product drops out. It helps to dip the container first for a short while in hot water to melt a tiny amount of gelatin that is attached to the container inside.

Note:

Whole pieces of meat such as pork butt or loin can be cured in brine and then cooked. Then they can be sliced and used as "show meat" in meat jellies. Cure #1 may be omitted but the color of the product will be gray.

Pennsylvania Scrapple

198 calories per 100 g serving

Pennsylvania Scrapple, also known as Pennsylvania Dutch Scrapple or Philadelphia Scrapple, is a delicious pork dish that was created by German settlers in Eastern Pennsylvania. The word scrapple comes from "scraps" which is the definition for leftover bits of food and pieces of animal fat or cracklings. The original Pennsylvania Deutsche (name changed in time to Pennsylvania Dutch) immigrants used less noble parts of a butchered pig (pork skins, jowls, snouts, ears, heart, tongue, brains, kidneys, head meat, liver, pork bones, some claim that pork neck bones are the best) to make scrapple. Those leftover meats were used for making original scrapple though today's recipes often call for parts like loin or picnic. Originally buckwheat was an essential part of the recipe although many of today's recipes call for a mixture of cornmeal and buckwheat half and half.

Meat	Metric	US
cooked pork picnic, jowls, hocks	650 g	1.43 lb.
buckwheat flour	100 g	3 ½ oz.
chopped medium onion	50 g	½ onion
meat stock	200 g	3/4 cup

Ingredients per 1000 g (1 kg) of meat:

salt	15 g	2½ tsp.
pepper	4.0 g	2 tsp.

Optional spices:

marjoram, crumbled	2 g	3 tsp.
thyme, crumbled	2 g	3 tsp.
nutmeg	2 g	1 tsp.
sage, ground	2 g	3 tsp.
mace	0.5 g	⅓ tsp.
red pepper	0.5 g	⅓ tsp.

Instructions:
1. Cover the meat and bones with water, add salt, pepper and onions and bring to a boil. Reduce heat, skim off the foam, cover with lid and simmer for 1-2 hours until meat is tender.
2. Scrape off the meat from the bones. Clarify the stock to remove fat.
3. Chop the meat very fine by hand or grind through 3/16" (5 mm) plate.
4. Place meat in stock, mix and taste. Add more salt or pepper if needed. Many recipes call for additional spices, now is the time to add them.
5. Make sure the stock with meat is hot and start adding buckwheat flour slowly, stirring the mixture with a paddle. Make sure it is smooth and thick - the paddle should stand up in the pot.
6. Pack the mixture into baking pans about 8 x 4 x 2" or 9 x 4 x 3". The pans should be either oiled or lined with wax paper. Cover and place in the refrigerator for 4 hours.
7. Cut into 1/2" individual slices. To freeze, place the slices between pieces of butcher paper.

Note:
Serve in a large skillet, brown scrapple slices on both sides in a hot oil until brown and crisp on each side. You can dredge the slices with flour and fry them.

Souse

130 calories per
100 g serving

Souse also known as Sulz is a head cheese to which vinegar has been added. It is a jellied meat sausage that is stuffed in a large diameter casing or simply as a jellied meat loaf. As most people add vinegar or squeeze some lemon juice into head cheese when eating it, so it should not be a surprise that producers add vinegar (5%) into the mix. This added the benefit of a longer shelf life of the product as all foods containing vinegar last longer. The reason is an increased acidity of the product which inhibits the growth of bacteria.

Meat	Metric	US
meat from cooked pig hocks	750 g	1.65 lb.
meat broth (from cooking hocks)	200 g	3/4 cup.
vinegar (5%)	50 g	0.11 lb.

Ingredients per 1000 g (1 kg) of meat:

salt	15 g	2½ tsp.
pepper	2.0 g	1 tsp.

Instructions:

1. Place 1 kg (2.2 lb.) pigs hocks, salt and pepper in a pot and cover with about two inches of water. Cook below the boiling point for about 2 hours or until meat separates easily from bones. Head cheese does not require much salt and a low sodium product can be made.

2. Strain liquid, filter and save for later.

3. Separate meats from bones. It is easier to perform this task when meats are still warm.

4. Cut meats into smaller pieces. It is easier to cut them when they are chilled. 5. Now you can choose from two different methods:

a. pour your souse into containers, let them sit for 2 hours at room temperature and then place in a refrigerator. Keep it there for 12 hours to give the souse time to set.

b. stuff with a ladle into large diameter waterproof casings, clip the ends and cook in hot water below the boiling point at 185° F (about 85° C). A rough estimate will be about 20 min for each 1/2" (12 mm) of diameter of a casing. Then place at room temperature for about 2 hours for gelatin to set. Place for 12 hours into refrigerator.

Notes:

Green peppers, pimentos or pickles are often added to souse to make it visually pleasing. You may add garlic, allspice, caraway, marjoram or other spices you like.

Sulz

130 calories per
100 g serving

Meat	Metric	US
meat from cooked pig hocks	750 g	1.65 lb.
meat broth (from cooking hocks)	200 g	3/4 cup.
vinegar (5%)	50 g	0.11 lb.

Ingredients per 1000 g (1 kg) of meat:

salt	15 g	2½ tsp.
whole pepper	2.0 g	1 tsp.
bay leaf	1 leaf	1 leaf
soup vegetables		

Instructions: think in terms of cooking a meat stock that is based on bones.

1. Place pigs feet in cold water, add whole peppercorns, bay leaf, carrot, onion and cook pigs feet until meat separates from bones. Use enough water just to cover the feet. This might take 3 hours.

2. Remove feet but save the stock. Remove fat from the top, then clarify meat stock by filtering it through cheese cloth. Add about 1.5% of vinegar which comes to about 1 teaspoon per liter of stock.

3. Separate meat from bones when feet are still hot.

4. Pour a little stock into the container.

5. Place meat on the bottom of the container.

6. Pour stock carefully into the container.

7. Place in refrigerator.

Notes:

Green peppers, scallions, pickles, pimentos, carrots, or sliced boiled eggs are often added to increase the attractiveness of a product.

The Polish popular product "Nózki w Galarecie" is processed in the above manner, the only difference is that vinegar is not added to stock. Instead each customer sprinkles his portion with vinegar or lemon juice according to his liking.

Chapter 13

Blood Sausages

Blood sausages have been made for thousands of years and every country has its own recipes. Whatever the name – Black pudding (UK, Ireland), Boudin noir (France), Blutwurst (Germany), Morcilla (Spain), Jelito (Czech), Kaszanka (Poland), or Mustamakkara (Finland), the main ingredients are as follows: blood – either from pig, sheep, lamb, cow, or goose (each author believing their choice is preferred); a filler that varies with region (e.g., oatmeal, buckwheat, breadcrumbs, barley, or other grains); onions and regional spices. All of these are typically smashed together and stuffed into a sausage casing.

Mention blood sausage or head cheese to an average American consumer and he is looking the other way. Yet mention blutwurst to a German, black pudding to an Englishman or la morcilla to a Spaniard and you will see a spark in the eye. In all areas of the world people love those products as they taste great. Unfortunately, many of us display a preconceived opinion on some names. When they hear blood sausage, they imagine that blood is bad and they look the other way. Then they go to a restaurant, order a medium rare steak and lick every drop of blood that is on the plate. Fully cooked blood in a sausage is not acceptable but raw fresh blood in a steak is fine...

Meat selection

Blood sausages were originally made from inexpensive raw materials such as pork head meat, jowls, tongues, groins, skins, pork or veal lungs, pork liver, beef and lamb liver, pork snouts, beef and liver lips, udders, beef and lamb tripe, veal casings, pork stomachs, pork heart, boiled bone meat and of course blood. This way any part of the animal was utilized and a highly nutritional product was made. In times of war and other hard times when meat was scarce, fillers were added to increase the volume of the sausage. Generally speaking a blood sausage is composed of diced, cooked fat pork and finely ground cooked meat and gelatin producing materials, mixed with beef or pork blood. The whole is spiced and stuffed into a casing. Sometimes pork or lamb tongues are included, in which instance the product is known as tongue and blood sausage.

Fat. Back fat is the best as it is hard and is less likely to smear. Fat from pork butt and jowl fat are also hard fats but belly fat (bacon) is soft. You can use any little fat pieces and fat trimmings. Sliceable blood sausage (without fillers) looks much nicer with visible pieces of white fat in it. To achieve this effect pork back fat should be cut into 4-5 mm (about 3/16") cubes which should be blanched briefly (5 min) in hot water (90°-95° C, 194°-203° F). This seals the surface of fat cubes and prevents blood from entering and discoloring it.

Skins. Skins are a very important ingredient as they contain a lot of collagen which will turn into gelatin during heat treatment. During subsequent cooling this gelatin will become a gel and that will create a better texture of the sausage. In sliceable blood sausages that are usually consumed cold, this will positively contribute to the sliceability of the sausage. In non-sliceable sausages (with fillers and consumed hot) this will add firmness to the sausage. Don't discard skin when trimming pork butts and freeze it for later use in head cheeses, blood or liver sausages.

Fillers. Many countries have their own traditionally used fillers that are added to a sausage mass:

England and Ireland - rusk, barley, rice, potatoes, flour, oatmeal.
Poland - buckwheat groats, barley, bread crumbs, rice, semolina.
Spain - milk, rice, eggs, cheese, almonds, pimentos, parsley, apples.
Sweden - rye meal, raisins.
Argentina - wheat gluten (seitan), corn flour, flour.

Filler material such as rice, barley or buckwheat groats must be pre-cooked. Groats can be found in supermarkets but they have been factory processed and are ill suited for making blood sausages. The real natural groats can be ordered from online distributors such as the Sausage Maker or Bulk Foods. Oatmeal is normally soaked overnight. The addition of filler material makes a sausage very economical. With such variety of filler materials, different meats that can be selected, and spices that can be chosen, it is hardly surprising to see the huge number of recipes floating around. And as we often repeat, it is not the recipe that makes a great sausage, but the way you make it.

Blood. Blood from any animal including poultry can be used for making blood sausage although pig and cow bloods are most often used. Pork blood is a better choice than beef blood as it is much lighter in color. Beef blood can be very dark red or almost black in color and was traditionally used in England. The amount of blood in a sausage can vary from 5%-60% and the more blood, the darker the sausage.

Sliceable blood sausages which are often eaten cold will contain less than 10% blood and will be much lighter in color than non-sliceable sausages (30% - 60% of blood) which will be darker. If an excessive amount of blood is added to a sliceable sausage, solid chunks of meats will have a tendency to sink down and accumulate in one area of the sausage. Blood sausages with filler material don't face this problem as the filler material acts like a sponge and more blood can be added making the sausage darker.

Blood coagulates easily and is stirred frequently when collected during the slaughter. It must be used within 1-2 days and should be cold when it is mixed with other ingredients. Before use it must be stirred again and filtered through a cheese cloth, otherwise the sausage may contain lumps of blood. If collecting blood during the slaughter of the pig keep on mixing it well, otherwise it will coagulate. Blood is a great food for the development of bacteria and it should be cooled down quickly and placed in a refrigerator. It is advisable to process blood no later than on the second day. If the refrigerator is capable of maintaining temperatures of 1° C (33° F) the blood may be kept for 2-4 days. Adding salt or nitrite is not effective in extending blood's shelf life but blood can be frozen for later use. In time blood plasma separates from the blood and water accumulates on top and the blood must be stirred before use. Commercial producers add anticoagulation chemicals like trisodium citrate to prevent the coagulation of blood. A good idea is to filter blood through a fine sieve or cheese cloth before use to eliminate larger condensed particles which may be visible in a sliced sausage. It is not easy to get blood in a metropolitan area. The best advice is to talk to the local butcher or a sausage maker. They make blood sausages and order frozen blood for themselves.

Blood, 100 g serving					
Animal	Protein (g)	Fat (g)	Sugar (g)	Salt (mg)	Water (g)	Cholesterol (mg)
Cattle	6.98	0.15	0.07	210	80.9	110
Swine	4.66	0.11	0.07	140	79.1	40
Sheep	6.48	0.09	0.07	210	82.2	160
Source: Abderhalden, Emil. Analysis of blood. Zeit, Physiol. Chem. 25: 65-115 (1898).						

1 g = 1000 mg

The data in the above table demonstrates that there is a little difference in blood originating from different animals. One 100 g serving provides about 30 calories.

Salt, Spices and Other Ingredients. Blood sausages are perishable products and contain a large amount of water (blood). Adding salt will have little effect on the preservation of the product and salt is used mainly as a flavoring ingredient (between 1.5 and 2.2%). The majority of sausage eating countries have a blood sausage based on pigs blood and most blood sausage recipes contain onion.

Blood sausages like highly aromatic spices such as: pepper, thyme, marjoram, caraway, pimento, cloves, nutmeg, allspice and coriander. Fresh onions are commonly added to blood sausages but they can impart a sourly taste to the product. To eliminate this danger, in most cases onions are fried in oil first until they become transparent-glassy looking and of light yellow color. Often apples, pine nuts, chestnuts, raisins and cream are added.

Manufacturing process

1. Cooking. Blood sausage, head cheese and liver sausage belong to a special group of sausages. What makes them different is that meats and fillers are pre-cooked before being minced, mixed and stuffed. The fat is not cooked but only scalded and diced into cubes. The blood is not cooked.

2. Grinding. Except fat, all other pre-cooked meats are cooled, ground through 1/8" (3 mm) plate and mixed together.

3. Mixing. Diced fat, blood, salt, and spices are added and everything is mixed together.

4. Stuffing. The blood sausage mass is much softer than the mixture for regular sausages. It is not stuffed with a stuffer but ladled into

the casing through any suitable funnel. Traditional blood sausages were stuffed into beef bungs or hog middles but any natural or synthetic casings will do. Prick any visible air pockets with a needle otherwise the sausages will swim up to the surface during cooking.
5. Cooking. The sausages are cooked in water for about 1 hour at 176-180° F (80-82° C). If they raise to the surface, remove air pockets with a needle.
6. Cooling. Chill in cold water, wipe off the moisture and store in a refrigerator.

If a smoked flavor is desired, add sodium nitrite (Cure #1) during mixing. Mix, stuff and cook the sausage, then follow with smoking. A simpler solution is to add liquid smoke during mixing. Cool and refrigerate. In a blood sausage the blood is boiled so the sausage is already cooked and needs only to be reheated. Fried blood changes its color to dark brown - black. In some countries, for example in England, black colorants like Black PN or Brilliant Black (E151) were added but these are no longer permitted in the EU. Blood sausages are made with filler material and its popularity varies from country to country.

Black pudding - UK, pigs blood, pork fat and cereal (oatmeal and or barley).

Boudin Noir - France, pigs blood, pork fat, bread crumbs.

Blutworst - Germany, pigs blood, diced bacon and lungs, barley.

Drisheen - Ireland, sheep blood, oatmeal or bread crumbs.

Kaszanka - Poland, pig blood, lungs, liver, buckwheat grouts.

Morcilla - Spain, pigs blood, pork fat, long grain rice.

Navajo Indian - USA, sheep blood, cornmeal.

White Blood Sausage

A white blood sausage is made from pork *without* blood. Many countries have their own versions:

England - White Pudding - diced pork, oats or bread, suet, sugar, onions, cinnamon.

France - Boudin Blanc - pork, milk, parsley, rice, pepper, onions. *Boudin blanc de Rethel* carries PGI certificate and must be made without filler material. Pork meat, fresh whole eggs and milk.

USA - Boudin Blanc, Cajun Style - pork meat, pork liver, rice, onions, parsley, garlic, pepper.

Poland-White Blood Sausage-pork, pork liver, rice, onions, marjoram.

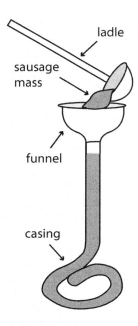

ladle

sausage mass

funnel

casing

Fig. 13.1 Stuffing blood sausage.

Photo 13.1 Blood sausage with buckwheat grouts.

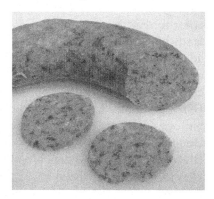

Photo 13.2 White Blood Sausage (no blood added) with rice.

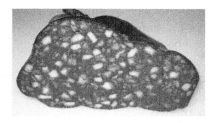

Photo 13.3 Blood sausages with diced fat.

Blood composition	Water	Protein	Fat	Ash
Beef blood	78.17%	21.31%	0	0.67%
Adapted from "Meat Through The Microscope", Institute of Meat Packing, The University of Chicago, Chicago, Illinois.				

The above data demonstrates that blood is a very nutritional product without any fat at all. A 100 g serving provides only 85 calories of energy. If no animal fat is added, the product can definitely be called a healthy sausage.

Black Pudding

132 calories per
100 g serving

Black Pudding is a blood sausage, very popular in Northern England, Scotland and Ireland.

Materials	Metric	US
pork blood	400 g	0.88 lb.
soy protein isolate	20 g	3 Tbsp.
textured vegetable protein	80 g	3 oz.
(water for TVP)	240 g	1 cup
flour	60 g	2 oz.
cooked oatmeal, barley or both	200 g	7 oz.

Ingredients per 1000 g (1 kg) of meat:

salt	15 g	2 ½ tsp.
carrageenan	10 g	2 tsp.
black pepper	2.0 g	1 tsp.
mace	1.0 g	½ tsp.
ground coriander	2.0 g	1 tsp.
onion, finely chopped	30 g	½ onion

Instructions:
1. Soak oatmeal overnight in water.
2. Soak TVP overnight in 1 cup of water.
3. Add salt to blood and stir.
3. Mix blood and all ingredients together.
2. Stuff into 32 - 36 mm hog casings.
3. Cook in hot water at 176° F (80° C) for about 40 minutes.
4. Store in refrigerator.

Drisheen

165 calories per
100 g serving

Drisheen is an Irish blood sausage similar to English black pudding, very popular in specialty stores in Cork or Dublin.

Materials	Metric	US
sheep blood	500 g	1.10 lb.
full cream milk	250 g	1 cup
bread crumbs	250 g	1 cup

Ingredients per 1000 g (1 kg) of meat:

salt	15 g	2½ tsp.
carrageenan	5.0 g	1 tsp.
black pepper	2.0 g	1 tsp.
mace	1.0 g	½ tsp.
thyme	2.0 g	1 tsp.

Instructions:

1. Add salt to blood and stir it.
2. Mix blood with cream, then add bread crumbs and other ingredients. Mix all together well.
3. Stuff into largest hog casings (38 - 42 mm).
4. Place sausages into boiling water and simmer at 80° - 85° C (176° - 185° F) for 40 minutes.
5. Cool and keep in refrigerator.
6. Drisheen is sliced and either fried or grilled, often with bacon, eggs and other sausages.

Notes:

If sheep blood can be hard to obtain use pork, veal or beef blood.
You can bake the batter in oven like a meat loaf. Put into greased glass pan and bake at 300° - 350° F (149° - 177° C) for about 1 hour.

Kaszanka - Polish Blood Sausage

138 calories per 100 g serving

Materials	Metric	US
lean pork	500 g	1.10 lb.
pork liver	50 g	0.11 lb.
pork skins*	50 g	0.11 lb.
blood	200 g	0.44 lb.
buckwheat or barley groats	200 g	0.44 lb.

Ingredients per 1000 g (1 kg) of meat:

salt	18 g	3 tsp.
carrageenan	5.0 g	1 tsp.
black pepper	2.0 g	1 tsp.
allspice	1.0 g	½ tsp.
marjoram	2.0 g	1 tsp.
chopped onion	30 g	½ onion

Instructions:

1. Slow cook meat (except liver) in a small amount of water:
   * skins at 203° F (95° C) until soft.
   * other meats at 176-185° F (80-85° C) until soft.
Spread meat apart on a flat surface to cool. Save stock.
2. Boil buckwheat or barley grouts in left over stock or water until semi-soft. Boil grouts for about ½ hr continuously stirring. After boiling leave for ½ to 1 hr covered.
3. Grind pork through 10 mm plate. Grind boiled skins through 3 mm plate. Grind raw liver through 3 mm plate.
4. Add salt and spices to ground meats, mix barley or buckwheat grouts with blood and then mix everything well together.
5. Stuff mixture loosely into pork middles, beef rounds or synthetic casings.
6. Place sausages in boiling water and poach at 176-185°F (80-85°C) for about 60
7. Place sausages for 5 min in cold running water, then spread them on a flat surface to cool down.
8. Store in refrigerator.

Notes:
* you may replace pork skins with 10 g (2½ tsp.) of gelatin powder.

Morcilla

87 calories per
100 g serving

Morcilla is a blood sausage, very popular in Spain and Latin America.

Materials	Metric	US
pork blood	250 g	0.55 lb.
soy protein concentrate	20 g	3 Tbsp.
textured vegetable protein	70 g	3 oz.
(water for TVP)	210 g	7 ½ oz.
rice	250 g	0.55 lb.
diced onions	200 g	0.44 lb.

Ingredients per 1000 g (1 kg) of meat:

salt	15 g	2½ tsp.
carrageenan	5.0 g	1 tsp.
black pepper	2.0 g	1 tsp.
Spanish paprika, sweet	10.0 g	5 tsp.
Spanish paprika, hot	10.0 g	5 tsp.
cinnamon	1.0 g	½ tsp.
cloves, ground	2.0 g	1 tsp.
oregano, ground	2.0 g	1 tsp.

Instructions:
1. Peel off onions and chop them finely. Mix them with rice and leave overnight in a suitable container. The rice will absorb onion juice and will increase in volume.
2. Soak TVP overnight in 210 g of water.
2. Stir blood with salt, add all ingredients and mix together. .
3. Stuff loosely into 32 - 36 mm hog casings as the rice may still increase in volume during cooking.
4. Cook in a hot water at 176° F (80° C) for about 60 minutes.
5. Cool and refrigerate.

Notes:
There is a morcilla variety where instead of rice bread crumbs are used. Everything else remains the same.
Pimenton is Spanish Smoked Paprika that gives chorizos or morcillas this particular flavor and deep red color.

Morcilla Blanca

180 calories per
100 g serving

Morcilla Blanca is Spanish sausage which is related to blood sausages, although it is made without blood. You may translate it as White Blood Sausage and this sausage type is quite common in countries such as England, France, Germany, Poland and Spain.

Meat	Metric	US
lean pork	700 g	1.54 lb.
cream	250 g	1 cup
potato flour	30 g	2 Tbsp.
non fat dry milk	20 g	2 Tbsp.

Ingredients per 1000 g (1 kg) of meat:

salt	15 g	2½ tsp.
white pepper	3.0 g	1 ½ tsp.
carrageenan	10 g	2 tsp.
cinnamon	1.0 g	½ tsp.
cloves, ground	1.0 g	½ tsp.
nutmeg	1.0 g	½ tsp.
whole egg	1	1
onion, finely chopped	60 g	1 small onion
parsley, finely chopped	1 Tbsp	1 Tbsp

Instructions:

1. Grind pork through 3/16" (5 mm) plate.
2. Mix the egg, cream and all ingredients in a blender. If no blender is available, mix manually.
3. Pour over meat and mix everything well together.
4. Stuff into 32-36 mm hog casings.
5. Place sausages into warm water, increase the temperature (around 176° F, 80° C) and simmer for 30 min.
6. Cool and store in a refrigerator.
7. To serve: fry in a skillet or grill.

Navajo Blood Sausage

145 calories per
100 g serving

Navajo Blood Sausage is a blood sausage, very popular among Navajo Indians in the USA. The Navajo Indians lived in Arizona, New Mexico, and Utah. During the 1600's the Navajo Indians began to raise sheep and this animal became a part of their diet. All of the sheep is eaten. A butchered sheep's blood is caught and mixed with corn meal, bits of fat, and potatoes to make blood sausage. The Navajo Indians in Utah reside on a reservation of more than 1,155,000 acres in the southeastern corner of the state.

Materials	Metric	US
sheep blood	500 g	1.10 lb.
cornmeal	200 g	0.44 lb.
textured vegetable protein	60 g	2 oz.
(water for TVP)	180 g	3/4 cup
cooked and diced potato	60 g	1

Ingredients per 1000 g (1 kg) of meat:

salt	18 g	3 tsp.
black pepper	2.0 g	1 tsp.
onion, finely chopped	30 g	½ onion
green chile	20 g	1

Instructions:
1. Soak TVP in 180 g of water for at least 30 minutes.
1. Add salt to blood and stir it.
2. Mix blood with all ingredients.
3. Stuff into large casings (38 - 42 mm).
4. Place sausages into boiling water and poach at 80° - 85° C (176° - 185° F) for about 40 minutes.
5. Cool and keep in refrigerator.

Note:
If sheep blood is hard to obtain use pork, veal or beef blood.
You may add mace (1.0 g, ½ tsp.).
To make the recipe more authentic a Navajo type of corn meal can be used if it can be obtained.

Chapter 14

Poultry-Fish-Game

Poultry Sausages

Poultry sausages are highly popular in regions where people for cultural or religious reasons do not eat pork. Chicken meat, including fat-rich chicken skin are the preferable meat in making these products. To cut down on cholesterol, chicken skins can be replaced with vegetable oil. Making poultry sausages follows the same manufacturing procedure as the production of other sausages. The most popular meats on the market are:

- Chicken.
- Turkey.
- Duck.
- Goose.

Chicken. Chicken is the most popular but does not necessarily mean that chicken meat is superior to goose. Roasted goose or duck are wonderful and no fat can come close to the taste of goose fat. Goose and duck livers produce the highest quality liver sausages. The reason those birds are less popular is that there is not enough profit in growing them on a large scale. Chicken occupies the # 1 spot as it is the most profitable poultry to raise. It needs less feed than other poultry types, its meat contains little fat and the bird is popular all over the world due to its *egg producing capabilities*. Everybody has eaten chicken in his life hundreds of times but how many times have we eaten a goose or a duck?

Chicken fat contains more water and less collagen structure than other fats which makes it soft and semi-liquid at room temperature due to its low melting point. When submitted to heat treatment, chicken fat will melt inside the sausage creating oily pockets and make the sausage seem like a fat product. For those reasons pork fat is often added, but this prevents the sausage from being classified as an all chicken sausage.

Nutritional Values of Poultry Meat

Meat (100 g serving)	Protein (g)	Fat (g)	Energy (cal)	Cholesterol (mg)
Chicken, leg, meat only, raw	20.13	3.81	120	80
Chicken, leg, meat and skin, raw	18.15	12.12	187	83
Chicken breast, meat only, raw	21.23	2.59	114	64
Chicken breast, meat and skin, raw	20.85	9.25	172	64
Chicken, skin only, raw	13.33	32.35	349	109
Chicken fat	0	99.80	900	85
Turkey, fryer-roaster, leg, meat only, raw	20.35	2.37	108	84
Turkey, fryer-roaster, leg, meat & skin, raw	20.13	3.57	118	87
Turkey, fryer-roaster, breast, meat only, raw	24.60	0.65	111	62
Turkey, fryer-roaster, breast, meat & skin, raw	23.76	2.65	125	70
Turkey, fryer-roaster, skin only, raw	16.60	23.54	283	139
Turkey fat	0	99.80	900	102
Goose, domesticated, meat only, raw	22.75	7.13	161	84
Goose, domesticated, meat and skin, raw	15.86	33.62	371	80
Goose fat	0	99.80	900	100
Duck, domesticated, meat only, raw	18.28	5.95	135	77
Duck, domesticated, meat and skin, raw	11.49	39.34	404	76
Duck fat	0	99.80	882	100
Duck, wild, breast, meat only, raw	19.85	4.25	123	77
Duck, wild, meat and skin, raw	17.42	15.20	211	80

Source: USDA Nutrient database

Selecting poultry meat for making sausages offers two main advantages:

- Poultry meat is less expensive than red meats.
- Poultry meat is much healthier than red meats.

To make a healthy sausage use only chicken meat, which is lean. Discard any visible fat and the skin which contains plenty of fat and cholesterol. Instead of pork fat, use vegetable oil. Although vegetable oil contains as much calories as solid fat, it does not contain cholesterol. Low myoglobin content of chicken meat results in a pale color of the finished product, especially if only breast meat is used. Leg meat is juicier than breast.

Chicken skins contain a lot of fat, collagen and most of the bacteria. *Campylobacter jejuni* is a typical pathogen found in poultry meat. Finely ground chicken skin promotes the binding of ingredients which results in a better texture of the finished product. For health reasons chicken skin should be avoided and the sausage texture can be improved by adding powdered gelatin. Using less salt is less noticeable in poultry sausages. It is not recommended to make poultry fresh sausages (uncooked) as fresh poultry does not keep well.

Turkey. Turkey is inexpensive and it has the biggest breast of all poultry. Turkey breast is a great cut for smoking. Being very lean, the breast should be pumped with curing solution. Other parts and turkey trimmings can be used for sausages.

Goose and Duck. These birds are much fatter, especially the skin which contains a lot of attached fat. As skin contains a lot of collagen, it can bind water and emulsify fats very well. Meats from those birds will make good sausages, in addition goose and duck livers are superior material for making liver sausages. Poultry meat is fine for making emulsified sausages that would be cooked in water. The best example is a variety of poultry hotdogs and frankfurters that are carried in our supermarkets.

Fish Sausages

Basic characteristics of fish when used for making sausages:

Cheap raw material. Easy to process. All fish varieties can be used, including de-boned meat.	For best results needs to be combined with pork or other meats. No *myoglobin* (white or grayish color). The final flavor is always fishy even when other meats were added.

Fish products and sausages are popular in countries such as the Philippines, Thailand, Malaysia, Japan, and China.

Making Fish Sausage

1. Grind skinless and boneless pieces of fish. Different species of fish can be mixed together. Adding pork fat will make a great sausage. Those who object to using pork, can add some vegetable oil (if needed). The flesh of the fish is very soft and it should be partly frozen for the clean cut.
2. Mix ground fish with all ingredients. Adding binders such as flour, cornstarch, bread crumbs or cooked rice, helps to develop a good texture. White of an egg is an excellent binder which is added to many sausages. Fish flesh is very light and white pepper will not be visible. Fish goes well with lemon so adding lemon salt or grated lemon zest is a good idea.
3. Stuff into casings.
4. Smoke (optional).
5. Cook to 145° F (63° C) internal meat temperature.
6. Store in refrigerator.

Wild Game Sausages

Wild game meat is lean and darker than other meats due to a lot of physical activity the animal is subjected to. This requires an increased supply of oxygen and as a result more myoglobin is developed. The more myoglobin is present the darker the color of the meat. Game meat is often tougher but is fine for sausages as grinding is a tenderizing step. Sausages made of venison are commercially made for sale in Canada and Alaska. Venison is lean meat and it should be mixed with pork back fat, fatty pork or a combination of pork and beef. A proportion of 60% venison to 40% other fatter meats is a good choice. You can add 30% of pork back fat or fat pork trimmings.

Venison	Good color, good price. Popular meat in Northwestern U.S. and Alaska.	Available during hunting season. Very lean, needs some pork fat or oil.

Chicken Apple Sausage
(Reduced-fat)

179 calories per
100 g serving

Materials	Metric	US
chicken (no skin)	700 g	1.54 lb.
oil emulsion*	200 g	0.44 lb.
dried apple powder	30 g	1 oz.
non-fat dry milk	20 g	2 Tbsp.
gelatin	10 g	2½ tsp.
water	40 g	1/6 cup

Ingredients per 1000 g (1 kg) of meat:

salt	12 g	2 tsp.
carrageenan	5.0 g	1 tsp.
pepper	2.0 g	1 tsp.
cinnamon	1.0 g	½ tsp.
nutmeg	1.0 g	½ tsp.
ginger, ground	0.5 g	1/4 tsp.
sage, dry	1.0 g	2 tsp.

Instructions:
1. Grind chicken meat through 3/16" (5 mm) plate.
2. Mix minced chicken meat with all ingredients together, except emulsion.
3. Add oil emulsion and remix all together.
4. Stuff into hog, synthetic or cellulose casings.
5. Cook in water at 176° F (80° C).
6. Store in refrigerator.

Notes:
Instead of dry apple powder, 50 g of dried apples can be used. Soak dried apples in water or chicken stock first.
Instead of dried apples, you may use 100 g of apple sauce. Don't add any water when apple sauce is used.
* oil emulsion: soy protein isolate/oil/water at 1:4:5.

Chicken Apple Sausage
(Non-fat)

128 calories per 100 g serving

Materials	Metric	US
chicken (no skin)	700 g	1.54 lb.
dried apple powder	50 g	2 oz.
soy protein concentrate	30 g	4 Tbsp.
non-fat dry milk	20 g	2 Tbsp.
potato starch	30 g	4 Tbsp.
gelatin	20 g	5 tsp.
water	150 g	½ cup

Ingredients per 1000 g (1 kg) of meat:

	Metric	US
salt	12 g	2 tsp.
carrageenan	5 g	1 tsp.
pepper	2.0 g	1 tsp.
cinnamon	1.0 g	½ tsp.
nutmeg	1.0 g	½ tsp.
ginger, ground	0.5 g	1/4 tsp.
sage, dry	1.0 g	2 tsp.

Instructions:
1. Grind chicken meat through 3/16" (5 mm) plate.
2. Mix minced chicken meat with all ingredients together.
3. Stuff into hog, synthetic or cellulose casings.
4. Cook in water at 176° F (80° C).
5. Store in refrigerator.

Notes:
Instead of dry apple powder, 50 g of dried apples can be used. Soak dried apples in water or chicken stock first.

Instead of dried apples, you may use 100 g of apple sauce. Add less water (80 g, 1/3 cup) when apple sauce is used.

Chicken Bologna

124 calories per
100 g serving

Materials	Metric	US
chicken meat	900 g	1.98 lb.
soy protein isolate	10 g	4 tsp.
non-fat dry milk	20 g	2 Tbsp.
cold water	70 g	1/3 cup

Ingredients per 1000 g (1 kg) of materials:

salt	15.0 g	2 ½ tsp.
cure #1	2.0 g	1/3 tsp
phosphate*	3.0 g	½ tsp.
sodium erythorbate*	0.3 g	use scale
**carrageenan	5 g	1 tsp.
gelatin	10 g	2½ tsp.
white pepper	2.0 g	1 tsp.
paprika	2.0 g	1 tsp.
allspice	2.0 g	1 tsp.
coriander	2.0 g	1 tsp.

Instructions:

1. Grind meats through a 3/16" (5 mm) plate.
2. In a food processor chop cold water, ground chicken, salt and phosphate for about 2 minutes.
3. Add soy protein isolate and all other ingredients and blend for 2 more minutes.
4. Stuff firmly into 40-60 mm beef middles, fibrous or cellulose casings.
5. Hang at room temperature for one hour.
6. When sausages feel dry to touch, apply hot smoke 50-60° C (120-140° F) for 2-3 hours.
7. Cook in smokehouse or in water to 160° F (72° C) internal meat temperature.
8. Shower with or immerse in cold water for 10 minutes.
9. Store in refrigerator.

Notes:

* Sodium erythorbate and phosphate are not absolutely necessary, although highly recommended.
**Adding of carrageenan improves texture and sliceability of the sausage.

Chicken Cilantro Sausage
(reduced-fat)

175 calories per
100 g serving

Materials	Metric	US
chicken (no skin)	700 g	1.54 lb.
oil emulsion*	200 g	0.44 lb.
non-fat dry milk	20 g	2 Tbsp.
water	80 g	1/3 cup

Ingredients per 1000 g (1 kg) of meat:

salt	12 g	2 tsp.
carrageenan	5.0 g	1 tsp.
white pepper	2.0 g	2 tsp.
cumin	2.0 g	1 tsp.
cayenne	1.0 g	1/2 tsp.
garlic	7.0 g	2 cloves
cilantro, ground	2.0 g	1 tsp.
lemon juice	15 g	1 Tbsp.

Instructions:
1. Grind chicken meat through 3/16" (5 mm) plate.
2. Mix minced chicken meat with all ingredients together.
3. Stuff into hog, synthetic or cellulose casings.
4. Cook in water at 176° F (80° C).
5. Store in refrigerator.

Notes:
* oil emulsion: soy protein isolate/oil/water at 1:4:5.

Chicken Curry

150 calories per
100 g serving

Materials	Metric	US
chicken breast (no skin)	850 g	1.87 lb.
SPI (soy protein isolate)	10 g	4 tsp.
vegetable oil	40 g	2½ Tbsp.
water	50 g	3 Tbsp.
potato starch	10 g	2 tsp.
white wine	40 g	2½ Tbsp.

Ingredients per 1000 g (1 kg) of meat:

salt	12 g	2½ tsp.
carrageenan	5.0 g	1 tsp.
white pepper	3.0 g	1½ tsp.
curry powder	4.0 g	3 tsp.
garlic	3.5 g	1 clove

Instructions:

1. Oil emulsion: chop SPI, and water in food processor for 1 minute. Add oil and chop for 2 minutes. Refrigerate.
2. Grind meat through 3/16" (5 mm) plate.
3. Mix ground meat with wine and all ingredients.
4. Add oil emulsion and mix everything together.
5. Stuff into 32 mm hog or cellulose casings.
6. Cook in water at 176° F (80° C).
7. Cool and store in a refrigerator.

Chicken Hot Dog
(reduced-fat, extended)

140 calories per
100 g serving

Materials	Metric	US
chicken breast	650 g	1.43 lb.
TVP (textured vegetable protein)	30 g	1 oz.
(water for TVP)	90 g	1/3 cup
oil emulsion*	100 g	0.22 lb.
potato starch	20 g	3 Tbsp
non-fat dry milk	20 g	2 Tbsp.
cold water	90 g	1/3 cup

Ingredients per 1000 g (1 kg) of materials:

salt	15.0 g	2 ½ tsp.
cure #1	2.0 g	1/3 tsp
sodium erythorbate**	0.10 g	use scale
phosphate**	2.0 g	½ tsp
carrageenan***	5.0 g	1 tsp.
white pepper	2.0 g	1 tsp.
paprika	2.0 g	1 tsp.
allspice	2.0 g	1 tsp.
coriander	2.0 g	1 tsp.

Instructions:
1. Soak TVP in cold water for 30 minutes.
2. Grind chicken breast through a small plate (3/16", 5 mm).
3. In a food processor chop cold water, ground chicken, salt, cure #1, carrageenan, phosphate and sodium erythorbate. Add potato starch, rehydrated TVP, non-fat dry milk, and chop. Add spices and fat emulsion and chop/ emulsify everything together.
4. Stuff into 22-26 mm sheep casings.
5. Hold at room temperature for 30 minutes.
6. Smoke at 65° C (150° F) for 30-40 minutes.
7. Cook sausage in water at 176° F (80° C), about 15-20 minutes.
8. Cold shower or cool in cold water. Store in refrigerator.

Notes:
* oil emulsion: soy protein isolate/oil/water at 1:4:5.
** Sodium erythorbate and phosphate are not absolutely necessary, although highly recommended.
***Adding carrageenan improves texture and sliceability of the sausage.

Deer Sausage
(reduced-fat)

175 calories per
100 g serving

Meat	Metric	US
deer meat	750 g	1.65 lb.
oil emulsion*	200 g	0.44 lb.
cold water	50 g	3 Tbsp.

Ingredients per 1000 g (1 kg) of meat:

salt	18.0 g	3 tsp.
Cure #1	2.5 g	½ tsp.
carrageenan	5.0 g	1 tsp.
mustard, ground	2.0 g	1 tsp.
rosemary, dried	1.0 g	1 tsp.
pepper	2.0 g	1 tsp.
marjoram, dry	3.0 g	2 tsp.
garlic	7.0 g	2 cloves

Instructions:
1. Grind meat through a 3/8" (10 mm) plate.
2. Mix ground meat with all ingredients adding 50 g cold water.
3. Stuff tightly into 32-36 mm hog casings. Make 6" long links.
4. Hang overnight in a cool place.
5. Preheat smoker to 130° F, (54° C) then apply hot smoke for 2-3 hours. In the last hour of smoking start slowly increasing the temperature to about 170° F, (77° C).
6. Stop cooking when internal meat temperature is 160° F, (71° C).
7. Shower sausages with cold water and hang them to further cool down.
8. Store in refrigerator.

Notes:
* oil emulsion: soy protein isolate/oil/water at 1:4:5.

Fish Links

118 calories per
100 g serving

Meat	Metric	US
raw fish	800 g	1.76 lb.
bread crumbs	40 g	4 Tbsp.
water (for bread crumbs)	80 g	1/3 cup
onion, finely chopped	30 g	½ onion
egg white	50 g	2 egg white

Ingredients per 1000 g (1 kg) of meat:

salt	12 g	2 tsp.
Sausage Maker fat replacer	4.0 g	1 tsp.
white pepper	4.0 g	2 tsp.
sugar	5.0 g	1 tsp.
grated lemon peel	½ lemon	½ lemon

Instructions:

1. Soak bread crumbs in cold water.
2. Grind boneless, skinless chunks of fish through ¼" (6 mm) grinder plate. Fish should be partially frozen for easy grind.
3. Mix ground fish with all ingredients.
4. Stuff into 24-26 mm sheep casings.
5. Refrigerate and fully cook before serving.

Note:

To make zest, lightly grate the outside of a lemon. Do not grate the bitter white under skin.

Fish Sausage

142 calories per
100 g serving

Meat	Metric	US
raw fish	750 g	1.65 lb.
oil emulsion*	100 g	0.33lb.
potato flour	20 g	3 tsp.
egg	50 g	2 egg white
water	80 g	2 Tbsp.

Ingredients per 1000 g (1 kg) of meat:

salt	15 g	2 ½ tsp.
Sausage Maker fat replacer	4.0 g	1 tsp.
white pepper	3.0 g	1½ tsp.
ginger, ground	0.5 g	⅓ tsp.
nutmeg	1.0 g	⅓ tsp.
fresh parsley, chopped	10 g	1 bunch
onion powder	6 g	2 ½ tsp.
grated lemon peel	¼ lemon	¼ lemon

Instructions:

1. Grind boneless, skinless chunks of fish through ¼" (6 mm) grinder plate. Fish should be partially frozen for easy grind.
2. Mix ground fish with all ingredients adding cold water.
3. Add oil emulsion and remix all together.
4. Stuff into 28-32 mm hog casings.
5. Smoke for 30 minutes with hot smoke. This is an optional step.
6. Cook in water at 176° F (80° C) for about 30 minutes.
7. Refrigerate.

Notes:

* oil emulsion: soy protein isolate/oil/water at 1:4:5.

Fish Sausage

172 calories per
100 g serving

Fish sausage made with oil instead of pork fat.

Meat	Metric	US
raw fish	800 g	1.76 lb.
olive oil	50 g	0.11 lb.
potato flour	50 g	3 Tbsp.
bread crumbs	20 g	2 Tbsp.
water	80 g	1/3 cup

Ingredients per 1000 g (1 kg) of materials:

salt	18 g	3 tsp.
Sausage Maker fat replacer	4.0 g	1 tsp.
pepper	4.0 g	2 tsp.
nutmeg	2.0 g	½ tsp.
coriander	2.0 g	1 tsp.
cumin	2.0 g	1 tsp.
turmeric	2.0 g	1 tsp.
red pepper, ground	0.5 g	⅓ tsp.
ginger, ground	0.5 g	½ tsp.
egg white	30 g	1 egg

Instructions:

1. Grind boneless, skinless chunks of fish through 3/16" (5 mm) grinder plate. Fish should be partially frozen for easy grind.
2. Mix salt, flour, oil, bread crumbs, spices and fish together adding as much water as necessary.
3. Stuff into 32-36 mm natural or synthetic casings of your choice.
4. Refrigerate and fully cook before serving.

Notes:

- Sausage should have a slight curry flavor as all above spices are used for making curry powder. Turmeric will add a yellowish color but it may be omitted from the recipe.
- Sausage may be cooked in water and will become a ready to eat sausage.
- Cooked rice can be used as a filler.

Rabbit Sausage
(reduced-fat)

184 calories per
100 g serving

Meat	Metric	US
rabbit	750 g	1.65 lb.
oil emulsion*	200 g	0.44 lb.
cold water	50 g	4 Tbsp.

Ingredients per 1000 g (1 kg) of meat:

	Metric	US
salt	18 g	3 tsp.
Cure #1	2.5 g	½ tsp.
carrageenan	5.0 g	1 tsp.
Sausage Maker fat replacer	4.0 g	1 tsp.
pepper	2.0 g	1 tsp.
allspice	2.0 g	1 tsp.
nutmeg	1.0 g	½ tsp.
sugar	2.0 g	½ tsp.

Instructions:

1. Grind all meats and fat through a ¼" (6 mm) plate.
2. Mix ground meat with all ingredients adding 50 g cold water.
3. Stuff tightly into 32-36 mm hog casings.
4. Hang for 1 hour until casings feel dry.
5. Preheat smoker to 130° F, (54° C) then apply hot smoke for 90 minutes.
6. Cook in hot water at 176° F (80° C). This will take about 30 minutes. Stop cooking when internal meat temperature is 160° F, (71° C).
7. Cool in cold water, then hang them to further cool down.
8. Store in refrigerator.

Notes:

* oil emulsion: soy protein isolate/oil/water at 1:4:5.

Turkey Plum Sausage

Plum puree or dry plum powder provide a subtle flavor and helps to retain moisture.

Materials	Low-Fat	Non-Fat
Turkey meat (no skin),	750 g (1.65 lb)	750 g (1.65 lb)
Dry plum powder, 5%	50 g	50 g
Soy protein isolate	20 g	20 g
Olive oil,	80 g (6 Tbsp)	
Non-fat dry milk,		30 g
Water	100 g (1 cup)	150 g (1 cup)
Ingredients per 1 kg of material:		
Salt,	12 g (2 tsp)	12 g (2 tsp)
Carrageenan	5 g (1 tsp.)	5 g (1 tsp.)
Pepper	2 g (1 tsp)	2 g (1 tsp)
Cinnamon	2 g (1 tsp)	2 g (1 tsp)
Nutmeg	1 g (½ tsp)	1 g (½ tap)
Cloves, ground	0.5 g (1/4 tsp)	0.5 g (1/4 tsp)
Ginger, ground	1 g (½ tsp)	1 g (½ tsp)
Calories per 100 g (3.5 oz) serving, about	188 cal	128 cal

Instructions - non-fat sausage
1. Grind meat through 3/8" (10 mm) plate.
2. Mix ground meat with all ingredients together.
3. Stuff into hog, synthetic or cellulose casings.
4. Store in refrigerator and serve within 3 days. For a longer storage place in the freezer.

Instructions - low-fat sausage
1. Grind meat through 3/8" (10 mm) plate.
2. In food processor cut oil, soy protein isolate and ½ cup water. Mix until emulsion is obtained.
3. Add ground meat, remaining water, all ingredients and emulsify together.
4. Stuff into hog, synthetic or cellulose casings.
5. Store in refrigerator and serve within 3 days. For a longer storage place in the freezer.

Turkey Sausage

176 calories per
100 g serving

Turkey sausage can be made from turkey meat and pork back fat. Pork and beef trimmings may also be added.

Meat	Metric	US
turkey meat	700 g	1.54 lb.
oil emulsion*	200 g	0.44 lb.
potato starch	20 g	3 Tbsp.
cold water	80 g	1/3 cup

Ingredients per 1000 g (1 kg) of meat:

salt	15.0 g	2 ½ tsp.
carrageenan	5.0 g	1 tsp.
gelatin	10 g	2 ½ tsp.
white pepper	2.0 g	1 tsp.
paprika	2.0 g	1 tsp.
nutmeg	1.0 g	½ tsp.
garlic	3.5 g	1 clove

Instructions:

1. Grind meat through 3/16" plate (5 mm). Refreeze and grind again.
2. Mix ground meat with water, salt and spices
3. Add oil emulsion and remix all together.
4. Stuff into 36 mm casings.
5. Cook sausage in water at 176° F (80° C), about 15-20 minutes.
6. Cold shower or cool in cold water. Store in refrigerator.

Notes:

* oil emulsion: soy protein isolate/oil/water at 1:4:5.

Wild Boar Sausage   169 calories per
100 g serving

Wild boar is a naturally lean meat and to make a good sausage pork meat (70/30) or pork fat must be added. In this recipe 300 g of oil emulsion corresponds to adding 12% of vegetable oil.

Meat	Metric	US
wild boar	700 g	1.43 lb.
oil emulsion*	20 g	0.66 lb.
water	100 g	0.11 lb.

Ingredients per 1000 g (1 kg) of meat:

salt	15 g	2 ½ tsp.
Cure #1	2.0 g	1/3 tsp.
carrageenan	5.0 g	1 tsp.
Sausage Maker fat replacer	8.0 g	2 tsp.
pepper	4.0 g	1 tsp.
dry juniper berries	2.0 g	1 tsp.
garlic	7.0 g	2 cloves

Instructions:
1. Grind meat through a 3/8" (10 mm) plate.
2. Mix ground meat with all ingredients adding 50 g cold water.
3. Add oil emulsion and remix all together.
4. Stuff tightly into 32-36 mm hog casings.
5. Hang for 1 hour until casings feel dry.
6. Preheat smoker to 130° F, (54° C) then apply hot smoke for 2 hours. In last hour of smoking start slowly increasing temperature to about 170° F, (77° C).
7. Stop cooking when internal meat temperature is 160° F (71° C).
8. Shower sausages with cold water and hang them to further cool down.
9. Store in refrigerator.

Notes:
* oil emulsion: soy protein isolate/oil/water at 1:4:5.
If available - at the beginning and at the end of smoking add some juniper branches into the fire.

Chapter 15

Extended Value Sausages

Sausages offer a great opportunity to create new products. Whereas whole meats such as hams, butts, loins, and bacon offer less room to improvise, sausages can be made from countless combinations of meats, spices and different fillers. Those fillers make it possible to produce nutritious, yet very inexpensive products. Take for example blood sausages which incorporate fillers such as rusk, barley, bread crumbs, or rice. Make your own version without blood, which for people living in large cities may be difficult to obtain anyhow. Potatoes are much cheaper than meat and you get a lot of value when making Swedish potato sausage which tastes wonderful. Boudin, the Cajun classical sausage is made with rice. Cajun cuisine is a great example how local conditions dictate the way meat products and sausage are made. A bit of history might strengthen the point.

Acadia (what is known today as New Brunswick, Nova Scotia and Prince Edward Island in Canada) was the first permanent French settlement in North America, established at Port-Royal in 1607. In what is known as the Great Expulsion (le Grand Dérangement) of 1755-1763, during the Seven Years War between England and France (1755-1763) the British ordered the mass deportation of the Acadians. More than 14,000 Acadians (three-quarters of the Acadian population in Nova Scotia) were expelled by the British. Their homes were burned and their lands confiscated. Families were split up, and the Acadians were dispersed throughout the lands in North America; thousands were transported to France. Gradually, some managed to make their way to Louisiana, creating the Cajun population and culture after mixing with others there. The land they settled on was nothing like the fertile soil of Acadia. The climate was hot and humid, coastal areas abounded with swamps, alligators and snakes.

The popular crops were wheat, rice, sugarcane, sweet potatoes, peas, cabbage, turnips, apples, and raised maize as a secondary crop. Barley, oats, and potatoes were planted as feed for the livestock, including cattle, pigs, and poultry. These animals provided a steady supply of meat to the former Acadians, which they supplemented with fish. Living in such conditions Cajuns created a wonderful cuisine which combined the cooking art of Spanish, French, local natives, Filipinos and other ethnic groups. They have invented a unique style of cooking where fillers play an important part in a sausage formula. Often the sausage became a filler itself and became an ingredient of a more elaborate dish, for example gumbo or jambalaya.

Here presents itself a very attractive solution for making healthy sausages; why not to incorporate fillers into a sausage? This is not a new invention, sausages enriched with a filler material have been produced from the beginning and there are some great, time proven recipes. Emulsified sausages can easily incorporate fillers, vegetable proteins, and other ingredients which will blend in within the sausage mass. Basically any combination of meats and filling material that can be stuffed into a casings, can be called a sausage. For example you have made a quantity of chili, which is basically ground meat, beans, and chili powder. If you stuff chili into a casing you will get chili sausage, won't you? If your chili is too thin, add some bread crumbs to it or flour. Throw it on the grill or frying pan and the kids are getting the same chili they have been eating, but in a different form.

For healthy individuals there is nothing wrong with eating moderate quantities of fat. People who are at cardiovascular risk may try to eliminate fat all together. This is where extended value added sausages start to shine as they are made with filler material. Because a significant amount of non-meat is added to the sausage, the amount of fat, cholesterol and calories becomes proportionally smaller.

Depending on their composition, extended value sausages may contain very little meat. If this remaining meat is removed, a vegetarian sausage will be created.

General Recommendations and Tips:

- Adding finely ground beef increases the water holding capacity of the sausage.
- You can add about 20% of precooked and minced tripe. This will make the sausage lighter.
- Good filler material: rice, potatoes, onions, bread crumbs, barley, rusk, oats, semolina flour. You can save natural bread rolls such as Portuguese rolls or French baquettes. They will dry out and will remain usable for a long time. Before use,

soak them in water or milk. Then mix with ground meat and other ingredients. Add an egg to combine the mass better.

- Soy protein concentrate (or isolate) is a natural product and helps to bind water and retain moisture during cooking. The sausage will look plumper.
- Non-fat dry milk binds water very well.
- White of an egg binds all ingredients well together.
- *Textured vegetable protein (TVP) is an excellent filler and protein extender.* It is inexpensive, tasteless, feels like meat, contains more than twice the protein than meat and none of the cholesterol.
- Adding carrageenan results in a better texture and improved sliceability. Carrageenan works well in the presence of milk protein, so using it with non-fat dry milk is a good idea.
- Konjac flour mixes with cold water extremely well and gelatinizes easily. It provides a slippery, fatty sensation, but it does not create as firm of a texture as carrageenan does.
- Don't add salt to cooking water when preparing rice, potatoes, barley or making meat stock. Salt will be added during mixing ingredients.

In addition to typical flours that we are accustomed to, there is a great variety of flours that are utilized in tropical countries. Thanks to the Internet they all can be easily obtained online. This allows us to create even more different food combinations, each with a slightly different characteristic.

- Gram flour is a flour made from ground chickpeas. It is also known as chickpea flour, garbanzo flour, or besan. Used in many countries, it is a staple ingredient in Indian, Pakistani and Bangladeshi cuisines, and comes in the form of a paste mixed with water or yoghurt. When mixed with an equal proportion of water, it can be used as *an egg-replacer in vegan cooking.* Chila, a pancake made with gram flour batter, is a popular street and fast food in India.
- African gari and tufu flours are made from yam.
- Cassava flour is made from cassava (yuca).

Incorporating filler material into sausages was practiced throughout history. It was common in Europe after the end of World War II and has been practiced in poor countries in South America and Asia. What in the past was looked down as inferior food by the well to do

Westerners, was actually a healthy sausage of the poor. They ate healthier food, being physically active they were thinner and fit. What's important is that they have had less problems with hypertension, cardiovascular diseases and cancer. The may live shorter than us, but that is not due to their diet, but to the lack of medical care that they don't have and which we take for granted. The time has come to re-think the way we look at meat in a supermarket display and to realize that combining meat with other ingredients can make a much healthier sausage. Our attitude towards foods has been recently changing and we start to accept and "love" foods on which we have looked in the past in disdain. The best example is a case of polenta.

From Wikipedia:

Polenta is made with ground yellow or white cornmeal (ground maize), which can be ground coarsely or finely depending on the region and the texture desired. Polenta was originally and still is classified as a peasant food. Since the late 20th century, polenta has found popularity as a gourmet food. Polenta dishes are on the menu in many high-end restaurants, and prepared polenta can be found in supermarkets in tubes or boxes at high prices. Many current polenta recipes have given new life to an essentially bland and simple food, enriching it with meat and mushroom sauces, and adding vegetables, beans or various cheeses into the basic mixture.

In smaller caliber low-cost products such as hotdogs, larger quantity of extenders such as re-hydrated TVP and coarse fillers (bread crumbs, rusk, flour) are added during the chopping procedure. Finely cut fillers such as flours and starches are usually added dry. Coarse fillers such as bread crumbs, rusk and cereals are usually re-hydrated. Coarse extenders such as textured vegetable protein are usually re-hydrated before adding them to a mix.

Beef and Bean Burrito
(Extended)

137 calories per
100 g serving

Materials	Metric	US
lean beef	500 g	1.10 lb.
bean paste*	300 g	0.66 lb.
potato flour	60 g	4 Tbsp.
non-fat dry milk	20 g	2 Tbsp.
water	120 g	½ cup

Ingredients per 1000 g of materials:

salt	12 g	2 tsp
pepper	2.0 g	1 tsp.
garlic, smashed	3.5 g	1 clove
medium onion, finely diced	30 g	½ onion
chili powder	4.0 g	2 tsp.
oregano, dried	1.0 g	1 tsp.
carrageenan	5.0 g	2 tsp.

Instructions

1. *Soak dry beans overnight. Simmer in a little water for a few hours until soft. Rinse and drain. You may simplify the process by using canned beans.
2. Grind beef through 3/16" (5 mm) plate.
3. Mix everything together.
4. Stuff into 36 mm casings.
5. Cook sausage in water at 176° F (80° C), about 15-20 minutes.
6. Cool in cold water.
7. Store in refrigerator.

Notes:

Carrageenan may be replaced with 10 g of powdered gelatin or egg white.

Beef Hotdog
(Extended)

175 calories per 100 g serving

Materials	Metric	US
lean beef	350 g	0.77 lb.
oil emulsion*	200 g	0.44 lb.
cold water	140 g	5/8 cup
textured vegetable protein (TVP)	60 g	2 oz.
water (for TVP)	180 g	3/4 cup
potato starch	50 g	1-3/4 oz.
non-fat dry milk	20 g	2 Tbsp.

Ingredients per 1000 g of materials:

salt	10 g	2-1/3 tsp
white pepper	2.0 g	1 tsp.
cure #1	1.0 g	1/4 tsp.
nutmeg, ground	1.0 g	½ tsp.
coriander, ground	1.0 g	½ tsp.
mustard, ground	1.5 g	½ tsp.
paprika	1.0 g	½ tsp.
garlic, smashed	3.5 g	1 clove
carrageenan	5.0 g	1 tsp.
sodium erythorbate**	0.1 g	use scale
phosphate**	2.0 g	½ tsp.

Instructions
1. Soak TVP in cold water for 30 minutes.
2. Grind beef through a small plate (1/8", 3 mm).
3. In a food processor chop cold water, ground meat, salt, phosphate, cure #1, and sodium erythorbate. Add potato starch, non-fat dry milk, carrageenan and chop. Add spices and fat emulsion and chop/emulsify everything together.
4. Stuff into 22-26 mm sheep casings.
5. Hold at room temperature for 30 minutes.
6. Smoke at 65° C (150° F) for 30-40 minutes.
7. Cook sausage in water at 176° F (80° C), about 15-20 minutes.
8. Cold shower or cool in cold water. Store in refrigerator.

Notes:
* oil emulsion: soy protein isolate/oil/water at 1:4:5.
** Sodium erythorbate and phosphate are not absolutely necessary, although highly recommended.

Chicken Hotdog
(Extended)

174 calories per
100 g serving

Materials	Metric	US
chicken meat (no skin)	450 g	0.99 lb.
oil emulsion*	200 g	0.44 lb.
cold water	110 g	110 ml
textured vegetable protein (TVP)	50 g	0.11 lb.
water (for TVP)	150 g	0.33 lb.
potato starch	40 g	3 Tbsp.
non-fat dry milk	20 g	2 Tbsp.

Ingredients per 1000 g of materials:

salt	10 g	2-½ tsp.
white pepper	2.0 g	1 tsp.
cure #1	1.0 g	1/4 tsp.
nutmeg, ground	1.0 g	½ tsp.
garlic, smashed	3.5 g	1 clove
sodium erythorbate**	0.1 g	use scale
phosphate**	2.0 g	½ tsp.
carrageenan	5.0 g	1 tsp.

Instructions
1. Soak TVP in cold water for 30 minutes.
2. Grind chicken meat through a small plate (1/8", 3 mm).
3. In a food processor chop cold water, ground meat, salt, phosphate, cure #1, and sodium erythorbate. Add potato starch, non-fat dry milk, and chop. Add spices and fat emulsion and chop/emulsify everything together.
4. Stuff into 22-26 mm sheep casings.
5. Hold at room temperature for 30 minutes.
6. Smoke at 65° C (150° F) for 30-40 minutes.
7. Cook sausage in water at 176° F (80° C), about 15-20 minutes.
8. Cold shower or cool in cold water. Store in refrigerator.

Notes:
* oil emulsion: soy protein isolate/oil/water at 1:4:5.
** Sodium erythorbate and phosphate are not absolutely necessary, although highly recommended.
The sausage will be of a light color, but a food coloring may be added.

Pork Sausage
(Extended)

195 calories per
100 g serving

Materials	Metric	US
lean pork	500 g	1.10 lb.
oil emulsion*	200 g	0.44 lb.
potato starch	30 g	2 Tbsp.
bread crumbs	30 g	3 Tbsp.
wheat flour	50 g	3 Tbsp..
egg white	50 g	2 egg whites
cold water	80 g	1/3 cup

Ingredients per 1000 g of materials:

salt	12 g	2 tsp
white pepper	2.0 g	1 tsp.
garlic, smashed	3.5 g	1 clove
marjoram	1.0 g	½ tsp.
coriander, ground	1.0 g	½ tsp.

Instructions
1. Soak bread crumbs in 60 g of cold water.
2. Grind meat through a small plate (1/8", 3 mm).
3. In a food processor chop cold water, ground pork and salt. Add potato starch, bread crumbs and wheat flour and chop. Add spices and fat emulsion and chop/emulsify everything together.
4. Stuff into 22-26 mm sheep casings.
Cool and place in refrigerator. The sausage must be fully cooked before serving *OR*
5. Cook sausage in water at 176° F (80° C), about 15-20 minutes.
6. Cold shower or cool in cold water. Store in refrigerator.

Notes:
* oil emulsion: soy protein isolate/oil/water at 1:4:5.
** phosphate is not absolutely necessary, although highly recommended.
rusk may be used instead of bread crumbs.

Swedish Potato Sausage

110 calories per
100 g serving

Swedish Potato Sausage (Potatis Korv) is a fresh sausage made with ground pork and beef that is mixed with potatoes, onions, salt and pepper. Most Swedish potato sausage recipes include allspice and the proportion of beef and pork vary from 75/50 - 50/50 - 50/75 pork to beef.

Materials	Metric	US
lean pork	300 g	0.66 lb.
lean beef	300 g	0.66 lb.
potatoes	300 g	0.66 lb.
small onion,	30 g	½ onion
water	70 g	1/3 cup

Ingredients per 1000 g (1 kg) of meat:

salt	12 g	2 tsp.
white pepper	4.0 g	2 tsp.
allspice, ground	1.0 g	½ tsp.
carrageenan	10 g	2 tsp.

Instructions:

1. Grind meats, potatoes and onions through ⅜" plate.
2. Mix water with salt, pepper and allspice and mix everything well together.
3. Stuff into 36 mm casings.
4. The sausage can be fried, baked or boiled. You may place it in a skillet with water to cover, bring it to a boil and then simmer on lower heat for about 20 minutes. Keep the cover on.
5. Store in refrigerator or freeze for later use.
6. Cook before serving.

Turkey & Pork Sausage
(reduced-fat)

126 calories per
100 g serving

Materials	Metric	US
lean pork	250 g	0.55 lb.
turkey	150 g	0.33 lb.
textured vegetable protein	100 g	3.5 oz.
(water for TVP)	300 g	300 ml
vital wheat gluten	50 g	2 oz.
potato flour	50 g	2 oz.
water	100 g	100 ml

Ingredients per 1000 g (1 kg) of materials:

salt	18.0 g	2 tsp.
cure #1	2.0 g	1/3 tsp.
carrageenan	10 g	2 tsp.
white pepper	2.0 g	1 tsp.
onion powder	1.0 g	½ tsp.
mustard, ground	1.0 g	½ tsp.
coriander, ground	2.0 g	1 tsp.
garlic	3.0 g	1 clove

Instructions:
1. Soak TVP in water for at least 30 minutes.
2. Grind meats through a 3/16" (5 mm) plate.
3. Mix meats with TVP. Add all remaining ingredients and mix everything together. Add only ½ water, then add more if needed.
4. Stuff into 32-36 mm casings.
5. Hold at room temperature for 30 minutes.
6. Smoke at 65° C (150° F) for 60 minutes.
7. Cook sausage in water at 176° F (80° C) for about 30 minutes.
8. Cool in cold water.
9. Store in refrigerator.

Chapter 16

Kosher Sausages

Well, the meat selection is pretty much defined by the Jewish Bible:

- You may eat any animal that has a split hoof and chews the cud: the cow, the sheep, the goat, the deer, and the antelope. The camel, rabbit and the coney cannot be eaten.
- Of all the creatures living in the water, you may eat any that have fins and scales. That means no eels, oysters or lobsters.
- You may eat all clean birds: chicken, poultry. Eating birds of prey such as eagle falcon or nighthawk is not permitted.

Pork is not permitted and that includes pork fat which is normally added to venison, poultry or fish sausages. This restriction puts certain limitations on the recipe as pork back fat is a superior ingredient that is added to most high quality products. This forces us to come up with some alternatives:

- Beef fat (suet).
- Vegetable oil.

Don't use lamb or venison fat as they don't taste right. Chicken fat tastes good, the only problem is that it melts at room temperature and you may end up with pockets of melted fat inside your sausage.

Adding vegetable or olive oil is a good choice and as long as you don't add more than 25%, the sausage will be of acceptable quality. Emulsifying olive oil with soy protein isolate is a great idea as it helps to hold the sausage together and increases its protein content. Sausages made with oil are lighter in color than those made with solid fat.

Vegetable oils are liquid at processing temperatures and this may cause their separation during processing and cooking with fat pockets as a result. Adding an emulsifier such as soy protein or caseinate will reduce the problem.

Kosher head cheese and meat jelly can easily be made. Chicken and fish look extremely attractive and taste wonderful when added to the natural clarified stock. It is easier to produce a natural chicken only gelatin when chicken claws are added to meat broth. Concentrated chicken broth takes the first place in nutritional value compared with broths from other meats. It is also distinguished by a pleasant flavor.

To produce fish stock with enough gelatin, fish parts that contain collagen (skin, bone and fins) must be used in making broth. This implies that after filleting the fish, the rest of the body with the head included is added to the pot.

What follows is a sampler of some Kosher recipes. By now you should be able to take any recipe and modify it so it will conform to the requirements of Jewish rules and tradition. The manufacturing process will basically remain the same. In most cases beef will be the material of choice and more water can be added due to beef's excellent water holding properties.

Additives

Konjac flour, carrageenan and microcrystalline cellulose are of plant origin so their use should not conflict with the rules of Kosher law. Xanthan gum is made by using bacteria to ferment sugars which should also be fine. Sausage Maker's fat replacer can be used to mimic the sensation of fat and develop a better texture in reduced fat sausages. It consists of konjac gum, xanthan gum and microcrystalline cellulose. Gelatin creates a problem; it is made from animal collagen, mainly pork skins and beef hides so it does not conform to the requirements of Kosher law.

Chicken Curry

167 calories per
100 g serving

Very original, yet simple to make sausage.

Meat	Metric	US
lean chicken	850 g	1.87 lb.
olive oil	50 g	0.11 lb.
potato flour	30 g	2 Tbsp.
white wine	50 g	3 Tbsp.
non-fat dry milk	15 g	5 tsp.
carrageenan	5 g	1 tsp.

Ingredients per 1000 g (1 kg) of meat:

salt	12 g	2½ tsp.
white pepper	3.0 g	1½ tsp.
curry powder	2.5 g	1 tsp.
garlic	3.5 g	1 clove

Instructions:
1. Grind meat and fat through 3/8" plate (8 mm).
2. Mix meats with all ingredients.
3. Stuff into 32-36 mm hog casings forming 4" (10 cm) links.
4. Keep in a refrigerator or freeze for later use.
5. Cook before use.

Chicken Hotdog

173 calories per 100 g serving

Meat	Metric	US
lean chicken	750 g	1.65 lb.
olive oil	60 g	4 Tbsp.
soy protein isolate	10 g	4 tsp.
potato starch	10 g	4 tsp.
non-fat dry milk	20 g	5 tsp.
dry apples, rehydrated	100 g	3 oz.
water	50 g	2 oz.

Ingredients per 1000 g (1 kg) of meat:

salt	12 g	2½ tsp.
carrageenan	5 g	1 tsp.
white pepper	3.0 g	1½ tsp.
sage, rubbed	1.0 g	2 tsp.
garlic	3.5 g	1 clove

Instructions:

1. Soak dry apples in water.
2. Grind meat through 3/14" plate (5 mm).
3. Mix meat with 50 g of water, starch, dry milk, rehydrated apples, carrageenan and all ingredients.
4. In food processor chop soy protein isolate for 1 minute with 50 g of water. Add oil and chop for 2 more minutes. Add meat batter and chop everything together.
5. Stuff into 24-26 mm cellulose casings.
6. Dry at room temperature for 30 minutes.
7. Smoke at 140-150° F (60-66° C) for 45 minutes.
8. Cook in water at 176° F (80° C) for 30 minutes.
9. Cool in cold water, air-dry.
10. Store in refrigerator.

Chicken Sausage

145 calories per
100 g serving

Chicken sausage is made from all chicken meat and then it is smoked and poached.

Meat	Metric	US
chicken breast	400 g	0.88 lb.
chicken thighs	400 g	0.88 lb.
oil emulsion*	100 g	0.22 lb.
non-fat dry milk	20 g	2 Tbsp.
water	80 g	1/3 cup

Ingredients per 1000 g (1 kg) of meat:

salt	18 g	3 tsp.
carrageenan	5 g	1 tsp.
Cure #1	2.5 g	½ tsp.
pepper	4.0 g	2 tsp.
paprika	4.0 g	2 tsp.
garlic	3.5 g	1 clove

Instructions:

1. Grind meats 3/16" plate (5 mm).
2. Chop meats in food processor adding cold water and all ingredients, except oil emulsion.
3. Add oil emulsion and blend all together.
4. Stuff firmly into 32-36 mm hog casings.
5. Hang on smokesticks for one hour.
6. When sausages feel dry apply hot smoke 60-68° C (140-150° F) for 60 min.
7. Cook in water at 80° C (176° F) for about 35 minutes..
8. Cool in cold water for 5 minutes.
9. Store in refrigerator.

Notes:

* oil emulsion: soy protein isolate/oil/water at 1:4:5.

Kosher Beef Sausage

152 calories per
100 g serving

Meat	Metric	US
lean beef, beef trimmings,	800 g	1.76 lb.
oil emulsion*	100 g	0.22 lb.
cold water	100 g	¼ cup

Ingredients per 1000 g (1 kg) of meat:

salt	18 g	3 tsp.
Cure #1	2.0 g	1/3 tsp.
carrageenan	5 g	1 tsp.
SM fat replacer	4.0 g	1 tsp.
pepper	2.0 g	1 tsp.
paprika	2.0 g	1 tsp.
garlic	3.5 g	1 clove

Instructions:
1. Grind meat with 3/8" (10 mm) plate.
2. Mix meat with all ingredients adding water.
3. Add oil emulsion and remix.
4. Stuff into 40-60 mm beef middles or fibrous synthetic casings.
5. Hang at room temperature for 1-2 hours.
6. Apply hot smoke at 140-150° F (40-50° C) for 120 minutes.
7. Increase temperature to 170° F (78° C) and bake the sausages for 30 minutes with or without smoke.
8. Shower with cold water for about 10 min, then let air-dry.
9. Store in refrigerator.

Notes:
* oil emulsion: soy protein isolate/oil/water at 1:4:5.

Kosher Liver Sausage

152 calories per
100 g serving

Meat	Metric	US
lean veal or beef	550 g	1.21 lb.
veal liver	250 g	0.55 lb.
oil emulsion*	100 g	0.22 lb.
stock	100 g	3 oz.

Ingredients per 1000 g (1 kg) of meat:

salt	18 g	3 tsp.
carrageenan	5 g	1 tsp.
white pepper	4.0 g	2 tsp.
coriander	2.0 g	1 tsp.
nutmeg	1.0 g	½ tsp.
ginger	0.5 g	⅓ tsp.
onion	30 g	1 onion

Instructions:

1. Slow cook meat (except liver) in water until soft. Save stock.
2. Cut raw liver into smaller slices.
3. Be sure it is cold. Grind through 3/16" (5 mm) plate.
4. In a food processor chop liver with salt. Add stock, ground meat, all ingredients and chop. Add oil emulsion and chop all together.
5. Stuff into 36-38 mm diameter beef, cellulose or fibrous synthetic casings.
6. Cook in water at 176° F (80° C) for about 40 minutes.
7. Cool in cold water for 10 minutes, then air-dry.
8. Store in refrigerator.

Notes:

* oil emulsion: soy protein isolate/oil/water at 1:4:5.

Kosher Sausage With Oil

173 calories per
100 g serving

Meat	Metric	US
lean beef	800 g	1.76 lb.
olive oil	60 g	1/4 cup
potato flour	20 g	4 tsp.
cold water	80 g	1/3 cup

Ingredients per 1000 g (1 kg) of meat:

salt	18 g	1 Tbs.
carrageenan	5 g	1 tsp.
pepper	4.0 g	2 tsp.
garlic	3.5 g	1 clove
marjoram, ground	2.0 g	1 tsp.

Instructions:

1. Grind beef with 3/16" (5 mm) plate.
2. Add cold water, salt, and all other ingredients and mix with ground beef. Add potato flour and oil and mix everything together.
3. Stuff into 32-36 mm beef, cellulose or fibrous synthetic casings.
4. Cook in water at 176° F (80° C) for 35 minutes.
5. Cool in cold water for 5 minutes, then air-dry.
6. Store in refrigerator.

Merguez

166 calories per
100 g serving

Merguez, the French transliteration of the Arabic word mirqaz, is a spicy, short sausage from North Africa made with lamb or beef, and flavored with spices. Spices such as paprika, cayenne or harissa, a hot chili paste that gives Merguez sausage its red color. Sold by street vendors in Paris, can also be found in London, Belgium and New York.

Meat	Metric	US
lean lamb	950 g	2.09 lb.
olive oil	30 g	2 Tbs.
water	20 g	1 Tbsp.

Ingredients per 1000 g (1 kg) of meat:

salt	18 g	3 tsp.
pepper	4.0 g	2 tsp.
garlic	7.0 g	2 cloves
cayenne pepper	4.0 g	2 tsp.
allspice, ground	1.0 g	½ tsp.
paprika	4.0 g	2 tsp.
cumin, ground	1.0 g	½ tsp.

Instructions:
1. Grind through 1/4" (6 mm) plate.
2. Mix ground meat with all ingredients and olive oil.
3. Stuff into 24-26 mm sheep casings.
4. Store in refrigerator.
5. Cook before serving.

Notes:
Some recipes call for a mixture of lamb and beef.
Merguez owes its red color due to the high amount of paprika.
Some recipes call for Harrisa Paste which is nothing more than a combination of the spices that are already listed above (garlic, cumin, olive oil, hot chili peppers) plus coriander.

Making Harrisa paste:

1. Place 4 oz of red hot chilies in a bowl and cover with hot water for two hours, then drain.

2. Process in a blender 1/4 cup garlic cloves, 1/4 cup ground cumin, 1/2 cup ground coriander, 1/4 cup salt, drained chilies and 1/2 cup olive oil. Add olive oil slowly until a thick paste is produced. For a finer consistency rub paste through a sieve.

You can make a smaller amount of paste: 1 garlic clove crushed and finely chopped, 1/2 Tbsp. salt, 2 Tbsp. olive oil, 1 tsp. cayenne pepper, 1/2 tsp. ground cumin, 1/4 tsp. ground coriander. Mix ingredients in a jar and shake well. Cover with a lid.

There are Merguez sausage recipes that include coriander, oregano, fennel seeds (used in Italian sausages) and even ground cinnamon. This is a spicy sausage and in addition to the spices listed in the ingredients above, please feel free to add any spices that you personally like.

Merguez is often made into hamburger patties or meat balls. It is served by frying in olive oil until well browned or grilled.

Podhalanska

164 calories per
100 g serving

Podhalanska Sausage is made with lamb and pork. This sausage comes from the Southern part of Poland known as "Podhale" where the Tatry Mountains are located.

Meat	Metric	US
lean lamb	850 g	1.87 lb.
oil emulsion*	100 g	3 oz..
water	50 g	3 Tbsp.

Ingredients per 1000 g (1 kg) of meat:

salt	18 g	3 tsp.
Cure #1	2.5 g	½ tsp.
carrageenan	5 g	1 tsp.
pepper	2.0 g	1 tsp.
herbal pepper **	2.0 g	1 tsp.
allspice	2.0 g	1 tsp.
garlic	3.5 g	1 clove

Instructions:

1. Grind lamb and pork meat a 3/8" (10 mm) plate.
2. Add water, salt, cure #1 and all ingredients and mix together.
3. Add oil emulsion and remix everything well together.
4. Stuff into 32-42 mm hog casings.
5. Hang for 1 hour at room temperature.
6. When sausages feel dry apply hot smoke 60-68° C (140-150° F) for 60 min. Increase temperature to 170° F (78° C) and bake for 30 minutes with or without smoke.
7. Shower for 5 minutes with cold water, the air dry.
8. Store in refrigerator.

Notes:

* oil emulsion: soy protein isolate/oil/water at 1:4:5.
** Herbal pepper is a mixture of mustard, caraway, marjoram, chili, sweet Hungarian paprika, hot paprika and bay leaves. There are different combinations of spices on the market, so choose something you like.

Another combination: coriander, caraway, marjoram, cayenne, mustard, dried horseradish, powdered onion.

Tatar Sausage

164 calories per
100 g serving

The name Tatar initially appeared amongst the nomadic Turkic peoples of northeastern Mongolia in the region around Lake Baikal in the beginning of the 5th century. As various of these nomadic groups became part of Genghis Khan's army in the early 13th century, a fusion of Mongol and Turkic elements took place and the invaders of Rus and Hungary became known to Europeans as Tatars (or Tartars). After the break up of the Mongol Empire, the Tatars became especially identified with the western part of the empire, which included most of European Russia and was known as the Golden Horde. The Tatar sausage was originally cold smoked and not cooked.

Meat	Metric	US
lamb	850 g	1.87 lb.
lamb hard fat (or oil emulsion*)	100 g	0.22 lb.
water	50 g	3 Tbsp.

Ingredients per 1000 g (1 kg) of meat:

salt	18 g	3 tsp.
Cure #1	2.5 g	½ tsp.
carrageenan	5 g	1 tsp.
pepper	2.0 g	1 tsp.
allspice	2.0 g	1 tsp.
caraway seed	2.0 g	1 tsp.
nutmeg	1.0 g	½ tsp.
garlic	3.5 g	1 clove

Instructions:

1. Grind meats with 3/8" (10 mm) plate. Cut fat into ⅛ " (3 mm) cubes.
2. Mix all ingredients with meat adding water. Then add diced fat and mix everything together.
3. Stuff into sheep casings 24-26 mm and form rings.
4. Hang at room temperature for 1 hours.
5. Apply hot smoke for 60-90 min until casings develop a brown color with a red tint.
6. In the last stage of smoking the sausage is baked at 167-194° F (75-90° C) until internal meat temperature is 68-70° C (154-158° F).
7. Shower with cold water for about 5 min, then lower sausage temperature to below 12° C (53° F).
8. Store in refrigerator.

Notes:
* oil emulsion: soy protein isolate/oil/water at 1:4:5.

Chapter 17

Vegetarian Sausages

Vegetarian sausages are much healthier as they don't contain animal fat or cholesterol. The amount of salt, oil and calories can be manipulated using the same rules that apply for making other healthy sausages. The hardest problem to solve is to duplicate the flavor of meat. No matter how well vegetarian sausages are made, they are not in the same class as regular or even reduced-fat sausages. The fact should be accepted that a sausage that is made without meat has a different flavor and cannot compete with a traditionally made meat product. However, it does have its own character and it does not need to imitate or compete with meat sausages. And... it is 100% healthy.

Materials

A veggie burger is a hamburger-style patty that does not contain meat. The patty of a veggie burger may be made, for example, from vegetables, textured vegetable protein (soy meat), legumes, nuts, dairy products, mushrooms, wheat, or eggs. It should be noted that a purist-vegan will not add milk caseinate or egg to his formulations as they are of animal origin. Nor will he use animal casings for stuffing sausages.

A vegetarian hot dog (sometimes referred to as a "veggie dog" or "not dog") is a hot dog produced completely from non-meat products. Vegetarian hot dogs are sometimes eaten by non-vegetarians because they are lower in fat, calories, and contain no cholesterol compared to hot dogs from animal meats. Unlike traditional home-made meat sausages, the casing is not made of intestine but of synthetic ingredients. Vegetarian hot dogs are usually based on some sort of soy protein, for example tofu. Some contain egg whites, which would make them unacceptable to purist-vegans. Like ordinary hot dogs, vegetarian hot dogs contain little fiber.

Oil emulsion (Chapter 8) which is used in many recipes in this book is well suited for making veggie sausages. It contains pure protein (soy protein isolate), vegetable oil and water. Textured vegetable protein (TVP) is a great soy product that can be added as a protein extender (50 % protein) and filler material. Its granules mimic the feel of ground meat particles. TVP is rehydrated with 3 parts of water, so adding 6% of rehydrated TVP accounts for 24% of the sausage mass. There is no problem in creating products with plenty of protein as adding tofu, grains and flours will further increase the protein content of the sausage. The harder task is to create proper texture of the sausage but this can be accomplished with wheat gluten, starch and carrageenan. All flours can be used for making vegetarian sausages, although soy flour may impart a "beany taste" to the product.

Gram flour is a flour made from ground chickpeas. It is also known as chickpea flour, garbanzo flour, or besan. In comparison to other common flours such as wheat, potato, rice, corn, and semolina, it has a relatively high proportion of protein. Used in many countries, it is a staple ingredient in Indian, Pakistani and Bangladeshi cuisines, and in the form of a paste with water or yoghurt. Moreover, when mixed with an equal proportion of water it can be used as an egg-replacer in vegan cooking. Chila (or chilla), a pancake made with gram flour batter, is a popular street and fast food in India.

Tofu is a very nutritional product, unfortunately it has a very bland flavor and should rather be considered a filler material. This can be made up by adding natural flavors that have always been popular in baking industries such as apple, plum, strawberry, tomato, or vegetable dry powders. In addition some of them exhibit strong water binding properties, for example plum and apple powder.

Tofu (100 g)						
Name	Protein (g)	Fat (g)	Carbohy-drates (g)	Salt (mg)	Energy (cal)	Cholesterol (mg)
Tofu, raw, regular	8.08	4.78	1.88	7	76	0
Tofu, raw, firm	15.78	8.72	4.27	14	145	0
						USDA Nutrient database

Vital wheat gluten is the natural protein of grain and is separated from whole wheat with pure water. It is responsible for the stretchiness of dough and for the shapes that baked goods hold.

Vital wheat gluten, 100 g serving					
Protein (g)	Fat (g)	Carbohydrates (g)	Salt (mg)	Energy (cal)	Choles- terol
55.5	0	33.3	0	388	0

Source: Arrowhead Mills

In vegetarian sausages we can use a true emulsion of vegetable oil, water and pure soy protein. Soy protein covers oil particles with a protein film and oil and water mix together becoming a true emulsion. Such emulsion looks, feels and tastes like fat, helps to achieve a better texture, provides plenty of protein and calories, but none of the cholesterol. And it mixes well with any ingredients.

Texture

Meat protein which are extracted from meat cells during cutting or grinding are "gluing" ground meat particles, fat, water and spices together. Many vegetarian sausages suffer from poor texture which is due to insufficient binding of the ingredients. It is not enough to throw a bunch of non-meat ingredients, mix them together and call it a sausage. The sausage must look and feel like a sausage. When it is cut across, each slice should keep together and hold its own. The casing should peel off easily. Would you buy sliced ham or bologna that would break into many individual pieces? A vegetarian sausage should also have a good texture and the sliced sausage should hold its form without breaking apart. This is very hard to accomplish with veggie sausages because traditionally used binders such as egg white, gelatin, or non fat dry milk will not be used by vegetarian purists as they are of animal origin.

Binding can be improved by using *vital wheat gluten, starch, carrageenan and konjac flour.* Konjac flour improves binding but makes the removal of the skin harder. Konjac flour binds plenty of water and provides a good mouthfeel. Upon contact with water, it becomes slippery and facilitates mixing and stuffing. However, it creates a texture that is not as firm as the one made with carrageenan. That is why it should be used together with carrageenan. Xanthan gum is made by fermenting sugars so it should be acceptable by vegetarians. In most cases it is used with konjac flour to provide an even stronger effect. In our tests the best results were obtained when **vital wheat gluten** and **carrageenan** were employed.

Adding carrageenan results in a firmer texture and improves slice-ability. Carrageenan must be heated to 180° F (82° C) before it forms a gel. The gel remains stable when the sausage cools down.

Most commercially produced vegetarian sausages are of emulsified type, eg. veggie hot dogs. It is much easier to chop everything in a food processor, then stuff the resulting paste into a casing. However, emulsified sausages account for only part of a great variety of sausages. In the USA hot dogs, frankfurters and bologna account for 50% of all total sausage sales. In Europe this percentage is much smaller as Europeans consume many types of sausages.

Vegetarian sausages which are not emulsified in a food processor are harder to make. The difficulty lies in controlling texture, it is much harder to produce a vegetarian sausage that contains rice, barley or oats and to bind those materials with spices in such a way that they will not crumble when the sausage is sliced. When the texture is under control, the sausage can contain an infinite number of materials, some of which may be considered "show" pieces. For example, slices of re-hydrated apples or plums, raisins, olives or nuts. Filler materials such as tofu, potatoes, barley, rice, oats, rusk, bread crumbs and soaked bread can be used. Potato flakes, potato flour, chickpea flour, semolina, rice flour, starches and textured vegetable protein can be added as well. Most people love bread pudding and bread pudding sausage can easily be made. There is no shortage of ingredients and hundreds of recipes can be created.

Protein

The leaner the meat, the more protein in it. About 20% is the upper limit and considering the fact that a sausage may contain 70% lean meat, its protein value will be 14%. About 14 g per 100 g serving. Most commercially produced meats are made with plenty of water so the number will be even lower.

Vegetarian sausages are made with soy derived products such as soy protein concentrate, soy protein isolate, textured vegetable protein and tofu, all of which are very rich in protein. Our recipes often call for oil emulsion which is soy protein isolate (92% protein) : oil : water at the ratio of 1:4:5. In 100 g serving there is 9.2 g of protein, 4 g (4%) of oil, the rest is water. Adding 20% oil emulsion provides more protein than a sausage made from meat, yet less calories and none of cholesterol. In addition to oil emulsion other ingredients that are rich in portein are added such as textured vegetable protein, flours and tofu.

Textured vegetable protein (TVP) is a great protein source, but its real value lies in its texture. When rehydrated it feels like small meat particles and its texture remains firm after cooking. To sum it all up, a vegetarian sausage can be protein loaded, calorie rich and still a healthy product.

Color

In meat products the characteristic pink color is obtained by adding sodium nitrite. Sodium nitrite (cure #1) reacts with meat myoglobin and after heat treatment the meat remains pink. There is no myoglobin in vegetarian products, so adding nitrite leads us nowhere. However, the color can be adjusted by adding natural products such as beet powder, turmeric, annatto, saffron or paprika. One of the most popular natural colorings is carmine. It is used in the manufacture of artificial flowers, paints, crimson ink, rouge, and other cosmetics, and is routinely added to food products such as yogurt and certain brands of juice, most notably those of the ruby-red variety. However, it is made from little bugs and may not conform to the requirements of pure vegetarians. Food colorings may be obtained online or in food supermarkets.

Salt

In processed meats salt is needed at 1.8-2% to extract meat proteins, provide safety against spoilage and pathogenic bacteria in semi-dry sausages (2.5%, summer sausage), or at 3% in traditionally made salami. As vegetarian sausages do not contain meat, salt is added for flavoring mainly, although commercial producers will add it for preservation purposes. Home made vegetarian sausages can be made with very little salt (< 1%). If Morton® Lite Salt is used, 50% less sodium is introduced and the salt level drops to only 0.5%. That comes to 500 mg of sodium per 100 g serving. In addition, potassium chloride accounts for half of Morton® Lite Salt and carrageenan, which is usually added to vegetarian sausages and is known to react better in the presence of potassium chloride.

About Recipes

Recipes call for cooking sausages briefly in hot water. This is not done for safety reasons as all ingredients are safe to eat to begin with. The step is needed to activate carrageenan, which gelatinizes at 180° F (82° C). It can be easily noticed; a sausage that feels soft after stuffing will become firm and plump after 10 minutes of treatment in hot water.

Starches need to be heated as well in order to gelatinize. After stuffing, the sausage does not necessarily have to be cooked and may be placed in a refrigerator. Keep in mind that its texture will be softer as carrageenan or starch need to be thermally heated in order to gelatinize. Then when it is heated, the additives will set and the sausage will become firmer.

The amounts of water given in recipes are not fixed in stone. When trying a new recipe, the addition of water should be performed last. Adding too much water during mixing ingredients will result in a watery texture and the finished product may end up too soft. Many ingredients such as textured vegetable protein, bread crumbs, and pre-soaked oats contain much water. This water will be absorbed by soy protein isolate (if added), flour, starch, bread crumbs, potatoes, rice and carrageenan during mixing. It is recommended to mix all ingredients well together first, and then add water in small amounts until the mixture feels right.

Many tests were performed and some recipes were tried in five or six different versions. Test sausages were made in 100 g weight. It would be torture to wash, clean and dry grinder plates, stuffing tubes or stuffing cylinders all those times. A simple method was used, the same that has been in service for hundreds of years: stuffing sausages through a funnel. The grinder was not used at all, a small food processor took care of all our cutting and mixing needs. Mixing and stuffing were accomplished with a bowl, spoon, sausage casing and a funnel.

Photo 17.1 Smaller amounts of vegetarian, emulsified, liver, head cheese and blood sausages can be efficiently stuffed through a common funnel.

Rice Sausage with Apple Sauce

115 calories per
100 g serving

Materials	Metric	US
rice, boiled	650 g	1.54 lb.
apple sauce	200 g	0.44 lb.
vital wheat gluten	80 g	3 oz.
soy protein isolate	20 g	3 Tbsp.
water as needed	(50 g)	3 Tbsp.

Ingredients per 1 kg (1000 g) of materials

cinnamon	2 g	1 tsp.
ground cloves	0.25 g	1/8 tsp
sugar	10 g	2 tsp
carrageenan	10 g	2 tsp

Instructions

1. Combine rice, apple sauce, soy protein isolate, carrageenan and spices.
2. Add wheat gluten and remix. Add as much water as needed and remix.
3. Stuff into 32 mm casings.
4. Cook sausages in water at 176° F (80° C), about 15-20 minutes.
5. Cool in cold water. Store in refrigerator.

Photo 17.2 & 17.3 This is an easy one man operation.

Potato Sausage

140 calories per
100 g serving

Materials	Metric	US
boiled potatoes	400 g	0.88 lb.
textured vegetable protein	100 g	0.22 lb.
(water for TVP)	300 g	0.66 lb.
vital wheat gluten	80 g	3 oz.
oil emulsion*	100 g	0.22 lb.
water	20 g	1 Tbsp.

Ingredients per 1 kg (1000 g) of materials

salt	10 g	1½ tsp.
white pepper	4 g	2 tsp.
allspice, ground	2 g	1 tsp.
carrageenan	10 g	2 tsp.

Instructions
1. Mix boiled potatoes, rehydrated TVP, carrageenan, spices and oil emulsion. Add wheat gluten and remix. Add as much water as necessary for the right texture.
2. Stuff into desired casings (32-36 mm).
3. Cook sausages in water at 176° F (80° C), about 30 minutes.
4. Cool in cold water.
5. Store in refrigerator.

Bean Frankfurter

183 calories per
100 g serving

Materials	Metric	US
cooked beans	500 g	1.10 lb.
potato flour	200 g	0.44 lb.
vital wheat gluten	100 g	3½ oz.
soy protein isolate	20 g	3 Tbsp.
water as needed	(180 g)	3/4 cup

Ingredients per 1 kg (1000 g) of materials

salt	12 g	2 tsp
pepper	2 g	1 tsp
chili powder	8 g	4 tsp
onion powder	5 g	2 tsp.
carrageenan	10 g	2 tsp.

Instructions

1. Soak beans in water for 4 hours. Drain, then slow cook until tender. Use enough water to cover the beans.
2. Add beans and 1/2 cup water into food processor and chop until a paste is obtained.
3. Add all ingredients except wheat gluten and emulsify.
4. Add vital wheat gluten and blend everything together. Add more water if necessary.
5. Stuff into desired casings (24-26 mm).
6. Cook sausages in water at 176° F (80° C), about 20 minutes.
7. Cool in cold water.
8. Store in refrigerator.

Garbanzo Sausage

199 calories per
100 g serving

Materials	Metric	US
chickpea (garbanzo) flour	225 g	0.50 lb.
tofu, regular	225 g	0.50 lb.
oil emulsion*	100 g	0.22 lb.
vital wheat gluten	50 g	2 oz.
textured vegetable protein	100 g	3½ oz.
(water for TVP)	300 g	1-1/4 cup

Ingredients per 1000 g (1 kg) of materials:

salt	10 g	1½ tsp.
pepper	2.0 g	1 tsp.
garlic	3.5 g	1 clove
nutmeg	2.0 g	1 tsp.
ginger	1.0 g	½ tsp.
carrageenan	10 g	2 tsp.

Instructions:
1. Soak TVP in water for at least 30 minutes.
2. Mix chickpea flour, TVP, starch, salt, carrageenan and spices.
3. Add oil emulsion and remix everything together. Add vital wheat gluten and remix.
4. Stuff into 32 mm casings.
5. Cook in water at 176° F (80° C) for 20 minutes.
6. Cool in cold water.
7. Keep refrigerated.

Notes:
* oil emulsion: soy protein isolate/oil/water at 1:4:5.

Tofu Sausage with Bread Crumbs
178 calories per 100 g serving

Materials	Metric	US
tofu, soft	500 g	1.10 lb.
bread crumbs	150 g	0.33 lb.
(water for bread crumbs)	150 g	150 ml
vital wheat gluten	80 g	3 oz.
oil emulsion*	100 g	3½ oz.
water, as needed	(20 g)	1 Tbsp.

Ingredients per 1000 g (1 kg) of materials:

salt	10 g	1½ tsp.
pepper	3.0 g	1½ tsp.
onion powder	2.5 g	1 tsp.
garlic	3.5 g	1 clove
nutmeg	2.0 g	1 tsp.
ginger	1.0 g	½ tsp.
carrageenan	10 g	2 tsp.

Instructions:
1. Soak bread crumbs in water.
2. Mix tofu, bread crumbs, carrageenan, salt and spices. Add oil emulsion and remix. Add vital wheat gluten and mix everything together.
3. Stuff into 32 mm casings.
4. Cook in water at 176° F (80° C) for 20 minutes.
5. Cool in cold water.
6. Keep refrigerated.

Notes:
* oil emulsion: soy protein isolate/oil/water at 1:4:5.

Tomato Sausage

167 calories per
100 g serving

Materials	Metric	US
textured vegetable protein	100 g	0.22 lb.
(water for TVP)	300 g	0.66 lb.
oil emulsion*	200 g	0.44 lb.
cracker meal	100 g	3½ oz.
finely diced tomatoes	300 g	0.66 lb.

Ingredients per 1000 g (1 kg) of materials:

salt	10 g	1½ tsp.
pepper	2.0 g	1 tsp.
garlic	3.5 g	1 clove
small chopped onion	50 g	1 onion
carrageenan	5 g	1 tsp.

Instructions:
1. Soak TVP in water for at least 30 minutes.
2. Mix cracker meal, TVP, starch, salt, carrageenan, salt, spices and tomatoes.
3. Add oil emulsion and remix everything together.
4. Stuff into 32 mm casings.
5. Cook in water at 176° F (80° C) for 20 minutes.
6. Cool in cold water.
7. Keep refrigerated.

Notes:
* oil emulsion: soy protein isolate/oil/water at 1:4:5.
Cracker meal is a type of coarse flour which is made from finely milled crackers. It is often used as a seafood fry mix. It can be replaced with bread crumbs.

Victor Sausage

177 calories per
100 g serving

Materials	Metric	US
bread crumbs	120 g	0.22 lb.
(water for bread crumbs)	200 g	0.44 lb.
textured vegetable protein	100 g	3½ oz.
(water for TVP)	300 g	0.66 lb.
oil emulsion*	200 g	0.44 lb.
potato starch	25 g	5 tsp.
small chopped onion	50 g	1 onion
carrageenan	5 g	1 tsp.

Ingredients per 1000 g (1 kg) of materials:

salt	10 g	1½ tsp.
pepper	2.0 g	1 tsp.
garlic	3.5 g	1 clove

Instructions:

1. Soak TVP in water for at least 30 minutes. Soak bread crumbs in water.
2. Mix bread crumbs, TVP, starch, salt, carrageenan and spices.
3. Add oil emulsion and remix everything together.
4. Stuff into 32 mm casings.
5. Cook in water at 176° F (80° C) for 20 minutes.
6. Cool in cold water.
7. Keep refrigerated.

Notes:

* oil emulsion: soy protein isolate/oil/water at 1:4:5.

White Pudding   190 calories per
                                    100 g serving

White pudding is a sausage popular in Ireland, Scotland and some parts of England. It consists of beef suet, oatmeal, and leeks or onions. If blood was added, the sausage could be called black pudding which is a blood sausage. In many cases it is not stuffed into casings becoming a breakfast dish which is served with bacon, fried eggs and often with black pudding. This is the veggie version.

Materials	Metric	US
oats, steel cut, soaked	300 g	0.66 lb.
tofu, regular	400 g	0.88 lb.
oil emulsion*	100 g	3½ oz.
potato flour	100 g	3½ oz.
vital wheat gluten	100 g	3½ oz.
water, as needed		

Ingredients per 1000 g (1 kg) of meat:

salt	15 g	2½ tsp.
pepper	2.0 g	1 tsp.
mace	1.0 g	½ tsp.
cloves, ground	0.5 g	1/4 tsp.
green scallions, chopped	50 g	½ stalk
carrageenan	10 g	2 tsp.

Instructions:
1. Soak oats in water overnight. Drain, but don't dry.
2. Mix moist oats with other ingredients, except oil emulsion.
3. Add oil emulsion and mix everything together.
4. Stuff into 32 mm casings.
5. Cook in water at 176° F (80° C) for 20 minutes.
6. Cool in cold water.
7. Keep refrigerated.

Notes:
* oil emulsion: soy protein isolate/oil/water at 1:4:5.
Natural oats are very hard and must be soaked before use. 100 g of oats soaked in water overnight, when drained, will weigh 300 g next day.

Recipe Index

Appendix

The following table includes caloric values of meats, flours, soy products and other ingredients that are listed in the book. This data is useful for those who want to calculate the amount of calories that a sausage contains. The serving amount is 100 g and can be easily re-calculated for other sizes. For example 100 g of ground pork 72/18 contains 314 calories and the recipe calls for 750 g of pork. Multiplying 314 x 7.5 will gives 2355 and this is the amount calories present in 750 g of 72/18 pork.

Let's assume that we add 50 g of potato flour and 100 g serving of potato flour contains 357 calories. Ten grams of flour contains 357/10 = 35.7 calories. Then, 50 grams of flour must contain five times more calories, eg., 35.7 x 5 = 178.5 calories.

Serving size 100 g (3.5 oz)			
Ingredient	Calories	Ingredient	Calories
Pork back fat, fresh, raw	812	Soy flour, full-fat	436
Pork belly, fresh raw	518	Soy flour, low-fat	375
Pork shoulder (Boston butt), fresh raw	186	Soy flour, de-fatted	330
Pork shoulder, arm picnic, fresh, raw	253	Soy protein isolate	338
Pork loin, center rib, boneless, lean only, raw	152	Soy protein concentrate	331
Pork leg (ham), whole, fresh, lean only	136	Textured vegetable protein	333
		Potatoes, boiled, without skin	86
Pork ground, 72% lean, 28% fat, raw	314	Potato flour	357
Pork, ground, 84% lean, 16% fat, raw	218	Potato starch	333
Pork ground, 96% lean, 4% fat, raw	121	Wheat flour, white,	364
Pork liver	134	Wheat flour, whole grain	340
Pork skin, raw	326		
Beef fat, tallow	902	Chickpea (besan) flour	387
Beef brisket, flat half, boneless, trimmed to 0", fresh	165	Rice flour, white	366
		Rice, white, cooked,	130
Beef chuck, shoulder clod, top blade, trimmed to 0", raw	182	Corn flour, whole grain, white	361
		Cornmeal, enriched, yellow	370
Beef, ground, 70% lean, 30% fat, raw	332	Semolina flour	360
		Vital wheat gluten	388
Beef ground, 85% lean, 15% fat, raw	215	Oats	389
		Cracker meal	406
Beef, ground, 95% lean, 5% fat, raw	137	Bread crumbs, dry, plain	395
		Onions, raw	40

Beef liver	135	Beans, kidney, boiled	123
		Buckwheat groats, cooked	92
		Barley, pearled, cooked	123
Beef tripe	85	Egg whole, raw	143
Veal breast, whole, boneless, raw	208	Egg, yolk, fresh	322
Veal, ground, raw	144	Egg white, raw	52
Veal liver	140	Egg, white, dried	382
Chicken, fat	900	Gelatin, dry powder	335
Chicken breast, meat only, raw	114	Vegetable oil	900
		Cream, fluid, half and half	130
Chicken, ground, raw	143	Milk, whole, 3.25% fat	61
		Pepper, black	251
Chicken liver	119	Pepper, white	296
Lamb, separable lean only	142	Pepper, red or cayenne	318
Turkey, all classes, dark meat, raw	125	Paprika, ground	282
Turkey, all classes, light meat, raw	115	Nutmeg, ground	525
Turkey fat	900	Mace, ground	475
Turkey, ground, 93% lean, 7% fat	150	Ginger, ground	335
Turkey liver, raw	228	Marjoram, dried	271
Duck liver	136	Curry powder	325
Goose liver	133	Onion powder	341
Fish, bass, freshwater. raw	114	Garlic powder	331
Fish, catfish, farmed, raw	119	Cinnamon, ground	247
Fish, cod, Atlantic, raw	82	Non-fat dry milk	535
Fish, salmon, pink, raw	127	Tofu, raw, regular	76
Fish, tuna, yellowfin, raw	109	Tofu, raw, firm	145
		Tomatoes, red, ripe, raw	18
Game meat, deer, raw	120	Sugar (sucrose), granulated	387
Game meat, boar, wild	122	Vinegar, red wine	19
Rabbit, raw, domesticated	136	Lemon juice	22
Rabbit, raw, wild	114		
Cheese, goat, hard type	452	Carrageenan	16
Cheese, goat, semisoft type	364		
Cheese, goat, soft type	268		

General rule: *1 tsp of dried ground spice weighs about 2 grams and provides around 5-6 calories.*

Useful Links and Resources

Sausage-Making Equipment and Supplies

The Sausage Maker Inc., 1500 Clinton St., Building 123
Buffalo, NY 14206, 888-490-8525; 716-824-5814
www.sausagemaker.com

Allied Kenco Sales, 26 Lyerly #1, Houston, TX 77022
713-691-2935; 800-356-5189
www.alliedkenco.com

The Sausage Source, 3 Henniker Road, Hillsboro, NH 03244
1-800-978-5465
www.sausagesource.com

Butcher & Packer Supply Co., 1468 Gratiot Avenue, Detroit,
MI 48207, 888-521-3188; 313-567-1250
www.butcher-packer.com

LEM Products, Inc., 107 May Drive, Harrison, Ohio 45030
1-877-536-7763
http://www.lemproducts.com

Meat Processing Products, PO Box 900163, Utah 84090
1-877-231-8589
http://www.meatprocessingproducts.com

The Ingredient Store, Division of Ames Company, Inc.
PO Box 46, New Ringgold, PA 17960
http://www.theingredientstore.com

Sausage-Stuffer, 1807 Bryn Mawhr Street
Alexandria, Lousiana 71301,
877-332-9990
http://www.sausage-stuffer.com

Northern Tool & Equipment - Food Processing
Catalog sales plus stores.
http://www.northerntool.com/shop/tools/category_food-processing

Specialized Equipment and Supplies

American Weigh Scales, Inc - http://www.awscales.com
Highly Accurate Digital Scales.

Will Powder www.willpowder.net Molecular gastronomy-gums
Chef Rubber http://www.chefrubber.com
Molecular gastronomy, fruit powders, egg white powder, baking supplies
Lepicerie - http://www.lepicerie.com
Gums, carrageenan, apple powder, egg white powder, gums, meat glue, baking supplies
Bulk Foods, http://www.bulkfoods.com
Grains, flours, starches, dried fruits, molecular gastronomy
Bob's Red Mill - http://www.bobsredmill.com
Grains, flours, starches, molecular gastronomy
Barry Farm Foods www.barryfarm.com
Flours and other ingredients
Konjac flour
Konjac Foods http://www.konjacfoods.com
http://www.miraclenoodle.com
konjac-glucomannan-flour.html
http://www.lowcarbshop.com/product/9/5/Konjac-Flour.html
Natural Grocers, http://www.naturalgrocers.com
- flours.
Pacific Pectin - http://pacificpectin.com
Pectins, LM pectin
FMC BioPolymer www.fmc.com
Avicel® PH Microcrystalline Cellulose
Amazon www.amazon.con a great variety of equipment and supplies

Information Sources

USDA Nutrient Database http://www.nal.usda.gov/fnic/foodcomp/search
FITDAY™ http://www.fitday.com
Calorie Control Council http://www.caloriecontrol.org
Dietary Guidelines for Americans
http://www.health.gov/dietaryguidelines/dga2005/document
USDA Agricultural Research Service
http://www.ars.usda.gov/main/main.htm

Index

Also by Stanley and Adam Marianski

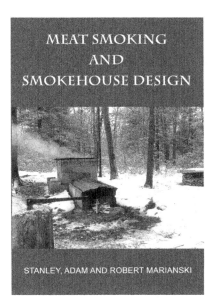

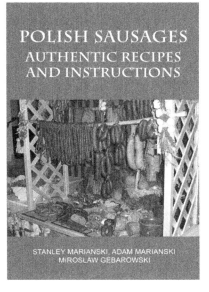

In Meat Smoking & Smokehouse Design readers are provided with detailed information about how to:

- Apply cures and make brines.
- Smoke meats, poultry, game and fish.
- Barbecue meats and build barbecues.
- Create your own recipes without adding chemicals.
- Design and build your own smokehouse.

The book explains differences between grilling, barbecuing and smoking. There are extensive discussions of curing as well as the particulars about smoking sausages, meat, fish, poultry and wild game.

ISBN: 978-0-9824267-0-8

Most books on sausage making are filled with unknown quality recipes, this book is different, it contains carefully compiled government recipes that were used by Polish meat plants between 1950-1990. Those recipes were not written by restaurant cooks or college students running web sites, but by the best professionals in meat science the country had. The recipes presented in *Polish Sausages* come from those government manuals and they were never published before. These are recipes and production processes of the products that were really made by Polish meat plants and sold to the public. Most of those sausages are still made and sold in Poland.

ISBN: 978-0-9824267-2-2

Learn more at: **www.bookmagic.com**

Also by Stanley and Adam Marianski

There has been a need for a comprehensive one-volume reference on the manufacture of meats and sausages at home. *Home Production of Quality Meats and Sausages* bridges the gap between technical textbooks and the requirements of the typical hobbyist. Along with 172 recipes you will discover how to:

- Apply cures and make brines.
- Smoke meats, poultry, game and fish.
- Create your own recipes.
- Conform to U.S. Government standards.
- Make fresh, smoked, emulsified and fermented sausages along with head cheeses, blood and liver sausages.
- Make hams, bacons and loins.
- Make jerky, pemmican and more...

ISBN: 978-0-9824267-3-9

In The Art of Making Fermented Sausages readers are provided with detailed information about how to:

- Control meat acidity and removal of moisture.
- Choose proper temperatures for fermenting, smoking and drying.
- Understand and control fermentation process.
- Choose proper starter cultures and make traditional or fast-fermented products.
- Choose proper equipment, and much more...

ISBN: 978-0-9824267-1-5

Learn more at: **www.bookmagic.com**

Also by Stanley and Adam Marianski

The Amazing Mullet offers
information that has been gathered
through time and experience.
Successful methods of catching,
smoking and cooking mullet are
covered in great depth. One will
learn the distinct characteristics that
make mullet such an exceptional
fish. Numerous filleting, cleaning,
cooking and smoking practices
are reviewed thoroughly. The
cooking section explains the best
methods for preparing fish and
the recipe section, in addition to
mullet recipes, includes detailed
information on making fish cakes,
ceviche, spreads and sauces.

ISBN: 978-0-9824267-8-4

Learn more at: **www.bookmagic.com**

CPSIA information can be obtained at www.ICGtesting.com
Printed in the USA
LVOW04s2002211114

414978LV00018B/929/P

9 780983 697305